HEAD *to* HEAD
SHEFFIELD WEDNESDAY

Peter Waring

breedon **books**
PUBLISHING

First published in Great Britain in 2004 by
The Breedon Books Publishing Company Limited
Breedon House, 3 The Parker Centre,
Derby, DE21 4SZ.

ISBN 1 85983 417 6

Printed and bound by Cromwell Press Ltd,
Trowbridge, Wiltshire.

Introduction

This book contains the results of all matches played by Sheffield Wednesday in the following competitions:
Premiership and Football League
FA Cup
League Cup
Football League play-offs and test matches
European Cup, Cup-Winners Cup and UEFA Cup

Some clubs have changed their names over the course of their history. Where this has happened, the results are nonetheless included under the club's current name, unless there have been no matches since the name change. Some of the more significant name changes are as follows:

Arsenal (known as Royal Arsenal until 1893, then Woolwich Arsenal until 1914)

Birmingham (known as Small Heath until 1905)

Gateshead (known as South Shields until 1930)

Leyton Orient (known as Clapton Orient until 1946, and Orient between 1967 and 1987)

Manchester City (known as Ardwick until 1894)

Manchester United (known as Newton Heath until 1902)

Furthermore, some clubs have merged, notably in Burton, Rotherham and Walsall, though these are explained under the relevant entries where applicable.

Notes on cups

FA Cup ties have always been straight knockout affairs, except in 1945-46, when all ties up to and including the quarter-finals were played over two legs. Between 1970 and 1974, the losing semi-finalists participated in third place play-offs. Penalty shoot-outs were introduced in 1991 to replace multiple replays.

League cup ties have been decided over one leg, with the following exceptions (played over two legs):
First round ties (1975-76 to 2000-01)
Second round ties (1979-80 to 2000-01)
Semi-finals (every season)

To give you some idea of exactly what stage of the competition each FA Cup tie was played, the following is a list of each season's round of 16 (ie. the round immediately preceding the quarter-finals):

1873-74 to 1875-76	Round 2
1876-77 to 1878-79	Round 3
1879-80 to 1883-84	Round 4
1884-85 to 1887-88	Round 5
1889-90 to 1904-05	Round 2
1905-06 to 1924-25	Round 3
1925-26 to present	Round 5

In the league cup, Round 4 has been the round of 16 every season.

An asterisk after a cup result denotes extra-time was played.

Two final points

The letters appearing after some final league positions denote the following:
P   club was promoted
R   club was relegated
F   club failed to retain league membership for the following season

In the lists entitled 'Played for both clubs', an entry reading, for example, Liverpool 1980-83 would indicate that the player first appeared in a league match for Liverpool in the 1980-81 season, and last appeared in the 1982-83 season. Only league matches are taken into consideration on these lists.

v. Accrington

Season	League	Date	Result	Home Wed'day	Accrington	Date	Result	Away Wed'day	Accrington	Final Positions Wed'day	Accrington
1892-93	Division 1	10 September	Won	5	2	24 September	Lost	2	4	12th	15thF

FA Cup

										Division	
1889-90	Round 2	1 February	Won	2	1					Non L Div 1	

Summary	P	W	D	L	F	A
Wednesday's home league record:	1	1	0	0	5	2
Wednesday's away league record:	1	0	0	1	2	4
Wednesday's cup record:	1	1	0	0	2	1
TOTAL:	3	2	0	1	9	7

Wednesday's top scorers vs Accrington
Bob Brown, Harry Davis, Sandy Rowan 2

v. Aldershot

		Home					Away		Final Positions	
Season	League	Date	Result	Wed'day	Aldershot	Date	Result	Wed'day	Aldershot	Wed'day	Aldershot
1975-76	Division 3	21 February	Won	3	1	15 November	Drew	1	1	20th	21stR

League Cup   *Division*

										Division	
1989-90	Round 2	20 September	Drew	0	0	3 October	Won	8	0	Div 1	Div 4

Summary	P	W	D	L	F	A
Wednesday's home league record:	1	1	0	0	3	1
Wednesday's away league record:	1	0	1	0	1	1
Wednesday's cup record:	2	1	1	0	8	0
TOTAL:	4	2	2	0	12	2

Wednesday's top scorers vs Aldershot
Steve Whitton 4
Dalian Atkinson 3

Wednesday hat-tricks vs Aldershot
3 Oct 1989 Steve Whitton (4) (cup)
3 Oct 1989 Dalian Atkinson (cup)

Played for both clubs

Bill Gowdy	Wednesday 1931-32	Aldershot 1938-39
Tom McAnearney	Wednesday 1952-65	Aldershot 1965-69
Bobby Brown	Wednesday 1974-76	Aldershot 1975-76
Richard Walden	Aldershot 1964-76	Wednesday 1975-78
Andy McCulloch	Wednesday 1979-83	Aldershot 1984-85

Tom McAnearney, who spent 14 years at Hillsborough then, later, four more at Aldershot, before returning to the Owls in October 1968 as coach.

v. Arsenal

Season	League	Date	Result	Home Wed'day	Arsenal	Date	Result	Away Wed'day	Arsenal	Final Positions Wed'day	Arsenal
1899-00	Division 2	17 March	Won	3	1	11 November	Won	2	1	1stP	8th
1904-05	Division 1	29 October	Lost	0	3	25 February	Lost	0	3	9th	10th
1905-06	Division 1	24 March	Won	4	2	18 November	Won	2	0	3rd	12th
1906-07	Division 1	1 January	Drew	1	1	29 March	Lost	0	1	13th	7th
1907-08	Division 1	31 December	Won	6	0	20 April	Drew	1	1	5th	14th=
1908-09	Division 1	28 December	Won	6	2	12 April	Lost	0	2	5th	6th
1909-10	Division 1	13 November	Drew	1	1	26 March	Won	1	0	11th	18th
1910-11	Division 1	18 March	Drew	0	0	12 November	Lost	0	1	6th	10th
1911-12	Division 1	6 April	Won	3	0	2 December	Won	2	0	5th	10th
1912-13	Division 1	23 November	Won	2	0	29 March	Won	5	2	3rd	20thR
1919-20	Division 1	27 December	Lost	1	2	20 December	Lost	1	3	22ndR	10th
1926-27	Division 1	12 March	Won	4	2	23 October	Lost	2	6	16th	11th
1927-28	Division 1	22 October	Drew	1	1	2 May	Drew	1	1	14th	10th
1928-29	Division 1	25 August	Won	3	2	29 December	Drew	2	2	1st	9th
1929-30	Division 1	7 September	Lost	0	2	4 January	Won	3	2	1st	14th
1930-31	Division 1	15 November	Lost	1	2	21 March	Lost	0	2	3rd	1st
1931-32	Division 1	5 December	Lost	1	3	16 April	Lost	1	3	3rd	2nd
1932-33	Division 1	2 January	Won	3	2	14 April	Lost	2	4	3rd	1st
1933-34	Division 1	2 September	Lost	1	2	6 January	Drew	1	1	11th	1st
1934-35	Division 1	22 September	Drew	0	0	2 February	Lost	1	4	3rd	1st
1935-36	Division 1	18 January	Won	3	2	14 September	Drew	2	2	20th	6th
1936-37	Division 1	13 February	Drew	0	0	10 October	Drew	1	1	22ndR	3rd
1950-51	Division 1	30 December	Lost	0	2	2 September	Lost	0	3	21stR	5th
1952-53	Division 1	2 March	Lost	1	4	11 October	Drew	2	2	18th	1st
1953-54	Division 1	20 March	Won	2	1	31 October	Lost	1	4	19th	12th
1954-55	Division 1	9 October	Lost	1	2	26 February	Lost	2	3	22ndR	9th
1956-57	Division 1	22 September	Lost	2	4	2 February	Lost	3	6	14th	5th
1957-58	Division 1	23 November	Won	2	0	22 March	Lost	0	1	22ndR	12th
1959-60	Division 1	19 December	Won	5	1	22 August	Won	1	0	5th	13th
1960-61	Division 1	23 December	Drew	1	1	26 December	Drew	1	1	2nd	11th
1961-62	Division 1	20 September	Drew	1	1	14 November	Lost	0	1	6th	10th
1962-63	Division 1	18 May	Lost	2	3	8 September	Won	2	1	6th	7th
1963-64	Division 1	30 March	Lost	0	4	24 March	Drew	1	1	6th	8th
1964-65	Division 1	2 September	Won	2	1	25 August	Drew	1	1	8th	13th
1965-66	Division 1	27 December	Won	4	0	28 December	Lost	2	5	17th	14th
1966-67	Division 1	13 May	Drew	1	1	6 September	Drew	1	1	11th	7th
1967-68	Division 1	4 May	Lost	1	2	30 April	Lost	2	3	19th	9th
1968-69	Division 1	1 March	Lost	0	5	11 January	Lost	0	2	15th	4th
1969-70	Division 1	20 December	Drew	1	1	6 September	Drew	0	0	22ndR	12th
1984-85	Division 1	25 November	Won	2	1	27 April	Lost	0	1	8th	7th
1985-86	Division 1	16 April	Won	2	0	14 September	Lost	0	1	5th	7th
1986-87	Division 1	14 February	Drew	1	1	2 September	Lost	0	2	13th	4th
1987-88	Division 1	30 April	Drew	3	3	5 December	Lost	1	3	11th	6th
1988-89	Division 1	24 September	Won	2	1	21 January	Drew	1	1	15th	1st

Season	League	Date	Result	Home Wed'day	Home Arsenal	Date	Result	Away Wed'day	Away Arsenal	Final Wed'day	Final Arsenal
1989-90	Division 1	17 February	Won	1	0	9 September	Lost	0	5	18thR	4th
1991-92	Division 1	23 November	Drew	1	1	15 February	Lost	1	7	3rd	4th
1992-93	Premiership	6 May	Won	1	0	29 August	Lost	1	2	7th	10th
1993-94	Premiership	21 August	Lost	0	1	12 December	Lost	0	1	7th	4th
1994-95	Premiership	4 February	Won	3	1	6 November	Drew	0	0	13th	12th
1995-96	Premiership	8 April	Won	1	0	21 November	Lost	2	4	15th	5th
1996-97	Premiership	26 December	Drew	0	0	16 September	Lost	1	4	7th	3rd
1997-98	Premiership	22 November	Won	2	0	28 March	Lost	0	1	16th	1st
1998-99	Premiership	27 September	Won	1	0	9 March	Lost	0	3	12th	2nd
1999-00	Premiership	3 January	Drew	1	1	9 May	Drew	3	3	19thR	2nd

FA Cup

Season	Round	Date	Result	Home Wed'day	Home Arsenal	Date	Result	Away Wed'day	Away Arsenal	Division Wed'day	Division Arsenal
1893-94	Round 1					27 January	Won	2	1	Div 1	Div 2
1906-07	Semi-Final	23 March				St Andrew's, Birmingham	Won	3	1	Div 1	Div 1
1934-35	Q'ter final	2 March	Won	2	1					Div 1	Div 1
1949-50	Round 3					7 January	Lost	0	1	Div 2	Div 1
1962-63	Round 4					12 March	Lost	0	2	Div 1	Div 1
1978-79	Round 3	6 January	Drew	1	1	9 January	Drew*	1	1	Div 3	Div 1
		15 January				Filbert Street (2nd replay)	Drew*	2	2		
		17 January				Filbert Street (3rd replay)	Drew*	3	3		
		22 January				Filbert Street (4th replay)	Lost	0	2		
1992-93	Final	15 May				Wembley	Drew*	1	1	Prem	Prem
		20 May				Wembley (replay)	Lost*	1	2		

League Cup

Season	Round	Date	Result	Home Wed'day	Home Arsenal	Date	Result	Away Wed'day	Away Arsenal	Division Wed'day	Division Arsenal
1982-83	Q'ter final					18 January	Lost	0	1	Div 2	Div 1
1987-88	Q'ter final	20 January	Lost	0	1					Div 1	Div 1
1992-93	Final	18 April				Wembley	Lost	1	2	Prem	Prem
1994-95	Round 4					30 November	Lost	0	2	Prem	Prem
1995-96	Round 4					29 November	Lost	1	2	Prem	Prem

Summary

	P	W	D	L	F	A
Wednesday's home league record:	54	24	15	15	91	73
Wednesday's away league record:	54	8	15	31	59	115
Wednesday's cup record:	17	3	5	9	18	26
TOTAL:	**125**	**35**	**35**	**55**	**168**	**214**

Wednesday's top scorers vs Arsenal
Andrew Wilson 11
Mark Hooper 9
David Hirst, Albert Quixall 5
Jack Ball, Frank Bradshaw, Harry Chapman, John Hickton, David McLean, Ellis Rimmer, Jimmy Stewart 4

Wednesday hat-tricks vs Arsenal
24 Mar 1906 Jimmy Stewart
31 Dec 1907 Frank Bradshaw
28 Dec 1908 Andrew Wilson
12 Mar 1927 Jimmy Trotter
27 Dec 1965 John Hickton

FACT FILE

- Arsenal and Sheffield Wednesday are the only teams ever to meet each other in both domestic cup finals in the same season and, unfortunately, Arsenal won them both. Andy Linighan scored the winner in the FA Cup final – in the last minute of extra-time in the replay. It is the closest the FA Cup Final has ever got to a penalty shoot-out.
- Wednesday have lost once in their last 16 league matches at home in the series.
- Arsenal have not lost in their last 27 home games, since Wednesday last won there in 1962.
- Wednesday won the first three cup ties between the sides, but Arsenal have won the last nine. They needed four replays against third division Wednesday in 1979. This was the last time that four replays were needed in any tie in the FA Cup competition proper.

Played for both clubs

Bill Gooing	Wednesday 1895-96	Arsenal 1901-05	
James Maxwell	Wednesday 1906-08	Arsenal 1908-09	
Frank Bradshaw	Wednesday 1905-10	Arsenal 1914-23	
George Drury	Wednesday 1936-38	Arsenal 1937-47	
George Hunt	Arsenal 1937-38	Wednesday 1946-48	
Brian Hornsby	Arsenal 1972-76	Wednesday 1977-82	
Brian Marwood	Wednesday 1984-88	Arsenal 1987-90	
Lee Chapman	Arsenal 1982-84	Wednesday 1984-88	
Siggi Jonsson	Wednesday 1984-89	Arsenal 1989-91	
Wilf Rostron	Arsenal 1974-77	Wednesday 1988-89	
Viv Anderson	Arsenal 1984-87	Wednesday 1990-93	

v. Aston Villa

Season	League	Home				Away				Final Positions	
		Date	Result	Wed'day	Villa	Date	Result	Wed'day	Villa	Wed'day	Villa
1892-93	Division 1	3 December	Won	5	3	7 January	Lost	1	5	12th	4th
1893-94	Division 1	6 January	Drew	2	2	9 December	Lost	0	3	12th	1st
1894-95	Division 1	3 November	Won	1	0	3 December	Lost	1	3	8th	3rd
1895-96	Division 1	18 January	Lost	1	3	14 March	Lost	1	2	7th	1st
1896-97	Division 1	14 November	Lost	1	3	21 November	Lost	0	4	6th	1st
1897-98	Division 1	27 September	Won	3	0	1 September	Lost	2	5	5th	6th
1898-99	Division 1	13 March	Won	4	1	25 March	Lost	1	3	18thR	1st
1900-01	Division 1	3 November	Won	3	2	9 March	Lost	1	2	8th	15th
1901-02	Division 1	22 February	Won	1	0	26 October	Lost	1	4	9th	8th
1902-03	Division 1	1 January	Won	4	0	26 December	Lost	0	1	1st	2nd
1903-04	Division 1	23 April	Won	4	2	26 December	Lost	1	2	1st	5th
1904-05	Division 1	24 September	Won	3	2	21 January	Won	2	0	9th	4th
1905-06	Division 1	10 February	Drew	2	2	7 October	Lost	0	3	3rd	8th
1906-07	Division 1	6 October	Won	2	1	9 February	Lost	1	8	13th	5th
1907-08	Division 1	19 October	Lost	2	3	15 February	Lost	0	5	5th	2nd
1908-09	Division 1	2 January	Won	4	2	5 September	Drew	1	1	5th	7th
1909-10	Division 1	30 October	Won	3	2	12 March	Lost	0	5	11th	1st
1910-11	Division 1	4 March	Won	1	0	29 October	Lost	1	2	6th	2nd
1911-12	Division 1	24 February	Won	3	0	21 October	Won	3	2	5th	6th
1912-13	Division 1	8 February	Drew	1	1	5 October	Lost	0	10	3rd	2nd
1913-14	Division 1	14 February	Lost	2	3	11 October	Lost	0	2	18th	2nd
1914-15	Division 1	12 September	Won	5	2	16 January	Drew	0	0	7th	14th
1919-20	Division 1	29 April	Lost	0	1	17 April	Lost	1	3	22ndR	9th
1926-27	Division 1	9 April	Won	3	1	20 November	Drew	2	2	16th	10th
1927-28	Division 1	5 May	Won	2	0	24 December	Lost	4	5	14th	8th
1928-29	Division 1	22 December	Won	4	1	4 May	Lost	1	4	1st	3rd
1929-30	Division 1	18 January	Won	3	0	14 September	Won	3	1	1st	4th
1930-31	Division 1	2 May	Won	3	0	1 September	Lost	0	2	3rd	2nd
1931-32	Division 1	3 October	Won	1	0	24 February	Lost	1	3	3rd	5th
1932-33	Division 1	15 April	Lost	0	2	3 December	Won	6	3	3rd	2nd
1933-34	Division 1	28 August	Lost	1	2	4 September	Lost	0	1	11th	13th
1934-35	Division 1	23 March	Won	2	1	10 November	Lost	0	4	3rd	13th
1935-36	Division 1	28 December	Won	5	2	31 August	Won	2	1	20th	21stR
1937-38	Division 2	18 September	Lost	1	2	29 January	Lost	3	4	17th	1stP
1950-51	Division 1	11 November	Won	3	2	31 March	Lost	1	2	21stR	15th
1952-53	Division 1	29 November	Drew	2	2	18 April	Lost	3	4	18th	11th
1953-54	Division 1	7 September	Won	3	1	31 March	Lost	1	2	19th	13th
1954-55	Division 1	28 August	Won	6	3	1 January	Drew	0	0	22ndR	6th
1956-57	Division 1	1 December	Won	2	1	13 April	Lost	0	5	14th	10th
1957-58	Division 1	7 December	Lost	2	5	19 April	Lost	0	2	22ndR	14th
1960-61	Division 1	26 November	Lost	1	2	29 April	Lost	1	4	2nd	9th
1961-62	Division 1	3 March	Won	3	0	16 October	Lost	0	1	6th	7th
1962-63	Division 1	10 November	Drew	0	0	13 April	Won	2	0	6th	15th
1963-64	Division 1	26 October	Won	1	0	7 March	Drew	2	2	6th	19th

			Home				Away			Final Positions	
Season	League	Date	Result	Wed'day	Villa	Date	Result	Wed'day	Villa	Wed'day	Villa
1964-65	Division 1	15 March	Won	3	1	19 September	Lost	0	2	8th	16th
1965-66	Division 1	27 April	Won	2	0	30 October	Lost	0	2	17th	16th
1966-67	Division 1	31 August	Won	2	0	22 August	Won	1	0	11th	21stR
1972-73	Division 2	23 December	Drew	2	2	24 April	Lost	1	2	10th	3rd
1973-74	Division 2	1 April	Lost	2	4	3 November	Lost	0	1	19th	14th
1974-75	Division 2	23 April	Lost	0	4	26 October	Lost	1	3	22ndR	2ndP
1984-85	Division 1	26 December	Drew	1	1	6 April	Lost	0	3	8th	10th
1985-86	Division 1	19 April	Won	2	0	16 November	Drew	1	1	5th	16th
1986-87	Division 1	6 December	Won	2	1	4 May	Won	2	1	13th	22ndR
1988-89	Division 1	1 October	Won	1	0	4 February	Lost	0	2	15th	17th
1989-90	Division 1	16 September	Won	1	0	10 February	Lost	0	1	18thR	2nd
1991-92	Division 1	17 August	Lost	2	3	18 January	Won	1	0	3rd	7th
1992-93	Premiership	5 December	Lost	1	2	20 March	Lost	0	2	7th	2nd
1993-94	Premiership	18 August	Drew	0	0	8 December	Drew	2	2	7th	10th
1994-95	Premiership	18 February	Lost	1	2	27 November	Drew	1	1	13th	18th
1995-96	Premiership	16 March	Won	2	0	6 March	Lost	2	3	15th	4th
1996-97	Premiership	17 August	Won	2	1	29 January	Won	1	0	7th	5th
1997-98	Premiership	2 May	Lost	1	3	27 September	Drew	2	2	16th	7th
1998-99	Premiership	29 August	Lost	0	1	28 December	Lost	1	2	12th	6th
1999-00	Premiership	5 April	Lost	0	1	18 December	Lost	1	2	19thR	6th

FA Cup

										Division	
1893-94	Q'ter final	24 February	Won*	3	2					Div 1	Div 1
1913-14	Q'ter final	7 March	Lost	0	1					Div 1	Div 1

League Cup

						Date	Result	Wed'day	Villa	Division	
1978-79	Round 2					30 August	Lost	0	1	Div 3	Div 1
1987-88	Round 4					18 November	Won	2	1	Div 1	Div 2
2001-02	Round 4					28 November	Won	1	0	Div 1	Prem

Summary	P	W	D	L	F	A
Wednesday's home league record:	64	38	8	18	132	88
Wednesday's away league record:	64	10	9	45	67	155
Wednesday's cup record:	5	3	0	2	6	5
TOTAL:	**133**	**51**	**17**	**65**	**205**	**252**

Wednesday's top scorers vs Villa

Andrew Wilson 14
Fred Spiksley 11
Harry Davis, Mark Hooper 8
Harry Chapman 6
Jack Allen, Harry Burgess, David Hirst,
David McLean, Albert Quixall, Ronnie Starling 4

Wednesday hat-tricks vs Villa

12 Sep 1914 David McLean

FACT FILE

- In October 1912, Villa condemned Wednesday to their biggest-ever league defeat. It is the only time Wednesday have conceded double figures in a league match.
- Wednesday lost their first 11 away matches against Villa.
- Villa have won their last five league matches against Wednesday.
- From 1897 to 1904, Wednesday won seven home games in a row in the series.
- From 1926 to 1931, they came within one win of equalling this achievement.
- Wednesday's win in April 1904 took them top of the table. When Manchester City lost to Everton two days later, Wednesday were champions for the second year in a row.
- In the 1898-99 season, English league history was created when, for the first and only time, a match started and ended on different days. On 26 November the match was abandoned after 79 minutes with Wednesday leading 3-1. The final 11 minutes, during which Wednesday scored again, were played on 13 March.

Played for both clubs

Horace Henshall	Villa 1910-11	Wednesday 1922-23
George Stephenson	Villa 1921-28	Wednesday 1930-33
George Beeson	Wednesday 1929-34	Villa 1934-37
Joe Nibloe	Villa 1932-34	Wednesday 1934-38
Jackie Palethorpe	Wednesday 1934-36	Villa 1935-36
Ronnie Starling	Wednesday 1932-37	Villa 1936-47
Frank Moss	Wednesday 1936-38	Villa 1938-55
Jackie Sewell	Wednesday 1950-56	Villa 1955-60
Mike Pinner	Villa 1954-57	Wednesday 1957-59
Tommy Craig	Wednesday 1968-75	Villa 1977-79
Gary Shelton	Villa 1978-82	Wednesday 1981-87
Pat Heard	Villa 1979-83	Wednesday 1982-85
Andy Blair	Villa 1981-84/85-88	Wednesday 1984-86
Simon Stainrod	Wednesday 1984-86	Villa 1985-88
Garry Thompson	Wednesday 1985-86	Villa 1986-89
Dalian Atkinson	Wednesday 1989-90	Villa 1991-95
Franz Carr	Wednesday 1989-90	Villa 1994-96
Phil King	Wednesday 1989-94	Villa 1994-95
Ian Taylor	Wednesday 1994-95	Villa 1994-2003
Guy Whittingham	Villa 1993-95	Wednesday 1994-99
Benito Carbone	Wednesday 1996-2000	Villa 1999-2000
Earl Barrett	Villa 1991-95	Wednesday 1997-99
Gilles De Bilde	Wednesday 1999-2001	Villa 2000-01
Simon Grayson	Villa 1997-99	Wednesday 2000-01
Tommy Johnson	Villa 1994-97	Wednesday 2001-02

v. Barnsley

		Home				Away				Final Positions	
Season	League	Date	Result	Wed'day	Barnsley	Date	Result	Wed'day	Barnsley	Wed'day	Barnsley
1899-00	Division 2	27 February	Won	5	1	24 March	Lost	0	1	1stP	16th
1920-21	Division 2	4 September	Drew	0	0	28 August	Drew	0	0	10th	16th
1921-22	Division 2	27 August	Lost	2	3	3 September	Lost	0	2	10th	3rd
1922-23	Division 2	23 December	Lost	2	3	16 December	Won	4	2	8th	9th
1923-24	Division 2	10 November	Won	1	0	3 November	Drew	0	0	8th	11th
1924-25	Division 2	28 March	Won	1	0	22 November	Lost	0	3	14th	15th
1925-26	Division 2	31 October	Won	3	0	13 March	Drew	1	1	1stP	18th
1937-38	Division 2	19 March	Lost	0	1	6 November	Lost	1	4	17th	21stR
1939-40	Division 2	28 August	Won	3	1						
1946-47	Division 2	2 September	Lost	2	4	9 September	Lost	1	4	20th	10th
1947-48	Division 2	6 September	Won	5	2	17 January	Lost	1	3	4th	12th
1948-49	Division 2	5 March	Drew	1	1	9 October	Lost	0	4	8th	9th
1949-50	Division 2	8 April	Won	2	0	3 December	Won	4	3	2ndP	13th
1951-52	Division 2	6 October	Won	2	1	16 February	Lost	4	5	1stP	20th
1955-56	Division 2	21 March	Won	3	0	5 November	Won	3	0	1stP	18th
1958-59	Division 2	25 April	Won	5	0	6 December	Won	1	0	1stP	22ndR
1979-80	Division 3	3 November	Lost	0	2	18 August	Won	3	0	3rdP	11th
1981-82	Division 2	24 November	Drew	2	2	22 September	Lost	0	1	4th	6th
1982-83	Division 2	4 April	Lost	0	1	27 December	Drew	0	0	6th	10th
1983-84	Division 2	5 November	Won	2	0	3 March	Won	1	0	2ndP	14th
1990-91	Division 2	27 April	Won	3	1	23 October	Drew	1	1	3rdP	8th
1997-98	Premiership	8 December	Won	2	1	11 April	Lost	1	2	16th	19thR
2000-01	Division 1	21 April	Won	2	1	18 November	Lost	0	1	17th	16th
2001-02	Division 1	24 October	Won	3	1	2 December	Lost	0	3	20th	23rdR
2003-04	Division 2	13 March	Won	2	1	13 December	Drew	1	1	16th	12th

FA Cup

										Division	
1922-23	Round 2	3 February	Won	2	1					Div 2	Div 2
1930-31	Round 4					24 January	Lost	1	2	Div 1	Div 2
1983-84	Round 3	7 January	Won	1	0					Div 2	Div 2

League Cup

										Division	
1982-83	Round 4	30 November	Won	1	0					Div 2	Div 2
1987-88	Round 3					27 October	Won	2	1	Div 1	Div 2

Summary	P	W	D	L	F	A
Wednesday's home league record:	25	16	3	6	53	27
Wednesday's away league record:	24	6	6	12	27	41
Wednesday's cup record:	5	4	0	1	7	4
TOTAL:	54	26	9	19	87	72

Wednesday's top scorers vs Barnsley
Redfern Froggatt 8
Roy Shiner 7
Jimmy Dailey 5
Andy Smailes 4

Wednesday hat-tricks vs Barnsley
27 Feb 1900 Jocky Wright
6 Sep 1947 Jimmy Dailey

FACT FILE

- Wednesday have won their last seven home games against their near neighbours.
- Had the 1923 FA Cup tie been played under current rules, Wednesday might not have won. With the score at 0-0, Barnsley scored direct from a corner, but this was against the rules of football at the time.

Played for both clubs

Harry Davis	Barnsley 1898-1900	Wednesday 1899-1907
William Simmons	Wednesday 1899-1900	Barnsley 1899-1900
Jack Beech	Wednesday 1896-1904	Barnsley 1904-06
Joe Ryalls	Wednesday 1902-04	Barnsley 1905-06
Ollie Tummon	Wednesday 1905-10	Barnsley 1920-21
Jimmy Spoors	Wednesday 1908-20	Barnsley 1920-22
Joe Harron	Wednesday 1922-25	Barnsley 1928-30
Brough Fletcher	Barnsley 1914-30	Wednesday 1925-26
Jack Breedon	Barnsley 1928-31	Wednesday 1930-34
Doug Hunt	Barnsley 1936-38	Wednesday 1937-40
John Logan	Barnsley 1936-47	Wednesday 1946-47
Donald Watson	Wednesday 1954-57	Barnsley 1961-62
Graham Pugh	Wednesday 1965-72	Barnsley 1976-80
Peter Springett	Wednesday 1967-75	Barnsley 1975-80
Mick Prendergast	Wednesday 1968-78	Barnsley 1977-79
Brian Joicey	Wednesday 1971-76	Barnsley 1976-79
Peter Fox	Wednesday 1972-77	Barnsley 1977-78
Rodger Wylde	Wednesday 1972-80	Barnsley 1984-88
Derek Bell	Wednesday 1975-76	Barnsley 1978-80
John Collins	Wednesday 1976-77	Barnsley 1976-80
Jimmy Hinch	Wednesday 1977-78	Barnsley 1977-78
Gordon Owen	Wednesday 1977-83	Barnsley 1984-86
Mark Smith	Wednesday 1977-87	Barnsley 1989-93
Mike Pickering	Barnsley 1974-77/83-84	Wednesday 1978-83
Peter Shirtliff	Wednesday 1978-86/89-93	Barnsley 1995-98
John Pearson	Wednesday 1980-85	Barnsley 1991-93
Tony Cunningham	Barnsley 1982-84	Wednesday 1983-84
Andy Blair	Wednesday 1984-86	Barnsley 1987-88
Siggi Jonsson	Wednesday 1984-89	Barnsley 1985-86
Glynn Snodin	Wednesday 1985-87	Barnsley 1993-95
Colin Walker	Barnsley 1980-83	Wednesday 1986-87
Larry May	Barnsley 1983-87	Wednesday 1986-88
Carl Bradshaw	Barnsley 1986-87	Wednesday 1986-89
David Hirst	Barnsley 1985-86	Wednesday 1986-98
Viv Anderson	Wednesday 1990-93	Barnsley 1993-94
Danny Wilson	Wednesday 1990-93	Barnsley 1993-95
Stuart Ripley	Wednesday 2000-01	Barnsley 2000-01
Ian Hendon	Barnsley 1992-93	Wednesday 2000-03
Paul Warhurst	Wednesday 1990-93	Barnsley 2003-04
Marlon Beresford	Wednesday 2000-01	Barnsley 2003-04
Garry Monk	Wednesday 2002-03	Barnsley 2003-04

v. Barrow

League Cup	Date	Result	Home Wed'day	Barrow						Division Wed'day	Barrow
1967-68 Round 3	11 October	Won	3	1						Div 1	Div 3

Summary	P	W	D	L	F	A
Wednesday's cup record:	1	1	0	0	3	1
TOTAL:	**1**	**1**	**0**	**0**	**3**	**1**

Wednesday's top scorers vs Barrow
John Fantham 2

Played for both clubs

Tom Brelsford	Wednesday 1919-24	Barrow 1924-25
Jimmy Short	Wednesday 1931-32	Barrow 1935-36
George Bratley	Wednesday 1932-33	Barrow 1936-38
Gavin Malloch	Wednesday 1931-36	Barrow 1937-38
Colin Whitaker	Wednesday 1951-52	Barrow 1964-65
Ronnie Codd	Wednesday 1952-53	Barrow 1954-56
Donald Watson	Wednesday 1954-57	Barrow 1964-65
Don McEvoy	Wednesday 1954-58	Barrow 1960-62
Ron Staniforth	Wednesday 1955-59	Barrow 1959-61

v. Belper Town

FA Cup					Date	Result	Away Belper	Barrow	Division Belper	Barrow
1887-88 Round 1					15 October	Won	3	2		

Summary	P	W	D	L	F	A
Wednesday's cup record:	1	1	0	0	3	2
TOTAL:	1	1	0	0	3	2

FACT FILE

● This is Belper's only ever match in the FA Cup competition proper.

Wednesday's top scorers vs Belper

T.E. Cawley 2

v. Birmingham City

Season	League	Date (Home)	Result	Wed'day	Birm'ham	Date (Away)	Result	Wed'day	Birm'ham	Final Positions Wed'day	Final Positions Birm'ham
1894-95	Division 1	26 December	Won	2	0	25 March	Drew	0	0	8th	12th
1895-96	Division 1	4 April	Won	3	0	8 February	Drew	1	1	7th	15thR
1899-00	Division 2	21 October	Won	4	0	24 February	Lost	1	4	1stP	3rd
1901-02	Division 1	19 April	Lost	1	2	21 December	Drew	1	1	9th	17thR
1903-04	Division 1	27 February	Won	3	2	31 October	Drew	0	0	1st	11th
1904-05	Division 1	18 March	Won	3	1	19 November	Lost	1	2	9th	7th
1905-06	Division 1	9 December	Won	4	2	14 April	Lost	1	5	3rd	7th
1906-07	Division 1	15 December	Lost	0	1	25 April	Drew	1	1	13th	9th
1907-08	Division 1	18 April	Lost	1	4	21 December	Lost	1	2	5th	20thR
1920-21	Division 2	23 October	Lost	1	2	30 October	Lost	0	4	10th	1stP
1926-27	Division 1	19 April	Drew	4	4	13 September	Drew	0	0	16th	17th
1927-28	Division 1	8 October	Lost	2	3	7 March	Lost	0	1	14th	11th
1928-29	Division 1	13 October	Won	3	0	23 February	Lost	1	4	1st	15th
1929-30	Division 1	28 April	Drew	1	1	26 October	Lost	0	1	1st	11th
1930-31	Division 1	13 December	Won	9	1	18 April	Lost	0	2	3rd	19th
1931-32	Division 1	7 November	Won	5	1	19 March	Won	2	1	3rd	9th
1932-33	Division 1	5 April	Drew	1	1	8 October	Lost	1	2	3rd	13th
1933-34	Division 1	2 January	Won	2	1	3 April	Lost	0	3	11th	20th
1934-35	Division 1	25 December	Won	2	1	26 December	Won	4	0	3rd	19th
1935-36	Division 1	19 October	Won	3	1	22 April	Lost	1	4	20th	12th
1936-37	Division 1	3 April	Lost	0	3	28 November	Drew	1	1	22ndR	11th
1946-47	Division 2	29 March	Won	1	0	23 November	Lost	1	3	20th	3rd
1947-48	Division 2	24 April	Drew	0	0	6 December	Lost	0	1	4th	1stP
1951-52	Division 2	3 September	Drew	1	1	12 September	Drew	0	0	1stP	3rd
1956-57	Division 1	29 April	Won	3	0	25 December	Lost	0	4	14th	12th=
1957-58	Division 1	28 September	Won	5	3	12 March	Lost	0	1	22ndR	13th
1959-60	Division 1	23 April	Lost	2	4	10 October	Drew	0	0	5th	19th

Trevor Francis had a full career at club and international level in between starting out at Birmingham as a 16-year-old scoring sensation and turning out for (as well as managing) the Owls 20 or more years later.

			Home				Away			Final Positions	
Season	League	Date	Result	Wed'day	Birm'ham	Date	Result	Wed'day	Birm'ham	Wed'day	Birm'ham
1960-61	Division 1	31 December	Won	2	0	27 August	Drew	1	1	2nd	19th
1961-62	Division 1	26 August	Won	5	1	23 December	Drew	1	1	6th	17th
1962-63	Division 1	15 September	Won	5	0	30 March	Drew	1	1	6th	20th
1963-64	Division 1	28 September	Won	2	1	8 February	Won	2	1	6th	20th
1964-65	Division 1	17 October	Won	5	2	27 February	Drew	0	0	8th	22ndR
1970-71	Division 2	13 February	Drew	3	3	12 October	Lost	0	1	15th	9th
1971-72	Division 2	29 April	Lost	1	2	11 December	Drew	0	0	14th	2ndP
1985-86	Division 1	8 March	Won	5	1	5 October	Won	2	0	5th	21stR
2000-01	Division 1	22 October	Won	1	0	24 March	Won	2	1	17th	5th
2001-02	Division 1	26 December	Lost	0	1	8 September	Lost	0	2	20th	5thP

FA Cup

										Division	
1891-92	Round 2	30 January	Won	2	0					Non L	Non L
1968-69	Round 4	25 January	Drew	2	2	28 January	Lost	1	2	Div 1	Div 2

League Cup

2000-01	Q'ter final					12 December	Lost	0	2	Div 1	Div 1

Summary	P	W	D	L	F	A
Wednesday's home league record:	37	22	6	9	95	50
Wednesday's away league record:	37	5	14	18	27	56
Wednesday's cup record:	4	1	1	2	5	6
TOTAL:	78	28	21	29	127	112

FACT FILE

- When the sides met in December 1930, Wednesday were striving for a third successive league title, and they annihilated the Midlanders 9-1. It is the only time Wednesday have scored nine in a league match, and they would have reached double figures but for a penalty save by Birmingham and England goalkeeper Harry Hibbs in the last few minutes.
- Wednesday failed to win in their first 15 away matches in the series.
- Wednesday were unbeaten in eight home games from 1928 to 1935.
- Wednesday were undefeated in 10 matches between 1960 and 1965.
- Between 1936 and 1963, Wednesday failed to win in 11 away games.

Wednesday's top scorers vs Birmingham

John Fantham 10

Andrew Wilson 7

Keith Ellis, Ellis Rimmer 6

Jack Ball, Mark Hooper 5

Wednesday hat-tricks vs Birmingham

13 Oct 1928 Jack Allen

13 Dec 1930 Mark Hooper

26 Dec 1934 Jackie Palethorpe

29 Apr 1957 Keith Ellis

26 Aug 1961 John Fantham

8 Mar 1986 Carl Shutt

Played for both clubs

Frank Foxall	Wednesday 1906-10	Birmingham 1910-11
Laurie Burkinshaw	Wednesday 1911-14	Birmingham 1919-22
Billy Walker	Birmingham 1913-20	Wednesday 1923-24
Bill Harvey	Wednesday 1919-20	Birmingham 1921-25
Jack Whitehouse	Birmingham 1919-23	Wednesday 1928-30
Bob Gregg	Wednesday 1928-31	Birmingham 1930-34
Tom Grosvenor	Birmingham 1931-36	Wednesday 1935-37
Walter Aveyard	Wednesday 1946-47	Birmingham 1947-48
Jimmy Dailey	Wednesday 1946-49	Birmingham 1948-52
Johnny Jordan	Birmingham 1948-50	Wednesday 1950-51
Steve Bryant	Birmingham 1974-76	Wednesday 1976-77
Bobby Hope	Birmingham 1972-76	Wednesday 1976-78
Trevor Matthewson	Wednesday 1980-83	Birmingham 1989-93
Paul Hart	Wednesday 1985-87	Birmingham 1986-87
Carl Shutt	Wednesday 1985-88	Birmingham 1993-94
Steve Whitton	Birmingham 1985-89	Wednesday 1988-91
Trevor Francis	Birmingham 1970-79	Wednesday 1989-94
John Sheridan	Wednesday 1989-97	Birmingham 1995-96
Paul Williams	Wednesday 1990-93	Birmingham 1994-95
Graham Hyde	Wednesday 1991-99	Birmingham 1998-2002
Peter Atherton	Wednesday 1994-2000	Birmingham 2000-01
Danny Sonner	Wednesday 1998-2000	Birmingham 2000-02
Barry Horne	Birmingham 1996-97	Wednesday 1999-2000
Terry Cooke	Birmingham 1996-97	Wednesday 2000-01/03-04
Ian Hendon	Birmingham 1994-95	Wednesday 2000-03
Jon McCarthy	Birmingham 1997-2002	Wednesday 2001-02
David Burrows	Birmingham 2000-02	Wednesday 2001-03
Allan Johnston	Birmingham 1999-2000	Wednesday 2002-03
Darryl Powell	Wednesday 2002-03	Birmingham 2002-03
Lee Bradbury	Birmingham 1998-99	Wednesday 2002-03
Mark Burchill	Birmingham 2000-01	Wednesday 2003-04

v. Blackburn Rovers

Season	League	Home Date	Result	Wed'day	Blackburn	Away Date	Result	Wed'day	Blackburn	Final Positions Wed'day	Blackburn
1892-93	Division 1	19 November	Lost	0	3	15 October	Won	2	0	12th	9th
1893-94	Division 1	30 September	Won	4	2	9 September	Lost	1	5	12th	4th
1894-95	Division 1	8 September	Won	4	1	29 September	Lost	1	3	8th	5th
1895-96	Division 1	11 January	Won	3	0	23 November	Lost	1	2	7th	8th
1896-97	Division 1	28 December	Won	6	0	19 September	Lost	0	4	6th	14th
1897-98	Division 1	13 November	Won	4	1	23 October	Drew	1	1	5th	15th
1898-99	Division 1	8 October	Lost	1	2	4 February	Lost	0	2	18thR	6th
1900-01	Division 1	16 February	Drew	1	1	13 October	Drew	2	2	8th	9th
1901-02	Division 1	22 March	Lost	0	1	23 November	Lost	0	2	9th	4th
1902-03	Division 1	14 March	Drew	0	0	15 November	Lost	1	2	1st	16th
1903-04	Division 1	23 January	Won	3	1	26 September	Drew	0	0	1st	15th
1904-05	Division 1	28 January	Lost	1	2	1 October	Won	1	0	9th	13th
1905-06	Division 1	25 November	Lost	0	1	31 March	Lost	0	1	3rd	9th
1906-07	Division 1	1 December	Won	3	1	6 April	Won	2	0	13th	12th
1907-08	Division 1	4 April	Won	2	0	7 December	Lost	0	2	5th	14th=
1908-09	Division 1	19 April	Lost	1	2	31 October	Drew	2	2	5th	4th
1909-10	Division 1	16 April	Won	2	1	4 December	Drew	0	0	11th	3rd
1910-11	Division 1	1 April	Won	1	0	26 November	Lost	1	6	6th	12th
1911-12	Division 1	8 April	Drew	1	1	25 December	Drew	0	0	5th	1st
1912-13	Division 1	2 September	Won	2	1	21 March	Won	1	0	3rd	6th
1913-14	Division 1	28 March	Won	3	1	22 November	Lost	2	3	18th	1st
1914-15	Division 1	24 October	Drew	1	1	27 February	Drew	1	1	7th	3rd
1919-20	Division 1	11 October	Drew	0	0	18 October	Lost	0	1	22ndR	20th
1926-27	Division 1	5 February	Lost	0	3	18 September	Drew	2	2	16th	18th
1927-28	Division 1	21 January	Won	4	1	10 September	Lost	1	3	14th	12th
1928-29	Division 1	5 January	Won	1	0	1 September	Lost	1	4	1st	7th
1929-30	Division 1	14 December	Won	4	0	19 April	Won	1	0	1st	6th
1930-31	Division 1	25 April	Lost	1	3	20 December	Lost	2	5	3rd	10th
1931-32	Division 1	2 January	Won	5	1	26 August	Won	6	1	3rd	16th
1932-33	Division 1	10 September	Drew	1	1	21 January	Drew	1	1	3rd	15th
1933-34	Division 1	3 February	Won	4	0	23 September	Lost	1	3	11th	8th
1934-35	Division 1	28 January	Drew	2	2	15 September	Lost	1	2	3rd	15th
1935-36	Division 1	11 April	Drew	0	0	7 December	Lost	2	3	20th	22ndR
1937-38	Division 2	19 April	Drew	1	1	18 April	Lost	0	1	17th	16th
1938-39	Division 2	8 September	Won	3	0	2 January	Won	4	2	3rd	1stP
1948-49	Division 2	13 November	Won	3	0	9 April	Lost	1	2	8th	14th
1949-50	Division 2	26 December	Won	2	0	27 December	Drew	0	0	2ndP	16th
1951-52	Division 2	20 October	Won	2	0	12 March	Drew	0	0	1stP	14th
1955-56	Division 2	27 December	Won	5	1	26 December	Drew	2	2	1stP	4th
1959-60	Division 1	16 January	Won	3	0	5 September	Lost	1	3	5th	17th
1960-61	Division 1	10 December	Won	5	4	1 April	Drew	1	1	2nd	8th
1961-62	Division 1	21 October	Won	1	0	26 April	Won	2	0	6th	16th
1962-63	Division 1	15 April	Won	4	0	12 April	Lost	0	3	6th	11th
1963-64	Division 1	28 March	Won	5	2	2 November	Drew	1	1	6th	7th

				Home					Away	Final Positions	
Season	League	Date	Result	Wed'day	Blackburn	Date	Result	Wed'day	Blackburn	Wed'day	Blackburn
1964-65	Division 1	22 August	Won	1	0	29 January	Won	1	0	8th	10th
1965-66	Division 1	4 December	Won	2	1	30 April	Won	2	1	17th	22ndR
1970-71	Division 2	29 August	Drew	1	1	3 April	Lost	2	3	15th	21stR
1979-80	Division 3	25 August	Lost	0	3	22 April	Won	2	1	3rdP	2ndP
1980-81	Division 2	7 October	Won	2	1	14 March	Lost	1	3	10th	4th
1981-82	Division 2	16 January	Drew	2	2	29 August	Won	1	0	4th	10th
1982-83	Division 2	15 February	Drew	0	0	2 October	Won	3	2	6th	11th
1983-84	Division 2	1 October	Won	4	2	4 February	Drew	0	0	2ndP	6th
1990-91	Division 2	10 April	Won	3	1	10 November	Lost	0	1	3rdP	19th
1992-93	Premiership	31 October	Drew	0	0	8 May	Lost	0	1	7th	4th
1993-94	Premiership	20 March	Lost	1	2	25 September	Drew	1	1	7th	2nd
1994-95	Premiership	2 November	Lost	0	1	12 February	Lost	1	3	13th	1st
1995-96	Premiership	23 August	Won	2	1	20 January	Lost	0	3	15th	7th
1996-97	Premiership	19 October	Drew	1	1	22 April	Lost	1	4	7th	13th
1997-98	Premiership	26 December	Drew	0	0	25 August	Lost	2	7	16th	6th
1998-99	Premiership	12 September	Won	3	0	20 February	Won	4	1	12th	19thR
2000-01	Division 1	28 August	Drew	1	1	13 January	Lost	0	2	17th	2ndP

FA Cup

										Division	
1880-81	Round 2	18 December	Won	4	0						
1881-82	Semi-Final	6 March				St John's, Huddersfield	Drew	0	0		
		15 March				Whalley Range, Manc'ter (rep)	Lost	1	5		
1889-90	Final	29 March				Kennington Oval	Lost	1	6	Non L	Div 1
1902-03	Round 1	7 February	Drew	0	0	12 February	Lost	0	1	Div 1	Div 1
1904-05	Round 1					4 February	Won	2	1	Div 1	Div 1
1959-60	Semi-Final	26 March				Maine Road	Lost	1	2	Div 1	Div 1
1965-66	Q'ter final					26 March	Won	2	1	Div 1	Div 1
1988-89	Round 4					28 January	Lost	1	2	Div 1	Div 2
1997-98	Round 4	26 January	Lost	0	3					Prem	Prem

League Cup

1981-82	Round 2	27 October	Lost	1	2	7 October	Drew	1	1	Div 2	Div 2
1992-93	Semi-Final	14 March	Won	2	1	10 February	Won	4	2	Prem	Prem
2001-02	Semi-Final	8 January	Lost	1	2	22 January	Lost	2	4	Div 1	Prem

Summary	P	W	D	L	F	A
Wednesday's home league record:	61	34	16	11	122	59
Wednesday's away league record:	61	14	16	31	70	111
Wednesday's cup record:	17	5	3	9	23	33
TOTAL:	**139**	**53**	**35**	**51**	**215**	**203**

FACT FILE

- Wednesday's first-ever FA Cup match was against Blackburn in 1880-81 (Wednesday were due to play Queen's Park from Glasgow in the first round, but the Scotsmen withdrew). A Gregory hat-trick helped them to a 4-0 win.
- Only once have Wednesday conceded six in an FA Cup match. Strangely, it happened in the final itself, against Blackburn in 1890.
- Between 1938 and 1965, Wednesday won 12 consecutive home games in the series. This was part of a run of 19 successive home games against Blackburn without defeat.
- Wednesday have won once in their last nine visits to Ewood Park.

Wednesday's top scorers vs Blackburn
John Fantham, Walter Millership 7
Fred Spiksley, Andrew Wilson 6
Redfern Froggatt, David McLean,
George Stephenson 5

Wednesday hat-tricks vs Blackburn
18 Dec 1880 R Gregory (cup)
28 Dec 1896 Bob Ferrier
29 Aug 1931 George Stephenson (4)
2 Jan 1932 Walter Millership
2 Jan 1939 Walter Millership

Played for both clubs

Tom Brandon	Blackburn 1889-91/93-1900	Wednesday 1892-93
Jack Darroch	Wednesday 1892-94	Blackburn 1901-02
Johnny McIntyre	Wednesday 1919-22	Blackburn 1921-28
Ted Harper	Blackburn 1923-28/33-35	Wednesday 1927-29
Charlie Luke	Wednesday 1935-38	Blackburn 1937-38
Eddie Quigley	Wednesday 1947-50	Blackburn 1951-56
Bobby Craig	Wednesday 1959-62	Blackburn 1961-63
Andy Burgin	Wednesday 1964-65	Blackburn 1974-76
Steve Downes	Wednesday 1969-72	Blackburn 1975-76
Ken Knighton	Blackburn 1969-71	Wednesday 1973-76
Neil Ramsbottom	Wednesday 1975-76	Blackburn 1978-79
Malcolm Darling	Blackburn 1965-70	Wednesday 1977-78
John Lowey	Wednesday 1978-80	Blackburn 1980-86
Paul Warhust	Wednesday 1990-93	Blackburn 1993-97
Stuart Ripley	Blackburn 1992-98	Wednesday 2000-01
Simon Grayson	Blackburn 1999-2000	Wednesday 2000-01
Steve Harkness	Blackburn 1999-2000	Wednesday 2000-01
Marlon Broomes	Blackburn 1997-2001	Wednesday 2001-02
Kevin Gallacher	Blackburn 1992-2000	Wednesday 2001-02

v. Blackpool

		Home				Away				Final Positions	
Season	League	Date	Result	Wed'day	Blackpool	Date	Result	Wed'day	Blackpool	Wed'day	Blackpool
1920-21	Division 2	7 February	Lost	0	1	5 February	Drew	1	1	10th	4th
1921-22	Division 2	26 November	Won	5	1	19 November	Won	2	0	10th	19th
1922-23	Division 2	6 January	Lost	2	3	30 December	Lost	0	3	8th	5th
1923-24	Division 2	6 October	Drew	2	2	13 October	Lost	0	1	8th	4th
1924-25	Division 2	25 December	Lost	2	6	26 December	Drew	2	2	14th	17th
1925-26	Division 2	1 May	Won	2	0	19 December	Lost	0	1	1stP	6th
1930-31	Division 1	29 November	Won	7	1	4 April	Won	4	0	3rd	20th
1931-32	Division 1	26 March	Won	3	0	14 November	Won	2	1	3rd	20th
1932-33	Division 1	27 August	Won	4	1	31 December	Won	4	3	3rd	22ndR
1950-51	Division 1	21 April	Won	3	1	2 December	Lost	2	3	21stR	3rd
1952-53	Division 1	14 March	Won	2	0	25 October	Won	1	0	18th	7th
1953-54	Division 1	6 March	Lost	1	2	17 October	Won	2	1	19th	6th
1954-55	Division 1	2 October	Won	2	1	19 February	Lost	1	2	22ndR	19th
1956-57	Division 1	20 October	Lost	1	2	2 March	Lost	1	3	14th	4th
1957-58	Division 1	12 October	Lost	0	3	22 February	Drew	2	2	22ndR	7th
1959-60	Division 1	12 September	Won	5	0	23 January	Won	2	0	5th	11th
1960-61	Division 1	15 October	Won	4	0	15 March	Won	1	0	2nd	20th
1961-62	Division 1	14 April	Won	3	2	25 November	Won	3	1	6th	13th
1962-63	Division 1	27 October	Drew	0	0	16 March	Won	3	2	6th	13th
1963-64	Division 1	7 December	Won	1	0	18 April	Drew	2	2	6th	18th
1964-65	Division 1	19 December	Won	4	1	29 August	Lost	0	1	8th	17th
1965-66	Division 1	4 April	Won	3	0	27 November	Lost	1	2	17th	13th
1966-67	Division 1	20 August	Won	3	0	17 December	Drew	1	1	11th	22ndR
1971-72	Division 2	8 January	Lost	1	2	28 August	Lost	0	1	14th	6th
1972-73	Division 2	28 February	Won	2	0	16 December	Won	2	1	10th	7th
1973-74	Division 2	1 September	Drew	0	0	1 January	Drew	0	0	19th	5th
1974-75	Division 2	8 February	Drew	0	0	2 November	Lost	1	3	22ndR	7th
1978-79	Division 3	17 May	Won	2	0	4 November	Won	1	0	14th	12th
1979-80	Division 3	22 March	Won	4	1	10 November	Drew	1	1	3rdP	18th
2003-04	Division 2	1 November	Lost	0	1	17 April	Lost	1	4	16th	14th

FA Cup

										Division	
1946-47	Round 3	11 January	Won	4	1					Div 2	Div 1
1952-53	Round 3	10 January	Lost	1	2					Div 1	Div 1

League Cup

1977-78	Round 2	5 September	Won	3	1	30 August	Drew	2	2	Div 3	Div 2
1988-89	Round 2	12 October	Won*	3	1	27 September	Lost	0	2	Div 1	Div 3

Summary

	P	W	D	L	F	A
Wednesday's home league record:	30	18	4	8	68	31
Wednesday's away league record:	30	12	7	11	43	42
Wednesday's cup record:	6	3	1	2	13	9
TOTAL:	**66**	**33**	**12**	**21**	**124**	**82**

FACT FILE

- Wednesday have lost two of their last 17 home games against Blackpool.
- Between 1926 and 1932, Wednesday won seven games in succession in the series.
- Between 1958 and 1964, Wednesday were unbeaten in 11 games home and away.

Wednesday's top scorers vs Blackpool
Harry Burgess, John Fantham 7
Mark Hooper 5
Alan Finney, Redfern Froggatt, Billy Griffin, Ellis Rimmer, Jackie Sewell 4

Wednesday hat-tricks vs Blackpool
29 Nov 1930 Mark Hooper
4 Apr 1931 Harry Burgess

Played for both clubs

Walter Miller	Wednesday 1907-08	Blackpool 1909-11
George Wilson	Blackpool 1911-20	Wednesday 1919-25
Jimmy Gill	Wednesday 1913-20	Blackpool 1925-26
Archie Ratcliffe	Blackpool 1920-21	Wednesday 1921-22
Johnny McIntyre	Wednesday 1919-22	Blackpool 1927-28
Matt Barrass	Blackpool 1919-25	Wednesday 1924-26
Sid Binks	Wednesday 1922-25	Blackpool 1925-27
George Ayres	Wednesday 1923-26	Blackpool 1926-28
Walter Rickett	Blackpool 1947-50	Wednesday 1949-53
Tony Coleman	Wednesday 1969-70	Blackpool 1970-71
Neil Ramsbottom	Blackpool 1970-72	Wednesday 1975-76
Gordon Simmonite	Wednesday 1976-77	Blackpool 1980-83
Gordon Owen	Wednesday 1977-83	Blackpool 1989-91
Ian Bailey	Wednesday 1982-83	Blackpool 1984-85
Tony Cunningham	Wednesday 1983-84	Blackpool 1987-89
Nigel Worthington	Wednesday 1983-94	Blackpool 1997-98
Paul Hart	Blackpool 1973-78	Wednesday 1985-87
Phil King	Wednesday 1989-94	Blackpool 1997-98
Julian Watts	Wednesday 1992-96	Blackpool 1998-99
Simon Grayson	Wednesday 2000-01	Blackpool 2002-04
Eric Nixon	Blackpool 1995-96	Wednesday 2003-04

v. Bolton Wanderers

		Home				Away			Final Positions	
Season	League	Date	Result	Wed'day	Bolton	Date	Result	Wed'day	Bolton	Wed'day	Bolton
1892-93	Division 1	5 November	Won	4	2	17 September	Lost	0	1	12th	5th
1893-94	Division 1	16 December	Won	2	1	25 December	Drew	1	1	12th	13th
1894-95	Division 1	22 September	Won	2	1	7 January	Drew	2	2	8th	10th
1895-96	Division 1	2 November	Drew	1	1	25 April	Lost	0	2	7th	4th
1896-97	Division 1	27 February	Drew	0	0	10 April	Lost	1	2	6th	8th
1897-98	Division 1	27 November	Won	3	0	9 October	Won	3	0	5th	11th
1898-99	Division 1	14 January	Won	1	0	17 September	Drew	0	0	18thR	17thR
1899-00	Division 2	16 September	Won	2	1	13 January	Lost	0	1	1stP	2ndP
1900-01	Division 1	8 September	Won	1	0	5 January	Drew	1	1	8th	10th
1901-02	Division 1	21 September	Won	5	1	18 January	Lost	1	3	9th	12th
1902-03	Division 1	3 January	Won	3	0	6 September	Won	2	0	1st	18thR
1905-06	Division 1	11 November	Lost	1	2	17 March	Lost	0	1	3rd	6th
1906-07	Division 1	16 March	Won	2	0	10 November	Drew	0	0	13th	6th
1907-08	Division 1	14 December	Won	5	2	11 April	Lost	1	2	5th	19thR
1909-10	Division 1	2 April	Drew	0	0	3 January	Won	2	0	11th	20thR
1911-12	Division 1	23 March	Lost	0	1	18 November	Lost	2	4	5th	4th
1912-13	Division 1	24 February	Drew	2	2	19 October	Lost	0	3	3rd	8th
1913-14	Division 1	29 December	Drew	1	1	1 September	Won	1	0	18th	6th
1914-15	Division 1	1 March	Won	7	0	17 October	Won	3	0	7th	17th
1919-20	Division 1	5 April	Lost	0	2	1 January	Lost	0	2	22ndR	6th
1926-27	Division 1	13 November	Won	2	1	2 April	Lost	2	3	16th	4th
1927-28	Division 1	17 September	Won	3	0	29 February	Lost	0	2	14th	7th
1928-29	Division 1	29 September	Drew	0	0	9 February	Drew	2	2	1st	14th
1929-30	Division 1	2 September	Won	1	0	25 September	Won	3	1	1st	15th
1930-31	Division 1	4 October	Won	1	0	7 February	Drew	2	2	3rd	14th
1931-32	Division 1	5 September	Won	7	1	16 January	Won	4	2	3rd	17th
1932-33	Division 1	29 April	Won	2	0	17 December	Lost	0	3	3rd	21stR
1935-36	Division 1	9 September	Drew	2	2	2 September	Drew	1	1	20th	13th
1936-37	Division 1	29 March	Won	2	0	26 March	Lost	0	1	22ndR	20th
1950-51	Division 1	25 November	Lost	3	4	14 April	Won	1	0	21stR	8th
1952-53	Division 1	11 April	Drew	1	1	22 November	Drew	1	1	18th	14th
1953-54	Division 1	16 September	Won	2	1	9 September	Lost	1	2	19th	5th
1954-55	Division 1	11 April	Won	3	2	8 April	Drew	2	2	22ndR	18th
1956-57	Division 1	3 November	Lost	1	2	16 March	Lost	2	3	14th	9th
1957-58	Division 1	15 March	Won	1	0	2 November	Lost	4	5	22ndR	15th
1959-60	Division 1	24 February	Won	1	0	3 October	Lost	0	1	5th	6th
1960-61	Division 1	29 October	Won	2	0	18 March	Won	1	0	2nd	18th
1961-62	Division 1	23 August	Won	4	2	30 August	Lost	3	4	6th	11th
1962-63	Division 1	18 August	Drew	1	1	6 May	Won	4	0	6th	18th
1963-64	Division 1	26 December	Won	3	0	28 December	Lost	0	3	6th	21stR
1970-71	Division 2	2 September	Drew	1	1	19 August	Lost	1	2	15th	22ndR
1973-74	Division 2	27 April	Won	1	0	16 February	Lost	2	4	19th	11th
1974-75	Division 2	26 December	Lost	0	2	14 September	Won	1	0	22ndR	10th
1980-81	Division 2	11 November	Won	2	0	19 August	Drew	0	0	10th	18th

Season	League	Date	Result	Home Wed'day	Bolton	Date	Result	Away Wed'day	Bolton	Final Positions Wed'day	Bolton
1981-82	Division 2	16 February	Lost	0	1	8 May	Lost	1	3	4th	19th
1982-83	Division 2	7 September	Won	3	1	9 April	Won	2	0	6th	22ndR
1995-96	Premiership	1 January	Won	4	2	23 March	Lost	1	2	15th	20thR
1997-98	Premiership	8 November	Won	5	0	14 March	Lost	2	3	16th	18thR
2000-01	Division 1	20 January	Lost	0	3	26 December	Lost	0	2	17th	3rdP

FA Cup

										Division	
1889-90	Semi-Final	8 March				Perry Barr, Birmingham	Won	2	1	Non L	Div 1
1891-92	Round 1	23 January	Won	4	1					Non L	Div 1
1893-94	Semi-Final	10 March				Fallowfield, Manchester	Lost	1	2	Div 1	Div 1
1895-96	Semi-Final	21 March				Goodison Park	Drew	1	1	Div 1	Div 1
		28 March				Town Ground, Nott'ham (rep)	Won	3	1		
1899-00	Round 1	27 January	Won	1	0					Div 2	Div 2
1953-54	Q'ter final	13 March	Drew	1	1	17 March	Won	2	0	Div 1	Div 1

League Cup

1972-73	Round 2	6 September	Won	2	0					Div 2	Div 3
1993-94	Round 2	6 October	Won	1	0	21 September	Drew	1	1	Prem	Div 1
1999-00	Round 4					30 November	Lost	0	1	Prem	Div 1

Summary

	P	W	D	L	F	A
Wednesday's home league record:	49	31	10	8	100	44
Wednesday's away league record:	40	12	11	26	63	79
Wednesday's cup record:	12	7	3	2	19	9
TOTAL:	**110**	**50**	**24**	**36**	**182**	**132**

John Sheridan, the stylish midfield player whose goal won the League Cup for the Owls in 1993. He spent two seasons at Bolton, during which time the Trotters took up residence at the Reebok Stadium.

FACT FILE

- Wednesday have enjoyed three five-goal victories in the Premiership. The most recent came against Bolton in 1997.
- The 1892 FA Cup tie was originally played a week earlier, with Wednesday winning 2-1. However, protests about the ground conditions led the FA to order a rematch.
- Wednesday were unbeaten in their first 13 home games in the series.
- Between 1926 and 1973, Wednesday lost twice in 24 home games against Bolton.

Wednesday's top scorers vs Bolton
Fred Spiksley 12
Harry Davis, Andrew Wilson 8
Harry Burgess, Keith Ellis, Jimmy Trotter 5

Wednesday hat-tricks vs Bolton
3 Jan 1903 Harry Davis
8 Nov 1997 Andy Booth

Played for both clubs

Bob Brown	Wednesday 1892-94	Bolton 1895-1902
Alec Gillies	Bolton 1895-96	Wednesday 1896-97
Laurie Bell	Wednesday 1895-97	Bolton 1899-1903
Jocky Wright	Bolton 1895-99/1902-04	Wednesday 1898-1902
Fred Kean	Wednesday 1920-29	Bolton 1928-31
Tom Grosvenor	Wednesday 1935-37	Bolton 1937-39
George Hunt	Bolton 1937-47	Wednesday 1946-48
Ronnie Codd	Bolton 1950-54	Wednesday 1952-53
Walter Bingley	Bolton 1949-55	Wednesday 1955-57
Malcolm Darling	Bolton 1973-74	Wednesday 1977-78
Ian Bailey	Bolton 1981-82/84-85	Wednesday 1982-83
Tony Cunningham	Wednesday 1983-84	Bolton 1990-91
David Reeves	Wednesday 1988-89	Bolton 1989-93
Franz Carr	Wednesday 1989-90	Bolton 1997-98
Jon Newsome	Wednesday 1989-91/95-2000	Bolton 1998-99
John Sheridan	Wednesday 1989-97	Bolton 1996-98
Paul Warhurst	Wednesday 1990-93	Bolton 1998-2003
Nigel Jemson	Bolton 1988-89	Wednesday 1991-94
Simon Coleman	Wednesday 1993-95	Bolton 1994-96
Matt Clarke	Wednesday 1996-98	Bolton 2000-01
Emerson Thome	Wednesday 1997-2000	Bolton 2003-04
Stuart Ripley	Bolton 1985-86	Wednesday 2000-01
Allan Johnston	Bolton 1999-2000	Wednesday 2002-03

v. AFC Bournemouth

				Home				Away		Final Positions	
Season	League	Date	Result	Wed'day	B'mouth	Date	Result	Wed'day	B'mouth	Wed'day	B'mouth
2003-04	Division 2	17 March	Lost	0	2	16 September	Lost	0	1	16th	9th

FA Cup										Division	
1927-28	Round 3	14 January	Won	3	0					Div 1	Div 3S
1931-32	Round 4	23 January	Won	7	0					Div 1	Div 3S

League Cup											
1969-70	Round 2	3 September	Drew	1	1	9 September	Lost	0	1	Div 1	Div 3
1973-74	Round 2	15 October	Drew	2	2	10 October	Drew	0	0	Div 2	Div 4
		29 October	Won	2	1	(replay)					

Summary	P	W	D	L	F	A
Wednesday's home league record:	1	0	0	1	0	2
Wednesday's away league record:	1	0	0	1	0	1
Wednesday's cup record:	7	3	3	1	15	5
TOTAL:	9	3	3	3	15	8

Wednesday's top scorers vs Bournemouth *Wednesday hat-tricks vs Bournemouth*

Walter Millership 4

Harry Burgess 3

23 Jan 1932 Walter Millership (4) (cup)

23 Jan 1932 Harry Burgess (3)

Played for both clubs

Frank Stringfellow	Wednesday 1908-11	Bournemouth 1925-29
Harry Kinghorn	Wednesday 1908-11	Bournemouth 1928-29
Jimmy Blair	Wednesday 1914-21	Bournemouth 1926-28
Joe Armstrong	Wednesday 1921-22	Bournemouth 1923-24
Ronnie Eyre	Wednesday 1923-24	Bournemouth 1924-33
Jack Whitehouse	Wednesday 1928-30	Bournemouth 1930-33
Dick Mellors	Wednesday 1926-31	Bournemouth 1934-38
Jack Surtees	Bournemouth 1933-34	Wednesday 1934-37
John Meredith	Wednesday 1960-61	Bournemouth 1969-71
Eddie Prudham	Wednesday 1970-75	Bournemouth 1980-81
Neil Ramsbottom	Wednesday 1975-76	Bournemouth 1983-84
Peter Feely	Bournemouth 1972-74	Wednesday 1975-77
Gordon Watson	Wednesday 1990-95	Bournemouth 1999-2000
Efan Ekoku	Bournemouth 1990-93	Wednesday 2000-02

v. Bradford City

Season	League	Date	Result	Home Wed'day	Bradf'd C	Date	Result	Away Wed'day	Bradf'd C	Final Positions Wed'day	Bradf'd C
1908-09	Division 1	20 March	Lost	0	2	14 November	Drew	0	0	5th	18th
1909-10	Division 1	28 March	Won	2	1	25 March	Lost	0	2	11th	7th
1910-11	Division 1	19 November	Lost	0	1	4 April	Lost	2	5	6th	5th
1911-12	Division 1	25 November	Won	4	2	30 March	Lost	1	5	5th	11th
1912-13	Division 1	5 April	Won	6	0	30 November	Drew	0	0	3rd	13th
1913-14	Division 1	15 November	Lost	1	3	21 March	Lost	1	3	18th	9th
1914-15	Division 1	12 December	Drew	3	3	17 April	Lost	0	1	7th	11th
1919-20	Division 1	26 December	Won	1	0	25 December	Drew	1	1	22ndR	15th
1922-23	Division 2	25 December	Drew	2	2	26 December	Drew	1	1	8th	15th
1923-24	Division 2	25 August	Drew	0	0	1 September	Lost	1	4	8th	18th
1924-25	Division 2	1 November	Drew	3	3	7 March	Lost	0	2	14th	16th
1925-26	Division 2	26 December	Won	5	1	25 December	Won	4	1	1stP	16th
1977-78	Division 3	21 March	Won	2	0	29 October	Lost	2	3	14th	22ndR
1999-00	Premiership	15 January	Won	2	0	14 August	Drew	1	1	19thR	17th
2001-02	Division 1	17 September	Drew	1	1	2 March	Won	2	0	20th	15th
2002-03	Division 1	19 October	Won	2	1	18 March	Drew	1	1	22ndR	19th

FA Cup

										Division	
1996-97	Round 5					16 February	Won	1	0	Prem	Div 1

League Cup

1994-95	Round 2	21 September	Won	2	1	4 October	Drew	1	1	Prem	Div 2

Summary	P	W	D	L	F	A
Wednesday's home league record:	16	8	5	3	34	20
Wednesday's away league record:	16	2	6	8	17	30
Wednesday's cup record:	3	2	1	0	4	2
TOTAL:	35	12	12	11	55	52

David Layne arrived at Hillsborough from Bradford City as a free-scoring centre-forward. He proved a big hit with Wednesday and it was a massive blow when 'Bronco' was banned from the game in 1964 following a betting scandal.

FACT FILE

- Wednesday are unbeaten in their last 11 home games against their Yorkshire rivals. Bradford's last away win was in 1913.
- Wednesday failed to win in their first 11 away games in the series.
- Wednesday are unbeaten in their last 10 games in the series.

Wednesday's top scorers vs Bradford

Andrew Wilson 6
David McLean, Jimmy Trotter 5
Andy Smailes 3

Played for both clubs

Billy Walker	Bradford 1911-13	Wednesday 1923-24
Colin McKay	Wednesday 1919-20	Bradford 1922-24
Ted Richardson	Wednesday 1924-25	Bradford 1926-28
Tommy Walker	Bradford 1924-26	Wednesday 1925-35
Ray Parker	Wednesday 1948-49	Bradford 1951-53
Jim McAnearney	Wednesday 1953-59	Bradford 1966-68
David Layne	Bradford 1960-62	Wednesday 1962-64
Allan Thompson	Wednesday 1970-76	Bradford 1979-82
Neil Ramsbottom	Wednesday 1975-76	Bradford 1980-83
Mike Pickering	Wednesday 1978-83	Bradford 1983-84
Ian Mellor	Wednesday 1979-82	Bradford 1982-84
Gavin Oliver	Wednesday 1980-85	Bradford 1985-95
Carl Shutt	Wednesday 1985-88	Bradford 1994-97
Wayne Jacobs	Wednesday 1987-88	Bradford 1994-2004
Greg Fee	Bradford 1982-84	Wednesday 1987-90
Gordon Watson	Wednesday 1990-95	Bradford 1996-99
Chris Waddle	Wednesday 1992-96	Bradford 1996-97
Ian Nolan	Wednesday 1994-2000	Bradford 2000-01
Peter Atherton	Wednesday 1994-2000	Bradford 2000-04
Dan Petrescu	Wednesday 1994-96	Bradford 2000-01
Benito Carbone	Wednesday 1996-2000	Bradford 2000-02
Matt Clarke	Wednesday 1996-98	Bradford 1999-2001
Simon Grayson	Wednesday 2000-01	Bradford 2001-02
Marlon Beresford	Wednesday 2000-01	Bradford 2003-04
Ashley Westwood	Bradford 1998-2000	Wednesday 2000-03
Dean Windass	Bradford 1998-2001/03-04	Wednesday 2001-02
Eric Nixon	Bradford 1986-87/96-97	Wednesday 2003-04

v. Bradford Park Avenue

				Home				Away		Final Positions	
Season	League	Date	Result	Wed'day	Bradf'd PA	Date	Result	Wed'day	Bradford PA	Wed'day	Bradf'd PA
1914-15	Division 1	26 September	Won	6	0	17 March	Drew	1	1	7th	9th
1919-20	Division 1	19 April	Lost	0	1	28 February	Lost	0	3	22ndR	11th
1921-22	Division 2	22 October	Won	2	1	29 October	Lost	1	2	10th	21stR
1937-38	Division 2	5 February	Won	1	0	25 September	Drew	1	1	17th	7th
1938-39	Division 2	4 February	Won	2	0	1 October	Lost	1	3	3rd	17th
1946-47	Division 2	5 October	Lost	1	2	12 March	Drew	1	1	20th	16th
1947-48	Division 2	7 February	Won	3	1	20 September	Lost	0	2	4th	14th
1948-49	Division 2	11 October	Won	2	1	7 May	Drew	1	1	8th	17th
1949-50	Division 2	24 December	Drew	1	1	27 August	Won	3	1	2ndP	22ndR

FA Cup

										Division	
1912-13	Round 3					22 February	Lost	1	2	Div 1	Div 2
1921-22	Round 1					7 January	Lost	0	1	Div 2	Div 2
1929-30	Round 5	15 February	Won	5	1					Div 1	Div 2
1951-52	Round 3					12 January	Lost	1	2	Div 2	Div 3N

Summary

	P	W	D	L	F	A
Wednesday's home league record:	9	6	1	2	18	7
Wednesday's away league record:	9	1	4	4	9	15
Wednesday's cup record:	4	1	0	3	7	6
TOTAL:	22	8	5	9	34	28

FACT FILE

- Wednesday failed to win in their first 10 away games in the series.
- Wednesday won seven out of 10 home games in the series.
- Bradford Park Avenue were elected out of the league in 1970, but still exist as a non-league side.

Wednesday's top scorers vs Park Avenue
David McLean, Eddie Quigley 3

Wednesday hat-tricks vs Park Avenue
26 Sep 1914 David McLean

Played for both clubs

Horace Nicholson	Wednesday 1913-14	Bradford PA 1920-23
David McLean	Wednesday 1910-20	Bradford PA 1919-22
Jack Burkinshaw	Wednesday 1913-20	Bradford PA 1920-21
Wally Dickinson	Bradford PA 1919-22	Wednesday 1922-23
Ernie Thompson	Wednesday 1921-22	Bradford PA 1922-24
Walter Millership	Bradford PA 1927-30	Wednesday 1929-39
Alf Strange	Wednesday 1926-35	Bradford PA 1935-36
Wilf Sharp	Wednesday 1934-36	Bradford PA 1936-37
Gerald Henry	Bradford PA 1947-50	Wednesday 1949-52
Colin Whitaker	Wednesday 1951-52	Bradford PA 1953-56
Albert Broadbent	Wednesday 1955-58	Bradford PA 1965-67

v. Brentford

Season	League	Date	Result	Home Wed'day	Brentf'd	Date	Result	Away Wed'day	Brentf'd	Final Positions Wed'day	Brentf;'d
1935-36	Division 1	8 February	Drew	3	3	5 October	Drew	2	2	20th	5th
1936-37	Division 1	28 December	Lost	0	2	25 October	Lost	1	2	22ndR	6th
1947-48	Division 2	12 April	Drew	1	1	25 October	Lost	0	1	4th	15th
1948-49	Division 2	28 August	Drew	0	0	1 January	Lost	1	2	8th	18th
1949-50	Division 2	18 February	Drew	3	3	1 October	Drew	1	1	2ndP	9th
1951-52	Division 2	14 April	Won	2	0	11 April	Won	3	2	1stP	10th
1978-79	Division 3	13 March	Won	1	0	17 April	Lost	1	2	14th	10th
1979-80	Division 3	8 September	Lost	0	2	19 January	Drew	2	2	3rdP	19th
2003-04	Division 2	10 April	Drew	1	1	4 October	Won	3	0	16th	17th

League Cup

Season	Round	Date	Result	Home Wed'day	Brentf'd	Date	Result	Away Wed'day	Brentf'd	Division Wed'day	Brentf'd
1985-86	Round 2	15 October	Won	2	0	25 September	Drew	2	2	Div 1	Div 3
1990-91	Round 2	26 September	Won	2	1	9 October	Won	2	1	Div 2	Div 3

Summary

	P	W	D	L	F	A
Wednesday's home league record:	9	2	5	2	11	12
Wednesday's away league record:	9	2	3	4	14	14
Wednesday's cup record:	4	3	1	0	8	4
TOTAL:	22	7	9	6	33	30

FACT FILE

- Wednesday failed to win in their first 10 games in the series.
- However, they have won seven times and lost only twice in their last 12 games.

Wednesday's top scorers vs Brentford
Lee Chapman, Derek Dooley 3

Wednesday hat-tricks vs Brentford
11 Apr 1952 Derek Dooley

Played for both clubs

Alf Capper	Wednesday 1914-21	Brentford 1921-24
George Kell	Wednesday 1920-21	Brentford 1922-25
Harry Anstiss	Brentford 1920-22	Wednesday 1926-27
Jack Allen	Brentford 1924-27	Wednesday 1926-31
William Smith	Wednesday 1929-33	Brentford 1933-34
George Kirby	Wednesday 1959-60	Brentford 1968-69
Andy McCulloch	Brentford 1975-79	Wednesday 1979-83
Wilf Rostron	Wednesday 1988-89	Brentford 1990-93
Paul Williams	Brentford 1987-88	Wednesday 1990-93
Andy Sinton	Brentford 1985-89	Wednesday 1993-96
Lloyd Owusu	Brentford 1998-2002	Wednesday 2002-04
Mickael Antoine-Curier	Brentford 2002-03	Wednesday 2003-04

v. Brighton & Hove Albion

			Home				Away		Final Positions	
Season	League	Date	Result	Wed'day	B & HA	Date	Result	Wed'day B & HA	Wed'day	B & HA
1958-59	Division 2	28 March	Won	2	0	11 October	Won	3 1	1stP	12th
1972-73	Division 2	17 March	Drew	1	1	21 October	Drew	3 3	10th	22ndR
1975-76	Division 3	23 August	Drew	3	3	24 April	Drew	1 1	20th	4th
1976-77	Division 3	8 January	Drew	0	0	3 May	Lost	2 3	8th	2ndP
1983-84	Division 2	25 February	Won	2	1	22 October	Won	3 1	2ndP	9th
1990-91	Division 2	13 March	Drew	1	1	3 October	Won	4 0	3rdP	6th
2002-03	Division 1	7 December	Drew	1	1	21 April	Drew	1 1	22ndR	23rdR
2003-04	Division 2	27 March	Won	2	1	20 September	Lost	0 2	16th	4thP

FA Cup									Division	
1913-14	Round 3	24 February	Won	3	0				Div 1	Non L
1926-27	Round 3	8 January	Won	2	0				Div 1	Div 3S
1982-83	Semi-Final	16 April	Highbury				Lost	1 2	Div 2	Div 1

Summary	P	W	D	L	F	A
Wednesday's home league record:	8	3	5	0	12	8
Wednesday's away league record:	8	3	3	2	17	12
Wednesday's cup record:	3	2	0	1	6	2
TOTAL:	19	8	8	3	35	22

FACT FILE

- Wednesday have never lost at home to Brighton.
- Wednesday were unbeaten in their first nine games in the series.

Wednesday's top scorers vs Brighton
Gary Bannister, John Fantham, Brian Joicey 2

Played for both clubs

Harry Bentley	Wednesday 1913-20	Brighton 1920-22
Dan Kirkwood	Wednesday 1926-28	Brighton 1928-33
Jimmy Short	Wednesday 1931-32	Brighton 1933-35
Alec Law	Wednesday 1933-35	Brighton 1935-39
Len Edwards	Wednesday 1951-52	Brighton 1954-55
Colin Dobson	Wednesday 1961-66	Brighton 1971-72
Howard Wilkinson	Wednesday 1964-66	Brighton 1966-81
Wilf Smith	Wednesday 1964-71	Brighton 1974-75
Peter Grummitt	Wednesday 1969-73	Brighton 1973-77
Eric Potts	Wednesday 1970-77	Brighton 1977-78
Ian Mellor	Brighton 1974-78	Wednesday 1979-82
Gavin Oliver	Wednesday 1980-85	Brighton 1985-86
Mark Chamberlain	Wednesday 1985-88	Brighton 1994-95
Larry May	Wednesday 1986-88	Brighton 1988-89
Phil King	Wednesday 1989-94	Brighton 1998-99
Danny Wilson	Brighton 1983-87	Wednesday 1990-93
Leon Knight	Wednesday 2002-03	Brighton 2003-04

v. Bristol City

Season	League	Date	Result (Home)	Wed'day	Bristol C	Date	Result (Away)	Wed'day	Bristol C	Wed'day	Bristol C
			Home				**Away**			*Final Positions*	
1906-07	Division 1	20 October	Won	3	0	24 April	Lost	0	2	13th	2nd
1907-08	Division 1	23 September	Won	5	3	14 September	Won	2	0	5th	10th
1908-09	Division 1	10 October	Won	2	0	13 February	Drew	1	1	5th	8th
1909-10	Division 1	22 January	Won	2	0	11 September	Drew	1	1	11th	16th
1910-11	Division 1	2 January	Won	2	1	26 December	Drew	2	2	6th	19thR
1920-21	Division 2	2 May	Drew	2	2	7 May	Won	1	0	10th	3rd
1921-22	Division 2	18 February	Won	1	0	25 February	Lost	1	3	10th	22ndR
1923-24	Division 2	21 April	Won	1	0	18 April	Won	3	2	8th	22ndR
1955-56	Division 2	18 February	Won	2	1	19 November	Lost	2	3	1stP	11th
1958-59	Division 2	15 November	Lost	2	3	4 April	Won	2	1	1stP	10th
1970-71	Division 2	27 February	Won	2	0	31 October	Won	2	1	15th	19th
1971-72	Division 2	21 August	Lost	1	5	18 March	Lost	0	1	14th	8th
1972-73	Division 2	14 March	Won	3	2	2 September	Won	2	1	10th	5th
1973-74	Division 2	10 February	Won	3	1	22 September	Lost	0	2	19th	16th
1974-75	Division 2	5 October	Drew	1	1	12 April	Lost	0	1	22ndR	5th
1980-81	Division 2	13 September	Won	2	1	7 February	Lost	0	1	10th	21stR
1990-91	Division 2	8 May	Won	3	1	8 December	Drew	1	1	3rdP	9th
2003-04	Division 2	28 February	Won	1	0	25 October	Drew	1	1	16th	3rd

FA Cup

Season	Round	Date	Result	Wed'day	Bristol C	Date	Result	Wed'day	Bristol C	Division	
1923-24	Round 2	2 February	Drew	1	1	6 February	Lost	0	2	Div 2	Div 2
1999-00	Round 3	11 December	Won	1	0					Prem	Div 2

League Cup

Season	Round	Date	Result	Wed'day	Bristol C	Date	Result	Wed'day	Bristol C	Division	
1982-83	Round 2	26 October	Drew	1	1	4 October	Won	2	1	Div 2	Div 4

Peter Grummitt appeared 130 times in the Wednesday goal, a much-respected keeper in the days when England had a crop of them that would be the envy of today's manager. Grummitt moved to the Goldstone Ground in December 1973 and enjoyed four seasons on the south coast.

Summary	P	W	D	L	F	A
Wednesday's home league record:	18	14	2	2	38	21
Wednesday's away league record:	18	6	5	7	21	24
Wednesday's cup record:	5	2	2	1	5	5
TOTAL:	41	22	9	10	64	50

FACT FILE

- Wednesday were unbeaten in their first 10 home games in the series.
- Between 1907 and 1922, Wednesday were unbeaten in 11 games.
- Wednesday are unbeaten in their last seven games against Bristol City.

Wednesday's top scorers vs Bristol City
Brian Joicey 5
Harry Chapman, Mick Prendergast,
Andrew Wilson 4

Wednesday hat-tricks vs Bristol City
18 Apr 1924 Sid Binks

Played for both clubs

Tom Marrison	Wednesday 1902-05	Bristol C 1912-13
Fred Dent	Wednesday 1920-21	Bristol C 1925-26
Billy Walker	Bristol C 1922-24	Wednesday 1923-24
Andy Smailes	Wednesday 1922-24	Bristol C 1923-29
Norman Jackson	Wednesday 1949-53	Bristol C 1954-56
Barry Watling	Bristol C 1967-69	Wednesday 1975-76
Gordon Owen	Wednesday 1977-83	Bristol C 1986-88
Gary Shelton	Wednesday 1981-87	Bristol C 1989-94
Carl Shutt	Wednesday 1985-88	Bristol C 1987-89
Julian Watts	Wednesday 1992-96	Bristol C 1998-99
Mark Robins	Bristol C 2002-03	Wednesday 2003-04

v. Bristol Rovers

Season	League	Date	Result	Wed'day	Bristol R	Date	Result	Wed'day	Bristol R	Wed'day	Bristol R
			Home				**Away**			*Final Positions*	
1955-56	Division 2	3 September	Won	**4**	**2**	31 December	Lost	**2**	**4**	1stP	6th
1958-59	Division 2	6 September	Won	**3**	**1**	30 April	Lost	**1**	**2**	1stP	6th
1974-75	Division 2	24 August	Drew	**1**	**1**	17 September	Drew	**1**	**1**	22ndR	19th
1980-81	Division 2	13 December	Won	**4**	**1**	18 October	Drew	**3**	**3**	10th	22ndR
1990-91	Division 2	23 March	Won	**2**	**1**	6 October	Won	**1**	**0**	3rdP	13th

FA Cup										Division	
1905-06	Round 1	13 January	Won	**1**	**0**					Div 1	Non L

Summary	P	W	D	L	F	A
Wednesday's home league record:	5	4	1	0	14	6
Wednesday's away league record:	5	1	2	2	8	10
Wednesday's cup record:	1	1	0	0	1	0
TOTAL:	**11**	**6**	**3**	**2**	**23**	**16**

FACT FILE

- **Wednesday have never lost at home in the series.**

Wednesday's top scorers vs Bristol Rovers
Andy McCulloch, Roy Shiner 3

Played for both clubs

Edward Harvey	Wednesday 1919-21	Bristol R 1921-22
Harry O'Neill	Wednesday 1919-22	Bristol R 1922-23
Harold Armitage	Wednesday 1920-22	Bristol R 1922-26
Fred Lunn	Wednesday 1921-22	Bristol R 1922-23
Jimmy Lofthouse	Wednesday 1920-23	Bristol R 1923-26
Jack Allen	Wednesday 1926-31	Bristol R 1934-35
Jimmy McCambridge	Bristol R 1933-36	Wednesday 1936-37
Idris Lewis	Wednesday 1938-40	Bristol R 1946-47
Don Megson	Wednesday 1959-70	Bristol R 1969-71
Colin Dobson	Wednesday 1961-66	Bristol R 1972-76
Wilf Smith	Wednesday 1964-71	Bristol R 1974-77
Alan Warboys	Wednesday 1968-71	Bristol R 1972-77
David Rushbury	Wednesday 1976-79	Bristol R 1986-87
Graham Hyde	Wednesday 1991-99	Bristol R 2002-04
Mark McKeever	Bristol R 1998-99/2000-03	Wednesday 1998-2000
Michaelli Di Piedi	Wednesday 2000-03	Bristol R 2002-03
Aaron Lescott	Wednesday 2000-02	Bristol R 2003-04
Craig Armstrong	Bristol R 1995-96	Wednesday 2001-04

v. Burnley

Season	League	Home Date	Result	Wed'day	Burnley	Away Date	Result	Wed'day	Burnley	Final Positions Wed'day	Burnley
1892-93	Division 1	1 October	Won	2	0	31 March	Lost	0	4	12th	6th
1893-94	Division 1	26 December	Lost	0	1	23 March	Won	1	0	12th	5th
1894-95	Division 1	6 October	Won	4	3	10 November	Lost	0	3	8th	9th
1895-96	Division 1	14 December	Won	1	0	4 January	Lost	0	2	7th	10th
1896-97	Division 1	6 March	Won	1	0	19 December	Drew	1	1	6th	16thR
1898-99	Division 1	1 April	Won	1	0	3 December	Lost	0	5	18thR	3rd
1913-14	Division 1	3 January	Lost	2	6	13 September	Lost	0	3	18th	12th
1914-15	Division 1	24 April	Drew	0	0	19 December	Won	3	2	7th	4th
1919-20	Division 1	24 January	Won	3	1	17 February	Lost	0	2	22ndR	2nd
1926-27	Division 1	23 April	Won	2	1	4 December	Lost	0	1	16th	5th
1927-28	Division 1	10 March	Won	5	0	29 October	Lost	1	3	14th	19th
1928-29	Division 1	27 April	Drew	1	1	15 December	Won	2	0	1st	19th
1929-30	Division 1	8 February	Won	4	1	5 October	Won	4	2	1st	21stR
1937-38	Division 2	30 April	Won	2	1	18 December	Drew	1	1	17th	6th
1938-39	Division 2	17 December	Won	4	1	22 April	Won	2	1	3rd	14th
1946-47	Division 2	19 October	Lost	1	2	22 February	Lost	0	2	20th	2ndP
1950-51	Division 1	26 August	Lost	0	1	23 December	Lost	0	1	21stR	10th
1952-53	Division 1	7 February	Lost	2	4	20 September	Drew	1	1	18th	6th
1953-54	Division 1	2 January	Won	2	0	29 August	Lost	1	4	19th	7th
1954-55	Division 1	23 October	Drew	1	1	12 March	Lost	0	2	22ndR	10th
1956-57	Division 1	9 February	Drew	0	0	29 September	Lost	1	4	14th	7th
1957-58	Division 1	7 April	Lost	1	2	4 April	Lost	0	2	22ndR	6th
1959-60	Division 1	14 November	Drew	1	1	2 April	Drew	3	3	5th	1st
1960-61	Division 1	24 September	Won	3	1	11 February	Won	4	3	2nd	4th
1961-62	Division 1	30 April	Won	4	0	26 December	Lost	0	4	6th	2nd

Sammy Todd appeared for the Clarets and the Owls but his best days were undoubtedly at Turf Moor.

Season	League	Date	Result	Home		Date	Result	Away		Final Positions	
				Wed'day	Burnley			Wed'day	Burnley	Wed'day	Burnley
1962-63	Division 1	23 April	Lost	0	1	29 December	Lost	0	4	6th	3rd
1963-64	Division 1	21 December	Won	3	1	31 August	Lost	1	3	6th	9th
1964-65	Division 1	23 September	Won	5	1	13 March	Lost	1	4	8th	12th
1965-66	Division 1	9 May	Lost	0	2	11 April	Lost	1	2	17th	3rd
1966-67	Division 1	6 May	Won	7	0	1 April	Lost	0	2	11th	14th
1967-68	Division 1	26 August	Won	2	1	23 December	Lost	1	2	19th	14th
1968-69	Division 1	21 September	Won	1	0	12 April	Lost	0	2	15th	14th
1969-70	Division 1	28 February	Won	2	0	18 October	Lost	2	4	22ndR	14th
1971-72	Division 2	6 November	Won	2	1	26 February	Lost	3	5	14th	7th
1972-73	Division 2	14 October	Lost	0	1	10 March	Won	1	0	10th	1stP
1982-83	Division 2	20 November	Drew	1	1	1 January	Lost	1	4	6th	21stR
2000-01	Division 1	17 March	Won	2	0	17 October	Lost	0	1	17th	7th
2001-02	Division 1	12 August	Lost	0	2	19 January	Won	2	1	20th	7th
2002-03	Division 1	5 October	Lost	1	3	26 April	Won	7	2	22ndR	16th

FA Cup
Division

										Division	
1892-93	Round 2	4 February	Won	1	0					Div 1	Div 1
1929-30	Round 3	11 January	Won	1	0					Div 1	Div 1
1934-35	Semi Final	16 March		Villa Park			Won	3	0	Div 1	Div 2
1937-38	Round 3	8 January	Drew	1	1	11 January	Lost	1	3	Div 2	Div 2
1960-61	Q'ter Final	4 March	Drew	0	0	7 March	Lost	0	2	Div 1	Div 1
1982-83	Q'ter Final	15 March	Won	5	0	12 March	Drew	1	1	Div 2	Div 2

Summary	P	W	D	L	F	A
Wednesday's home league record:	39	22	6	11	73	42
Wednesday's away league record:	39	9	4	26	45	92
Wednesday's cup record:	9	4	3	2	13	7
TOTAL:	**87**	**35**	**13**	**39**	**131**	**141**

FACT FILE

- In 2002-03, Wednesday hit their best form of the season only after they were already doomed to relegation. The highlight was a 7-2 win at Burnley, where Wednesday's goals were scored by seven different men (one of whom was a Burnley player). It was the first time Wednesday had ever scored seven goals in an away match in 111 years of league football!
- Wednesday lost 11 consecutive games at Turf Moor between 1961 and 1972.
- At the same time, Wednesday won nine out of 11 home games in the league.
- Wednesday were unbeaten in 10 home games from 1915 to 1938.
- The draw at home in April 1929, coupled with the fact that both Aston Villa and Leicester failed to win on the same day, handed Sheffield Wednesday their third league title.

Wednesday's top scorers vs Burnley

John Fantham 8
Ellis Rimmer 6
Doug Hunt, Jack Whitham 5
Jack Allen, Colin Dobson, John Sissons 4

Wednesday hat-tricks vs Burnley

23 Sep 1964 John Fantham
 6 May 1967 David Ford
26 Feb 1972 John Sissons

Played for both clubs

Alec Brady	Burnley 1888-89	Wednesday 1892-99
Bob Brown	Wednesday 1892-94	Burnley 1896-97
William Smith	Wednesday 1929-33	Burnley 1936-39
George Nevin	Wednesday 1932-33	Burnley 1935-37
Sydney Chedgzoy	Burnley 1933-34	Wednesday 1937-38
David Cargill	Burnley 1953-56	Wednesday 1956-58
Sammy Todd	Burnley 1963-70	Wednesday 1970-73
Eric Potts	Wednesday 1970-77	Burnley 1980-82
Paul Bradshaw	Burnley 1974-77	Wednesday 1976-78
David Reeves	Burnley 1987-88	Wednesday 1988-89
Alan Harper	Wednesday 1988-90	Burnley 1994-96
Chris Woods	Wednesday 1991-96	Burnley 1997-98
Chris Waddle	Wednesday 1992-96	Burnley 1997-98
Mike Williams	Wednesday 1992-97	Burnley 1997-99
Lee Briscoe	Wednesday 1993-2000	Burnley 2000-03
Danny Sonner	Burnley 1990-93	Wednesday 1998-2000
Marlon Beresford	Burnley 1992-98/2001-03	Wednesday 2000-01
David Johnson	Wednesday 2001-02	Burnley 2001-02
Craig Armstrong	Burnley 1994-95	Wednesday 2001-04
Paul Smith	Burnley 1993-2001	Wednesday 2003-04

John Fantham scored eight times against the Clarets.

ck Whitham netted five
nes against Burnley.

v. Burton Swifts

			Home				Away		Final Positions	
Season	League	Date	Result	Wed'day	Burton S	Date	Result	Wed'day	Burton S	Wed'day	Burton S
1899-00	Division 2	12 March	Won	6	0	7 October	Won	5	0	1stP	15th

Summary	P	W	D	L	F	A
Wednesday's home league record:	1	1	0	0	6	0
Wednesday's away league record:	1	1	0	0	5	0
TOTAL:	2	2	0	0	11	0

FACT FILE

- In 1901, Swifts merged with Burton Wanderers to form Burton United, hence the inclusion of Jack Reynolds in the list below.

Wednesday's top scorers vs Swifts
Tommy Crawshaw, Jocky Wright 2

Played for both clubs
Sandy Rowan	Wednesday 1892-94	Burton Sw 1893-94
Jack Reynolds	Burton Utd 1903-04	Wednesday 1905-07

v. Bury

Season	League	Date	Result	Wed'day	Bury	Date	Result	Wed'day	Bury	Wed'day	Bury
			Home				**Away**			*Final Positions*	
1895-96	Division 1	22 February	Lost	1	3	9 November	Lost	1	6	7th	11th
1896-97	Division 1	17 April	Won	2	0	17 October	Drew	1	1	6th	9th
1897-98	Division 1	20 November	Won	3	0	11 September	Lost	0	3	5th	14th
1898-99	Division 1	15 October	Won	3	2	2 January	Drew	0	0	18thR	10th
1900-01	Division 1	12 January	Lost	1	2	15 September	Lost	0	2	8th	5th
1901-02	Division 1	16 November	Won	4	1	15 March	Lost	0	2	9th	7th
1902-03	Division 1	8 November	Won	2	0	6 April	Lost	0	4	1st	8th
1903-04	Division 1	19 September	Drew	1	1	16 January	Lost	0	1	1st	12th
1904-05	Division 1	14 January	Won	4	0	17 September	Won	4	1	9th	17th
1905-06	Division 1	6 January	Drew	1	1	9 September	Drew	2	2	3rd	17th
1906-07	Division 1	29 December	Lost	1	2	1 September	Drew	0	0	13th	16th
1907-08	Division 1	8 February	Won	2	0	12 October	Won	2	0	5th	7th
1908-09	Division 1	19 December	Won	4	3	24 April	Lost	2	4	5th	17th
1909-10	Division 1	18 September	Lost	1	4	9 March	Lost	2	3	11th	13th
1910-11	Division 1	18 February	Won	1	0	15 October	Drew	1	1	6th	18th
1911-12	Division 1	18 March	Won	2	1	9 September	Drew	2	2	5th	20thR
1920-21	Division 2	23 April	Won	2	0	30 April	Drew	1	1	10th	11th
1921-22	Division 2	22 April	Won	4	1	15 April	Won	2	1	10th	11th
1922-23	Division 2	20 January	Won	2	0	27 January	Lost	0	4	8th	6th
1923-24	Division 2	19 April	Drew	1	1	12 April	Lost	0	5	8th	2ndP
1926-27	Division 1	1 January	Lost	1	3	25 December	Lost	0	2	16th	19th
1927-28	Division 1	5 November	Won	4	0	17 March	Lost	2	4	14th	5th
1928-29	Division 1	2 March	Won	3	1	20 October	Won	4	0	1st	21stR
1937-38	Division 2	11 December	Won	2	0	23 April	Lost	0	2	17th	10th
1938-39	Division 2	27 August	Won	2	0	24 December	Won	3	2	3rd	16th
1946-47	Division 2	26 December	Lost	2	5	25 December	Lost	2	4	20th	17th
1947-48	Division 2	15 September	Drew	2	2	10 September	Won	2	1	4th	20th
1948-49	Division 2	13 September	Lost	1	2	8 September	Lost	1	2	8th	12th
1949-50	Division 2	10 April	Won	1	0	7 April	Drew	0	0	2ndP	18th
1951-52	Division 2	17 November	Won	2	1	5 April	Won	2	1	1stP	17th
1955-56	Division 2	29 October	Drew	3	3	21 April	Won	5	2	1stP	15th
1975-76	Division 3	17 April	Won	1	0	26 December	Drew	0	0	20th	13th
1976-77	Division 3	25 January	Won	1	0	6 November	Won	3	1	8th	7th
1977-78	Division 3	28 January	Won	3	2	3 September	Lost	0	3	14th	15th
1978-79	Division 3	26 September	Drew	0	0	1 May	Drew	0	0	14th	19th
1979-80	Division 3	5 February	Won	5	1	12 April	Lost	0	1	3rdP	21stR

FA Cup   *Division*

Season	League	Date	Result	Wed'day	Bury					Div	Div
1900-01	Round 1	9 February	Lost	0	1					Div 1	Div 1
1977-78	Round 1	26 November	Won	1	0					Div 3	Div 3

League Cup

Season	League					Date	Result	Wed'day	Bury	Div	Div
2001-02	Round 1					21 August	Won	3	1	Div 1	Div 2

Summary	P	W	D	L	F	A
Wednesday's home league record:	36	23	6	7	75	42
Wednesday's away league record:	36	9	10	17	44	68
Wednesday's cup record:	3	2	0	1	4	2
TOTAL:	75	34	16	25	123	112

FACT FILE

● Wednesday are unbeaten in their last nine home games against Bury. Bury's last win there was in 1948.
● Between 1897 and 1904, Wednesday failed to score in six away matches against Bury.
● Wednesday were unbeaten in nine games in the series from 1910 to 1923.

Wednesday's top scorers vs Bury

Andrew Wilson 8
Jack Allen, Frank Bradshaw, Harry Davis,
Fred Spiksley, Jimmy Stewart 4

Wednesday hat-tricks vs Bury

14 Jan 1905 Jimmy Stewart
20 Oct 1928 Jack Allen (4)

Played for both clubs

Jack Darroch	Wednesday 1892-94	Bury 1896-1902
Harry Millar	Bury 1894-98	Wednesday 1899-1901
Sam Kirkman	Wednesday 1909-20	Bury 1920-21
Jimmy Trotter	Bury 1919-22	Wednesday 1921-29
George Bargh	Wednesday 1935-36	Bury 1936-39/46-47
Ernie Matthres	Bury 1935-38	Wednesday 1937-38
Jack Lindsay	Wednesday 1946-47	Bury 1946-47
Frank Slynn	Wednesday 1946-51	Bury 1950-53
Eddie Quigley	Bury 1946-48/56-57	Wednesday 1947-50
Eddie Kilshaw	Bury 1937-49	Wednesday 1948-49
Doug Fletcher	Wednesday 1948-50	Bury 1951-56
Donald Watson	Wednesday 1954-57	Bury 1957-62
Peter Swan	Wednesday 1955-64/72-73	Bury 1973-74
Billy Griffin	Wednesday 1958-63	Bury 1962-66
Roy McLaren	Bury 1955-59	Wednesday 1958-64
Eric Potts	Wednesday 1970-77	Bury 1982-84
Neil Ramsbottom	Bury 1965-71	Wednesday 1975-76
Malcolm Darling	Wednesday 1977-78	Bury 1977-78
Terry Curran	Bury 1977-78	Wednesday 1978-82
Trevor Matthewson	Wednesday 1980-83	Bury 1994-96
Tony Cunningham	Wednesday 1983-84	Bury 1989-91
John Ryan	Wednesday 1984-85	Bury 1993-94
Dean Barrick	Wednesday 1988-90	Bury 1998-2001
Danny Wilson	Bury 1977-80	Wednesday 1990-93
Nigel Jemson	Wednesday 1991-94	Bury 1997-99
Brian Linighan	Wednesday 1993-94	Bury 1999-2000
Danny Sonner	Bury 1992-93	Wednesday 1998-2000
Marlon Beresford	Bury 1989-90	Wednesday 2000-01
David Johnson	Bury 1995-98	Wednesday 2001-02

v. Cambridge United

			Home				Away		Final Positions	
Season	League	Date	Result	Wed'day	Cambridge	Date	Result	Wed'day	Cambridge	Wed'day	Cambridge
1977-78	Division 3	22 April	Drew	0	0	3 December	Lost	0	3	14th	2ndP
1980-81	Division 2	18 April	Won	4	1	24 January	Won	2	0	10th	13th
1981-82	Division 2	17 April	Won	2	1	21 September	Won	2	1	4th	14th
1982-83	Division 2	26 February	Won	3	1	16 October	Drew	2	2	6th	12th
1983-84	Division 2	6 September	Won	1	0	17 March	Won	2	1	2ndP	22ndR

FA Cup *Division*

						Date	Result				Division
1982-83	Round 5					19 February	Won	2	1	Div 2	Div 2
1990-91	Round 5					16 February	Lost	0	4	Div 2	Div 3
1992-93	Round 3					13 January	Won	2	1	Prem	Div 1

League Cup

						Date	Result				
1998-99	Round 2	16 September	Lost	0	1	22 September	Drew	1	1	Prem	Div 3

Summary	P	W	D	L	F	A
Wednesday's home league record:	5	4	1	0	10	3
Wednesday's away league record:	5	3	1	1	8	7
Wednesday's cup record:	5	2	1	2	5	8
TOTAL:	**15**	**9**	**3**	**3**	**23**	**18**

FACT FILE

- **Wednesday were unbeaten in 10 games against Cambridge from 1978 to 1984.**
- **The defeat to Cambridge in 1998-99 was one of Wednesday's most embarrassing cup exits in their history, coming as it did to a side three divisions below them.**

Wednesday's top scorers vs Cambridge
Andy McCulloch 6
Gary Bannister 4

Wednesday hat-tricks vs Cambridge
18 Apr 1981 Andy McCulloch

Played for both clubs

Robin Hardy	Wednesday 1961-64	Cambridge 1970-71
David Rushbury	Wednesday 1976-79	Cambridge 1986-87
Colin Walker	Cambridge 1985-86	Wednesday 1986-87
Dean Barrick	Wednesday 1988-90	Cambridge 1993-95
Andy Sinton	Cambridge 1982-86	Wednesday 1993-98
Richie Humphreys	Wednesday 1995-2001	Cambridge 2000-01
Scott Oakes	Wednesday 1996-99	Cambridge 2000-01

v. Cardiff City

Season	League	Date	Result	Home Wed'day	Home Cardiff	Date	Result	Away Wed'day	Away Cardiff	Final Positions Wed'day	Final Positions Cardiff
1920-21	Division 2	4 December	Lost	0	1	11 December	Lost	0	1	10th	2ndP
1926-27	Division 1	29 November	Won	3	0	16 April	Lost	2	3	16th	14th
1927-28	Division 1	3 September	Drew	3	3	7 January	Drew	1	1	14th	6th
1928-29	Division 1	27 October	Won	1	0	9 March	Lost	1	3	1st	22ndR
1947-48	Division 2	13 September	Won	2	1	31 January	Lost	1	2	4th	5th
1948-49	Division 2	16 April	Drew	1	1	20 November	Drew	1	1	8th	4th
1949-50	Division 2	29 August	Drew	1	1	22 August	Lost	0	1	2ndP	10th
1951-52	Division 2	9 February	Won	4	2	29 September	Lost	1	2	1stP	2ndP
1952-53	Division 1	3 January	Won	2	0	30 August	Lost	0	4	18th	12th
1953-54	Division 1	5 December	Won	2	1	24 April	Drew	2	2	19th	10th
1954-55	Division 1	2 April	Drew	1	1	13 November	Lost	3	5	22ndR	20th
1956-57	Division 1	12 September	Won	5	3	5 September	Lost	1	2	14th	21stR
1958-59	Division 2	11 April	Won	3	1	22 November	Drew	2	2	1stP	9th
1960-61	Division 1	31 August	Won	2	0	24 August	Won	1	0	2nd	15th
1961-62	Division 1	3 April	Won	2	0	11 November	Lost	1	2	6th	21stR
1970-71	Division 2	26 August	Lost	1	2	9 January	Lost	0	4	15th	3rd
1971-72	Division 2	25 March	Drew	2	2	11 September	Lost	2	3	14th	19th
1972-73	Division 2	14 April	Won	1	0	9 December	Lost	1	4	10th	20th
1973-74	Division 2	16 March	Won	5	0	20 October	Won	1	0	19th	17th
1974-75	Division 2	7 September	Lost	1	2	22 March	Drew	0	0	22ndR	21stR
1975-76	Division 3	17 March	Lost	1	3	18 October	Lost	0	2	20th	2ndP
1980-81	Division 2	11 October	Won	2	0	4 March	Drew	0	0	10th	19th
1981-82	Division 2	10 October	Won	2	1	27 February	Won	2	0	4th	20thR
1983-84	Division 2	17 December	Won	5	2	12 May	Won	2	0	2ndP	15th

John Pearson, a Sheffield lad who never quite fulfilled his early potential, later played for Cardiff City.

						Away		Division	
FA Cup			*Date*	*Result*	Wed'day	Cardiff	Wed'day	Cardiff
1947-48 Round 3			10 January	Won*	**2**	**1**	Div 2	Div 2

Summary	*P*	*W*	*D*	*L*	*F*	*A*
Wednesday's home league record:	24	15	5	4	52	27
Wednesday's away league record:	24	4	6	14	25	44
Wednesday's cup record:	1	1	0	0	2	1
TOTAL:	**49**	**20**	**11**	**18**	**79**	**72**

FACT FILE

- From 1926 to 1962, Wednesday were unbeaten in 14 home games in the series.
- Wednesday failed to win in their first 13 league games at Ninian Park.
- Wednesday have five wins and a draw from their last six games against Cardiff.

Wednesday's top scorers vs Cardiff
Jackie Sewell 9
Redfern Froggatt 6
Roy Shiner 4

Wednesday hat-tricks vs Cardiff
9 Feb 1952 Jackie Sewell (4)

Played for both clubs

Jimmy Gill	Wednesday 1913-20	Cardiff 1920-26
Jimmy Blair	Wednesday 1914-21	Cardiff 1920-26
Harry O'Neill	Wednesday 1919-22	Cardiff 1931-32
Paddy McIlvenny	Cardiff 1924-25	Wednesday 1925-26
Jimmy McCambridge	Cardiff 1930-33	Wednesday 1936-37
Ernie Blenkinsop	Wednesday 1922-34	Cardiff 1937-38
Keith Thomas	Wednesday 1950-52	Cardiff 1952-54
Keith Ellis	Wednesday 1954-64	Cardiff 1964-65
Jack Whitham	Wednesday 1966-70	Cardiff 1973-75
Alan Warboys	Wednesday 1968-71	Cardiff 1970-73
Peter Rodrigues	Cardiff 1963-66	Wednesday 1970-75
Jimmy Mullen	Wednesday 1970-80	Cardiff 1981-86
David Grant	Wednesday 1977-82	Cardiff 1983-85
Gordon Owen	Wednesday 1977-83	Cardiff 1983-84
Andy McCulloch	Cardiff 1972-74	Wednesday 1979-83
John Pearson	Wednesday 1980-85	Cardiff 1994-95
Tony Simmons	Wednesday 1981-83	Cardiff 1986-87
Pat Heard	Wednesday 1982-85	Cardiff 1990-92
Garry Thompson	Wednesday 1985-86	Cardiff 1993-95
Dave Bennett	Cardiff 1981-83	Wednesday 1988-90
Alan Harper	Wednesday 1988-90	Cardiff 1995-96
Richie Humphreys	Wednesday 1995-2001	Cardiff 1999-2000

v. Carlisle United

Season	League	Date (Home)	Result	Wed'day	Carlisle	Date (Away)	Result	Wed'day	Carlisle	Wed'day	Carlisle
				Home				**Away**		*Final Positions*	
1970-71	Division 2	26 September	Won	3	0	1 May	Lost	0	3	15th	4th
1971-72	Division 2	20 October	Won	2	1	29 January	Drew	2	2	14th	10th
1972-73	Division 2	23 April	Drew	0	0	30 September	Drew	1	1	10th	18th
1973-74	Division 2	15 September	Won	1	0	12 January	Drew	2	2	19th	3rdP
1977-78	Division 3	5 November	Won	3	1	2 January	Lost	0	1	14th	13th
1978-79	Division 3	14 October	Drew	0	0	24 February	Drew	0	0	14th	6th
1979-80	Division 3	3 May	Drew	0	0	26 February	Won	2	0	3rdP	6th
1982-83	Division 2	22 January	Drew	1	1	28 September	Lost	2	4	6th	14th
1983-84	Division 2	3 September	Won	2	0	31 December	Drew	1	1	2ndP	7th

FA Cup

			Date	Result	Wed'day	Carlisle	Division	
1979-80	Round 2		15 December	Lost	0	3	Div 3	Div 3
1996-97	Round 4		25 January	Won	2	0	Prem	Div 3

League Cup

			Date	Result	Wed'day	Carlisle	Division	
1971-72	Round 2		7 September	Lost	0	5	Div 2	Div 2

Summary

	P	W	D	L	F	A
Wednesday's home league record:	9	5	4	0	12	3
Wednesday's away league record:	9	1	5	3	10	14
Wednesday's cup record:	3	1	0	2	2	8
TOTAL:	**21**	**7**	**9**	**5**	**24**	**25**

Tommy Craig started in 92 games and a further six as substitute for Carlisle United. Born in Glasgow, he signed for Newcastle United in a £100,000 deal from Sheffield Wednesday, and was moved on to Aston Villa for £270,000. He won a Scottish cap in 1976.

FACT FILE

- Carlisle have not won at Hillsborough in nine attempts. They have scored only three goals in total in those matches.
- Wednesday did not win in their first eight away matches in the series.

Wednesday's top scorers vs Carlisle
Mick Prendergast 5
John Sissons 3

Played for both clubs

Tony Leach	Wednesday 1926-34	Carlisle 1936-38
Jack Lindsay	Wednesday 1946-47	Carlisle 1947-51/54-55
Vin Kenny	Wednesday 1946-55	Carlisle 1955-58
Tommy Craig	Wednesday 1968-75	Carlisle 1981-85
Eddie Prudham	Wednesday 1970-75	Carlisle 1974-77
David Rushbury	Wednesday 1976-79	Carlisle 1981-85
Brian Hornsby	Wednesday 1977-82	Carlisle 1982-84
Gordon Owen	Wednesday 1977-83	Carlisle 1990-91
Peter Shirtliff	Wednesday 1978-86/89-93	Carlisle 1996-97
John Pearson	Wednesday 1980-85	Carlisle 1993-95
Ian Bailey	Carlisle 1976-77	Wednesday 1982-83
Ian Knight	Wednesday 1985-89	Carlisle 1992-93
Steve McCall	Wednesday 1987-91	Carlisle 1989-90
David Reeves	Wednesday 1988-89	Carlisle 1993-97
Paul Warhurst	Wednesday 1990-93	Carlisle 2003-04
Steve Harkness	Carlisle 1988-89	Wednesday 2000-01
Jon McCarthy	Wednesday 2001-02	Carlisle 2002-03
Eric Nixon	Carlisle 1986-87	Wednesday 2003-04

v. Charlton Athletic

Season	League	Date (Home)	Result	Wed'day	Charlton	Date (Away)	Result	Wed'day	Charlton	Wed'day	Charlton
1936-37	Division 1	6 March	Won	3	1	31 October	Lost	0	1	22ndR	2nd
1950-51	Division 1	9 September	Lost	1	2	13 January	Lost	1	2	21stR	17th
1952-53	Division 1	6 September	Lost	0	3	17 January	Lost	0	3	18th	5th
1953-54	Division 1	5 September	Lost	1	2	16 January	Lost	2	4	19th	9th
1954-55	Division 1	27 December	Drew	2	2	25 December	Lost	0	3	22ndR	15th
1956-57	Division 1	12 January	Won	3	1	8 September	Drew	4	4	14th	22ndR
1958-59	Division 2	27 February	Won	4	1	8 November	Drew	3	3	1stP	8th
1970-71	Division 2	15 August	Won	1	0	17 October	Won	3	2	15th	20th
1971-72	Division 2	10 April	Won	2	1	9 October	Drew	2	2	14th	21stR
1981-82	Division 2	6 March	Drew	1	1	17 October	Lost	0	3	4th	13th
1982-83	Division 2	3 January	Won	5	4	4 September	Won	3	0	6th	17th
1983-84	Division 2	11 February	Won	4	1	10 September	Drew	1	1	2ndP	13th
1986-87	Division 1	24 January	Drew	1	1	23 August	Drew	1	1	13th	19th
1987-88	Division 1	26 September	Won	2	0	20 February	Lost	1	3	11th	17th
1988-89	Division 1	4 March	Won	3	1	29 October	Lost	1	2	15th	14th
1989-90	Division 1	11 November	Won	3	0	28 April	Won	2	1	18thR	19thR
1990-91	Division 2	19 January	Drew	0	0	8 September	Won	1	0	3rdP	16th
1998-99	Premiership	12 December	Won	3	0	16 May	Won	1	0	12th	18thR

Home / **Away** / *Final Positions*

FA Cup

Season	Round	Date	Result	Wed'day	Charlton	Division (Wed'day)	Division (Charlton)
1975-76	Round 3	3 January	Lost	1	2	Div 3	Div 2
1995-96	Round 3	6 January	Lost	0	2	Prem	Div 1

Summary

	P	W	D	L	F	A
Wednesday's home league record:	18	11	4	3	39	21
Wednesday's away league record:	18	5	5	8	26	35
Wednesday's cup record:	2	0	0	2	1	4
TOTAL:	**38**	**16**	**9**	**13**	**66**	**60**

Bob Bolder, Charlton custodian from 1986 to 1993, previously kept goal in over 200 games for Wednesday.

FACT FILE

- Wednesday have won six and drawn one of their last seven league games against Charlton. Charlton have scored just twice in this run.
- Wednesday have not lost in their last 14 home games in the series.
- Between 1950 and 1954, Wednesday lost seven games in a row.

Wednesday's top scorers vs Charlton

David Hirst 5
Roy Shiner 4
Gary Bannister, Lee Chapman, Alan Finney,
Redfern Froggatt 3

Played for both clubs

George Ayres	Charlton 1922-24	Wednesday 1923-26
George Stephenson	Wednesday 1930-33	Charlton 1934-39
Bob Bolder	Wednesday 1977-83	Charlton 1986-93
Peter Shirtliff	Wednesday 1978-86/89-93	Charlton 1986-89
John Pearson	Wednesday 1980-85	Charlton 1985-87
Lawrie Madden	Charlton 1977-82	Wednesday 1983-91
Steve MacKenzie	Charlton 1987-91	Wednesday 1990-92
Paul Williams	Charlton 1987-90/95-96	Wednesday 1990-93
Gordon Watson	Charlton 1989-91	Wednesday 1990-95
Chris Bart-Williams	Wednesday 1991-95	Charlton 2001-03
Mark Bright	Wednesday 1992-97	Charlton 1996-99
Paolo DiCanio	Wednesday 1997-99	Charlton 2003-04
Robbie Mustoe	Charlton 2002-03	Wednesday 2003-04

v. Chelsea

Season	League	Home Date	Result	Wed'day	Chelsea	Away Date	Result	Wed'day	Chelsea	Final Positions Wed'day	Chelsea
1907-08	Division 1	16 November	Won	3	1	14 March	Lost	1	3	5th	13th
1908-09	Division 1	22 March	Won	5	1	17 October	Drew	2	2	5th	11th
1909-10	Division 1	27 November	Won	4	1	9 April	Lost	1	4	11th	19thR
1912-13	Division 1	22 March	Won	3	2	16 November	Won	4	0	3rd	18th
1913-14	Division 1	26 October	Won	3	0	25 December	Lost	1	2	18th	8th
1914-15	Division 1	10 April	Won	3	2	5 December	Drew	0	0	7th	19th
1919-20	Division 1	6 April	Lost	0	2	20 March	Drew	1	1	22ndR	3rd
1924-25	Division 2	17 January	Won	2	1	13 September	Drew	0	0	14th	5th
1925-26	Division 2	28 November	Won	4	1	10 April	Drew	0	0	1stP	3rd
1930-31	Division 1	8 September	Drew	1	1	15 September	Drew	0	0	3rd	12th
1931-32	Division 1	21 September	Drew	2	2	9 September	Won	3	2	3rd	12th
1932-33	Division 1	1 April	Drew	2	2	19 November	Won	2	0	3rd	18th
1933-34	Division 1	4 November	Won	2	1	17 March	Won	1	0	11th	19th
1934-35	Division 1	3 September	Won	3	1	29 August	Won	2	1	3rd	12th
1935-36	Division 1	30 November	Won	4	1	7 March	Won	2	1	20th	8th
1936-37	Division 1	20 February	Drew	1	1	17 October	Drew	1	1	22ndR	13th
1950-51	Division 1	24 February	Drew	2	2	19 August	Lost	0	4	21stR	20th
1952-53	Division 1	1 November	Won	1	0	21 March	Lost	0	1	18th	19th
1953-54	Division 1	10 October	Won	2	0	27 February	Won	1	0	19th	8th
1954-55	Division 1	20 November	Drew	1	1	23 April	Lost	0	3	22ndR	1st
1956-57	Division 1	22 August	Won	4	0	19 September	Drew	0	0	14th	12th=
1957-58	Division 1	15 February	Lost	2	3	5 October	Lost	0	1	22ndR	11th
1959-60	Division 1	27 February	Drew	1	1	5 December	Won	4	0	5th	18th
1960-61	Division 1	25 February	Won	1	0	26 April	Won	2	0	2nd	12th
1961-62	Division 1	7 December	Won	5	3	24 February	Lost	0	1	6th	22ndR
1963-64	Division 1	29 February	Won	3	2	19 October	Won	2	1	6th	5th
1964-65	Division 1	16 September	Lost	2	3	9 September	Drew	1	1	8th	3rd
1965-66	Division 1	2 May	Drew	1	1	15 September	Drew	1	1	17th	5th
1966-67	Division 1	31 December	Won	6	1	27 August	Drew	0	0	11th	9th
1967-68	Division 1	6 April	Drew	2	2	11 November	Lost	0	3	19th	6th
1968-69	Division 1	9 October	Drew	1	1	28 August	Lost	0	1	15th	5th
1969-70	Division 1	8 November	Lost	1	3	25 March	Lost	1	3	22ndR	3rd
1980-81	Division 2	10 January	Drew	0	0	22 November	Lost	0	2	10th	12th
1981-82	Division 2	1 May	Drew	0	0	5 December	Lost	1	2	4th	12th
1982-83	Division 2	25 September	Won	3	2	2 May	Drew	1	1	6th	18th
1983-84	Division 2	17 September	Won	2	1	21 January	Lost	2	3	2ndP	1stP
1984-85	Division 1	8 December	Drew	1	1	6 May	Lost	1	2	8th	6th
1985-86	Division 1	17 August	Drew	1	1	14 December	Lost	1	2	5th	6th
1986-87	Division 1	30 August	Won	2	0	7 February	Lost	0	2	13th	14th
1987-88	Division 1	16 January	Won	3	0	15 August	Lost	1	2	11th	18thR
1989-90	Division 1	14 January	Drew	1	1	26 August	Lost	0	4	18thR	5th
1991-92	Division 1	7 December	Won	3	0	29 February	Won	3	0	3rd	14th
1992-93	Premiership	22 August	Drew	3	3	30 January	Won	2	0	7th	11th
1993-94	Premiership	30 March	Won	3	1	28 August	Drew	1	1	7th	14th

			Home				Away			Final Positions	
Season	League	Date	Result	Wed'day	Chelsea	Date	Result	Wed'day	Chelsea	Wed'day	Chelsea
1994-95	Premiership	29 October	Drew	1	1	14 January	Drew	1	1	13th	11th
1995-96	Premiership	17 April	Drew	0	0	4 November	Drew	0	0	15th	11th
1996-97	Premiership	7 September	Lost	0	2	28 December	Drew	2	2	7th	6th
1997-98	Premiership	20 December	Lost	1	4	19 April	Lost	0	1	16th	4th
1998-99	Premiership	25 April	Drew	0	0	28 November	Drew	1	1	12th	3rd
1999-00	Premiership	15 April	Won	1	0	29 December	Lost	0	3	19thR	5th

FA Cup

			Home				Away			Division	
1912-13	Round 2	5 February	Won	6	0	1 February	Drew	1	1	Div 1	Div 1
1931-32	Round 5	13 February	Drew	1	1	17 February	Lost	0	2	Div 1	Div 1
1938-39	Round 5	13 February	Drew*	0	0	11 February	Drew	1	1	Div 2	Div 1
		20 February				Highbury (2nd replay)	Lost	1	3		
1965-66	Semi-Final	23 April				Villa Park	Won	2	0	Div 1	Div 1
1966-67	Q'ter final					8 April	Lost	0	1	Div 1	Div 1
1967-68	Round 5	9 March	Drew	2	2	12 March	Lost	0	2	Div 1	Div 1
1972-73	Round 5	24 February	Lost	1	2					Div 2	Div 1
1974-75	Round 3					4 January	Lost	2	3	Div 2	Div 1
1993-94	Round 4	9 February	Lost*	1	3	29 January	Drew	1	1	Prem	Prem
1998-99	Round 5	13 February	Lost	0	1					Prem	Prem

League Cup

			Home				Away			Division	
1970-71	Round 2	9 September	Drew	1	1	22 September	Lost	1	2	Div 2	Div 1
1984-85	Q'ter final	30 January	Drew	4	4	28 January	Drew	1	1	Div 1	Div 1
		(2nd replay)				6 February	Lost	1	2		
1990-91	Semi-Final	27 February	Won	3	1	24 February	Won	2	0	Div 2	Div 1

Summary

	P	W	D	L	F	A
Wednesday's home league record:	50	25	19	6	102	60
Wednesday's away league record:	50	12	17	21	50	66
Wednesday's cup record:	23	4	9	10	32	34
TOTAL:	123	41	45	37	184	160

It was against Chelsea, at Villa Park in an FA Cup semi-final in 1966, that Vic Mobley of the Owls was unlucky to be injured. The knock ended his season and put him out of the final with Everton.

FACT FILE

- Nobody has faced Wednesday more often in cup games than Chelsea.
- One of these cup matches was an epic at Hillsborough in 1985. Wednesday led 3-0 at half-time, only to trail 4-3 with just seconds left. However, with the final whistle imminent, Wednesday won a penalty which Mel Sterland converted. The sides met again in a second replay, which Chelsea won.
- Wednesday were unbeaten in 16 home games from 1925 to 1956.
- Between 1981 and 1996, Wednesday lost once in 17 home games, and that defeat was only after extra time.
- Wednesday were unbeaten in 18 league games from 1924 to 1937.
- Wednesday have won twice in their last 24 league visits to Stamford Bridge.

Wednesday's top scorers vs Chelsea

Andrew Wilson 12
John Fantham 10
Ellis Rimmer 8
David McLean 7
Alan Finney, David Hirst, Albert Quixall 5

Wednesday hat-tricks vs Chelsea

5 Feb 1913 David McLean (cup)
28 Nov 1925 Harold Hill

Played for both clubs

English McConnell	Wednesday 1908-10	Chelsea 1909-11
Bob Gregg	Wednesday 1928-31	Chelsea 1933-38
Harry Burgess	Wednesday 1929-35	Chelsea 1934-40
Mike Pinner	Wednesday 1957-59	Chelsea 1961-62
Jim McCalliog	Chelsea 1964-66	Wednesday 1965-69
John Sissons	Wednesday 1970-74	Chelsea 1974-75
Peter Feely	Chelsea 1970-73	Wednesday 1975-77
Darren Wood	Chelsea 1984-89	Wednesday 1988-90
Dan Petrescu	Wednesday 1994-96	Chelsea 1995-2000
Emerson Thome	Wednesday 1997-2000	Chelsea 1999-2001

v. Chester City

Season	League	Date	Result	Wed'day	Chester	Date	Result	Wed'day	Chester	Wed'day	Chester
				Home				**Away**		*Final Positions*	
1975-76	Division 3	31 January	Won	2	0	21 October	Lost	0	1	20th	17th
1976-77	Division 3	5 October	Won	3	0	15 February	Lost	0	1	8th	13th
1977-78	Division 3	7 March	Drew	1	1	14 September	Lost	1	2	14th	5th
1978-79	Division 3	9 December	Drew	0	0	28 April	Drew	2	2	14th	16th
1979-80	Division 3	19 April	Won	3	0	1 December	Drew	2	2	3rdP	9th

FA Cup										*Division*	
1938-39	Round 4	21 January	Drew	1	1	25 January	Drew*	1	1	Div 2	Div 3N
		30 January				Maine Road (2nd replay)	Won	2	0		
1986-87	Round 4	4 February	Won	3	1	31 January	Drew	1	1	Div 1	Div 3

Summary	P	W	D	L	F	A
Wednesday's home league record:	5	3	2	0	9	1
Wednesday's away league record:	5	0	2	3	5	8
Wednesday's cup record:	5	2	3	0	8	4
TOTAL:	**15**	**5**	**7**	**3**	**22**	**13**

FACT FILE

- **Neither side has ever lost at home, in seven matches apiece.**
- **Wednesday are unbeaten in their last six games in the series.**

Wednesday's top scorers vs Chester
Lee Chapman, Terry Curran, Jackie Robinson,
Tommy Tynan, Rodger Wylde 2

Played for both clubs

Alec Law	Wednesday 1933-35	Chester 1939-40
George Davies	Wednesday 1950-55	Chester 1956-58
Graham Birks	Wednesday 1962-63	Chester 1969-72
Graham Pugh	Wednesday 1965-72	Chester 1974-77
Brian Woodall	Wednesday 1967-70	Chester 1970-71
Barry Watling	Chester 1975-76	Wednesday 1975-76
Brian Hornsby	Wednesday 1977-82	Chester 1981-82
John Lowey	Wednesday 1978-80	Chester 1987-88
Ian Mellor	Chester 1977-79	Wednesday 1979-82
Gary Shelton	Wednesday 1981-87	Chester 1994-99
Earl Barrett	Chester 1985-86	Wednesday 1997-99
Manuel Agogo	Wednesday 1997-99	Chester 1999-2000

v. Chesterfield

Season	League	Date (Home)	Result	Wed'day	Chesterf'd	Date (Away)	Result	Wed'day	Chesterf'd	Wed'day	Chesterf'd
		Home						**Away**		*Final Positions*	
1899-00	Division 2	2 September	Won	5	1	30 December	Lost	0	1	1stP	7th
1937-38	Division 2	1 January	Won	1	0	28 August	Lost	0	1	17th	11th
1938-39	Division 2	20 March	Drew	0	0	17 September	Lost	1	3	3rd	6th
1946-47	Division 2	21 September	Lost	0	1	7 June	Lost	2	4	20th	4th
1947-48	Division 2	29 March	Won	1	0	26 March	Won	2	0	4th	16th
1948-49	Division 2	19 April	Drew	0	0	15 April	Drew	1	1	8th	6th
1949-50	Division 2	3 September	Won	4	2	31 December	Won	2	1	2ndP	14th
1975-76	Division 3	24 March	Lost	1	3	24 September	Lost	0	1	20th	14th
1976-77	Division 3	18 September	Won	4	1	26 February	Lost	0	2	8th	18th
1977-78	Division 3	8 October	Won	1	0	4 March	Drew	2	2	14th	9th
1978-79	Division 3	14 April	Won	4	0	26 December	Drew	3	3	14th	20th
1979-80	Division 3	16 February	Drew	3	3	29 September	Lost	1	2	3rdP	4th
2003-04	Division 2	20 December	Drew	0	0	7 March	Lost	1	3	16th	20th

FA Cup — *Division*

Season	Round	Date (Home)	Result	Wed'day	Chesterf'd	Date (Away)	Result	Wed'day	Chesterf'd	Division	
1932-33	Round 3	14 January	Drew	2	2	18 January	Lost	2	4	Div 1	Div 2
1953-54	Round 4	30 January	Drew	0	0	3 February	Won	4	2	Div 1	Div 3N

Summary	P	W	D	L	F	A
Wednesday's home league record:	13	7	4	2	24	11
Wednesday's away league record:	13	2	3	8	15	24
Wednesday's cup record:	4	1	2	1	8	8
TOTAL:	**30**	**10**	**9**	**11**	**47**	**43**

FACT FILE

- On 2 September 1899, Chesterfield became Wednesday's first opponents at their new ground, Owlerton, and were beaten 5-1 by their hosts. In 1912, the ground was renamed Hillsborough. Over the years, it has become one of the major stadiums in England. Only Villa Park has been used more often for FA Cup semi-finals. It has also been used for two League Cup final replays (most recently in 1997), as well as matches in the 1966 World Cup and Euro '96.
- There have been no away wins in the last 10 matches between the sides.

Wednesday's top scorers vs Chesterfield
Rodger Wylde 6
Eddie Quigley 5
Redfern Froggatt 4

Wednesday hat-tricks vs Chesterfield
3 Sep 1950 Eddie Quigley (4)

Played for both clubs

Bill Gooing	Wednesday 1895-96	Chesterfield 1899-1902
Robert Hutton	Wednesday 1898-1902	Chesterfield 1903-04
Tommy Crawshaw	Wednesday 1894-1908	Chesterfield 1908-09
Percy Reed	Wednesday 1919-21	Chesterfield 1921-22
Joe Cooper	Wednesday 1920-21	Chesterfield 1921-23
Arnold Birch	Wednesday 1919-23	Chesterfield 1923-27
Horace Henshall	Wednesday 1922-23	Chesterfield 1923-24
Sam Taylor	Wednesday 1920-25	Chesterfield 1929-31
Sid Binks	Wednesday 1922-25	Chesterfield 1930-32
Frank Froggatt	Wednesday 1921-28	Chesterfield 1931-34
Bernard Oxley	Chesterfield 1925-28	Wednesday 1933-35
Harold Hill	Wednesday 1924-29	Chesterfield 1932-33
George Beeson	Chesterfield 1927-29	Wednesday 1929-34
George Bargh	Wednesday 1935-36	Chesterfield 1939-40
Charlie Luke	Wednesday 1935-38	Chesterfield 1938-39
Jack Thompson	Wednesday 1933-46	Chesterfield 1948-53
George Hunt	Chesterfield 1929-30	Wednesday 1946-48
Keith Bannister	Wednesday 1946-53	Chesterfield 1953-54
Dennis Woodhead	Wednesday 1946-55	Chesterfield 1955-56
Ray Parker	Chesterfield 1947-48	Wednesday 1948-49
Hugh McJarrow	Chesterfield 1946-50	Wednesday 1949-52
Brian Slater	Wednesday 1952-53	Chesterfield 1957-58
Ivor Seemley	Wednesday 1953-55	Chesterfield 1957-59
Terry Whitham	Wednesday 1956-59	Chesterfield 1961-64
John Meredith	Wednesday 1960-61	Chesterfield 1962-64
Wilf Smith	Wednesday 1964-71	Chesterfield 1976-77
Kenny Burton	Wednesday 1968-72	Chesterfield 1973-79
Steve Downes	Wednesday 1969-72	Chesterfield 1972-74
Jackie Sinclair	Wednesday 1969-73	Chesterfield 1972-73
Colin Prophett	Wednesday 1969-73	Chesterfield 1978-80
Derek Ball	Wednesday 1975-76	Chesterfield 1983-84
Malcolm Darling	Chesterfield 1974-77	Wednesday 1977-78
David Grant	Wednesday 1977-82	Chesterfield 1983-84
Brian Hornsby	Wednesday 1977-82	Chesterfield 1983-84
Gordon Owen	Wednesday 1977-83	Chesterfield 1982-83
Mark Smith	Wednesday 1977-87	Chesterfield 1992-93
John Lowey	Wednesday 1978-80	Chesterfield 1986-87
Terry Curran	Wednesday 1978-82	Chesterfield 1987-88
Jeff King	Wednesday 1979-82	Chesterfield 1983-84
Charles Williamson	Wednesday 1979-84	Chesterfield 1985-87
Lawrie Madden	Wednesday 1983-91	Chesterfield 1993-96
John Ryan	Wednesday 1984-85	Chesterfield 1989-91
Des Hazel	Wednesday 1987-88	Chesterfield 1995-96
Greg Fee	Wednesday 1987-90	Chesterfield 1992-93
David Reeves	Wednesday 1988-89	Chesterfield 1997-2004
Danny Wilson	Chesterfield 1980-83	Wednesday 1990-93
Paul Warhurst	Wednesday 1990-93	Chesterfield 2003-04
Graham Hyde	Wednesday 1991-99	Chesterfield 2001-02
Manuel Agogo	Wednesday 1997-99	Chesterfield 1999-2000

v. Colchester United

Season	League	Date	Result	Home Wed'day	Colchester	Date	Result	Away Wed'day	Colchester	Final Positions Wed'day	Colchester
1975-76	Division 3	27 March	Won	1	0	6 December	Lost	1	2	20th	22ndR
1977-78	Division 3	3 December	Lost	1	2	29 April	Drew	1	1	14th	8th
1978-79	Division 3	26 August	Drew	0	0	18 November	Lost	0	1	14th	7th
1979-80	Division 3	2 February	Won	3	0	15 September	Drew	0	0	3rdP	5th
2003-04	Division 2	24 April	Lost	0	1	15 November	Lost	1	3	16th	11th

Summary	P	W	D	L	F	A
Wednesday's home league record:	5	2	1	2	5	3
Wednesday's away league record:	5	0	2	3	3	7
TOTAL:	10	2	3	5	8	10

Wednesday's top scorers vs Colchester
Mark Smith 2

Played for both clubs

Bob Curry	Wednesday 1937-38	Colchester 1950-51
Reg Stewart	Wednesday 1946-47	Colchester 1950-57
Joe Locherty	Wednesday 1948-50	Colchester 1950-51
Paul Taylor	Wednesday 1971-73	Colchester 1973-74
Danny Cameron	Wednesday 1973-76	Colchester 1974-75
Steve Whitton	Wednesday 1988-91	Colchester 1993-98
Con Blatsis	Wednesday 2000-01	Colchester 2001-02

Steve Whitton, who spent five years at Layer Road in the mid-1990s and was once an Owl.

v. Coventry City

		Home			Away		Final Positions	
Season	League	Date	Result Wed'day Coventry		Date	Result Wed'day Coventry		Wed'day Coventry

Season	League	Date	Result	W	C	Date	Result	W	C	Wed'day	Coventry
1920-21	Division 2	25 September	Won	3	0	2 October	Won	3	2	10th	21st
1921-22	Division 2	13 March	Won	3	2	24 December	Drew	2	2	10th	20th
1922-23	Division 2	14 April	Won	3	0	21 April	Drew	1	1	8th	18th
1923-24	Division 2	26 December	Won	2	0	25 December	Lost	1	5	8th	19th
1924-25	Division 2	18 October	Won	2	0	21 February	Drew	1	1	14th	22ndR
1937-38	Division 2	2 April	Won	2	1	20 November	Won	1	0	17th	4th
1938-39	Division 2	22 October	Drew	2	2	25 February	Lost	0	1	3rd	4th
1946-47	Division 2	30 November	Won	4	2	5 April	Lost	1	5	20th	8th
1947-48	Division 2	10 April	Drew	1	1	22 November	Lost	1	3	4th	10th
1948-49	Division 2	5 February	Won	2	1	18 September	Won	4	3	8th	16th
1949-50	Division 2	22 April	Drew	1	1	11 February	Lost	0	3	2ndP	12th
1951-52	Division 2	1 December	Won	3	1	19 April	Won	2	0	1stP	21stR
1967-68	Division 1	7 October	Won	4	0	24 February	Lost	0	3	19th	20th
1968-69	Division 1	17 August	Won	3	0	8 March	Lost	0	3	15th	20th
1969-70	Division 1	28 January	Lost	0	1	14 March	Drew	1	1	22ndR	6th
1984-85	Division 1	2 March	Won	1	0	27 October	Lost	0	1	8th	18th
1985-86	Division 1	12 October	Drew	2	2	15 March	Won	1	0	5th	17th
1986-87	Division 1	25 October	Drew	2	2	7 March	Lost	0	1	13th	10th
1987-88	Division 1	31 August	Lost	0	3	13 February	Lost	0	3	11th	10th
1988-89	Division 1	10 September	Lost	1	2	2 January	Lost	0	5	15th	7th
1989-90	Division 1	30 September	Drew	0	0	17 March	Won	4	1	18thR	12th
1991-92	Division 1	7 March	Drew	1	1	8 April	Drew	0	0	3rd	19th
1992-93	Premiership	2 September	Lost	1	2	3 March	Lost	0	1	7th	15th
1993-94	Premiership	30 November	Drew	0	0	16 April	Drew	1	1	7th	11th
1994-95	Premiership	28 December	Won	5	1	15 April	Lost	0	2	13th	16th
1995-96	Premiership	3 December	Won	4	3	21 October	Won	1	0	15th	16th
1996-97	Premiership	1 February	Drew	0	0	26 October	Drew	0	0	7th	17th
1997-98	Premiership	20 September	Drew	0	0	7 February	Lost	0	1	16th	11th
1998-99	Premiership	3 April	Lost	1	2	18 October	Lost	0	1	12th	15th
1999-00	Premiership	23 October	Drew	0	0	6 May	Lost	1	4	19thR	14th
2001-02	Division 1	29 March	Won	2	1	27 October	Lost	0	2	20th	11th
2002-03	Division 1	5 March	Won	5	1	18 September	Drew	1	1	22ndR	20th

FA Cup										Division	
1910-11	Round 1	14 January	Lost	1	2					Div 1	Non L
1973-74	Round 3	5 January	Drew	0	0	8 January	Lost	1	3	Div 2	Div 1
1981-82	Round 3					2 January	Lost	1	3	Div 2	Div 1
1983-84	Round 4	30 January	Won	3	2					Div 2	Div 1
1986-87	Q'ter final	14 March	Lost	1	3					Div 1	Div 1

League Cup											
1990-91	Q'ter final					23 January	Won	1	0	Div 2	Div 1

Summary	P	W	D	L	F	A
Wednesday's home league record:	32	16	11	5	60	32
Wednesday's away league record:	32	7	8	17	27	57
Wednesday's cup record:	7	2	1	4	8	13
TOTAL:	**71**	**25**	**20**	**26**	**95**	**102**

FACT FILE

- Between 1920 and 1968, Wednesday were unbeaten in 14 home games against Coventry.
- Wednesday have failed to win in their last six games at Highfield Road.
- Wednesday have only lost once in their last nine home games in the series.

Wednesday's top scorers vs Coventry
Johnny McIntyre 5
Charles Binney, Derek Dooley, Eddie Quigley,
Guy Whittingham 4

Wednesday hat-tricks vs Coventry
25 Sep 1920 Johnny McIntyre
13 Mar 1922 Charles Binney

Played for both clubs

Billy Walker	Coventry 1919-20	Wednesday 1923-24
Jack Bellas	Wednesday 1920-23	Coventry 1924-26
Ernie Toseland	Coventry 1928-29	Wednesday 1938-40
Charlie Wilson	Wednesday 1927-32	Coventry 1934-35
Tommy Davison	Wednesday 1930-32	Coventry 1932-35
George Kirby	Wednesday 1959-60	Coventry 1963-65
Wilf Smith	Wednesday 1964-71	Coventry 1970-75
Dave Clements	Coventry 1964-72	Wednesday 1971-74
Brian Joicey	Coventry 1969-72	Wednesday 1971-76
Neil Ramsbottom	Coventry 1972-75	Wednesday 1975-76
Gary Bannister	Coventry 1978-81/87-90	Wednesday 1981-84
Andy Blair	Coventry 1978-81	Wednesday 1984-86
Garry Thompson	Coventry 1977-83	Wednesday 1985-86
Dave Bennett	Coventry 1983-89	Wednesday 1988-90
Steve Whitton	Coventry 1979-83	Wednesday 1988-91
Carlton Palmer	Wednesday 1988-94/2000-02	Coventry 1999-2001
Roland Nilsson	Wednesday 1989-94	Coventry 1997-99/2001-02
Andy Pearce	Coventry 1990-93	Wednesday 1993-96
Peter Atherton	Coventry 1991-94	Wednesday 1994-2000
Trond Egil Soltvedt	Coventry 1997-99	Wednesday 2000-03
Kevin Gallacher	Coventry 1989-93	Wednesday 2001-02
Paul Heald	Coventry 1991-92	Wednesday 2001-02
David Burrows	Coventry 1994-2000	Wednesday 2001-03

v. Crewe Alexandra

Season	League	Date	Result	Home Wed'day	Crewe	Date	Result	Away Wed'day	Crewe	Final Positions Wed'day	Crewe
2000-01	Division 1	6 May	Drew	0	0	25 November	Lost	0	1	17th	14th
2001-02	Division 1	12 January	Won	1	0	18 August	Won	2	0	20th	22ndR

FA Cup — *Division*

Season	Round	Date	Result	Home Wed'day	Crewe	Date	Result	Away Wed'day	Crewe	Division Wed'day	Crewe
1935-36	Round 3	15 January	Won	3	1	11 January	Drew	1	1	Div 1	Div 3N
2001-02	Round 3					15 January	Lost	1	2	Div 1	Div 1

League Cup

Season	Round	Date	Result	Home Wed'day	Crewe	Date	Result	Away Wed'day	Crewe	Div Wed'day	Crewe
1995-96	Round 2	4 October	Won	5	2	19 September	Drew	2	2	Prem	Div 2

Summary	P	W	D	L	F	A
Wednesday's home league record:	2	1	1	0	1	0
Wednesday's away league record:	2	1	0	1	2	1
Wednesday's cup record:	5	2	2	1	12	8
TOTAL:	9	4	3	2	15	9

Wednesday's top scorers vs Crewe
Mark Bright, Marc Degryse 3

Wednesday hat-tricks vs Crewe
4 Oct 1995 Mark Bright (cup)

Played for both clubs

Harry Anstiss	Wednesday 1926-27	Crewe 1933-34
Len Edwards	Wednesday 1951-52	Crewe 1955-57
Brian Woodall	Wednesday 1967-70	Crewe 1970-71
Colin Prophett	Wednesday 1969-73	Crewe 1979-81
Neil Ramsbottom	Crewe 1971-72	Wednesday 1975-76
Julian Watts	Wednesday 1992-96	Crewe 1997-98
Wayne Collins	Crewe 1993-96/2001-02	Wednesday 1996-98
Marlon Beresford	Crewe 1990-91	Wednesday 2000-01
Ashley Westwood	Crewe 1995-98	Wednesday 2000-03

Colin Prophett, a tall central defender, was discovered playing junior football in Crewe. He was later to return to his home town to play for the Alex.

v. Crusaders

							Away	
FA Cup				*Date*		*Result*	Wed'day	Crusaders
1887-88 Round 4				7 December		Won	**1**	**0**

Summary	P	W	D	L	F	A
Wednesday's cup record:	1	1	0	0	1	0
TOTAL:	1	1	0	0	1	0

FACT FILE

- This was as far as the East London team ever got in the FA Cup, but a Hiller goal prevented any further progress.

v. Crystal Palace

		Home				Away				Final Positions	
Season	League	Date	Result	Wed'day	Palace	Date	Result	Wed'day	Palace	Wed'day	Palace
1921-22	Division 2	1 October	Won	1	0	24 September	Drew	2	2	10th	14th
1922-23	Division 2	4 November	Won	3	1	11 November	Lost	0	2	8th	16th
1923-24	Division 2	22 December	Won	6	0	15 December	Lost	0	3	8th	15th
1924-25	Division 2	27 December	Lost	0	1	30 August	Won	1	0	14th	21stR
1969-70	Division 1	25 October	Drew	0	0	21 February	Won	2	0	22ndR	20th
1973-74	Division 2	29 September	Won	4	0	22 December	Drew	0	0	19th	20thR
1975-76	Division 3	7 April	Won	1	0	27 September	Drew	1	1	20th	5th
1976-77	Division 3	9 November	Won	1	0	23 April	Lost	0	4	8th	3rdP
1981-82	Division 2	5 September	Won	1	0	19 January	Won	2	1	4th	15th
1982-83	Division 2	14 May	Won	2	1	11 December	Lost	0	2	6th	15th
1983-84	Division 2	28 April	Won	1	0	26 November	Lost	0	1	2ndP	18th
1989-90	Division 1	25 November	Drew	2	2	24 February	Drew	1	1	18thR	15th
1991-92	Division 1	5 October	Won	4	1	25 April	Drew	1	1	3rd	10th
1992-93	Premiership	20 February	Won	2	1	25 August	Drew	1	1	7th	20thR
1994-95	Premiership	3 December	Won	1	0	14 March	Lost	1	2	13th	19thR
1997-98	Premiership	25 October	Lost	1	3	10 May	Lost	0	1	16th	20thR
2000-01	Division 1	14 April	Won	4	1	4 November	Lost	1	4	17th	21st
2001-02	Division 1	2 February	Lost	1	3	29 September	Lost	1	4	20th	10th
2002-03	Division 1	25 September	Drew	0	0	22 February	Drew	0	0	22ndR	14th

FA Cup

										Division	
1972-73	Round 4	3 February	Drew	1	1	6 February	Drew*	1	1	Div 2	Div 1
		19 February				Villa Park (2nd replay)	Won	3	2		

League Cup

										Division	
1982-83	Round 3					9 November	Won	2	1	Div 2	Div 2
2001-02	Round 3	10 October	Drew*	2	2					Div 1	Div 1
		(won 3-1 pens)									

Summary

	P	W	D	L	F	A
Wednesday's home league record:	19	13	3	3	35	14
Wednesday's away league record:	19	3	7	9	14	30
Wednesday's cup record:	5	2	3	0	9	7
TOTAL:	43	18	13	12	58	51

(+one penalty shoot-out victory)

FACT FILE

- Between 1973 and 1994, Wednesday won nine and drew one of their 10 home games against Palace.
- Wednesday have not won in their last 10 away games in the series.
- Palace scored only four goals in their first 12 matches at Hillsborough.

Wednesday's top scorers vs Palace

Sid Binks 5
Gary Bannister, Mick Prendergast 4
David Hirst, Brian Joicey 3

Wednesday hat-tricks vs Palace

22 Dec 1923 Sid Binks (4)
19 Feb 1973 Brian Joicey (cup)
29 Sep 1973 Mick Prendergast

Played for both clubs

Jimmy Gill	Wednesday 1913-20	Palace 1928-29
William Smith	Wednesday 1929-33	Palace 1933-36
Jackie Palethorpe	Wednesday 1934-36	Palace 1936-38
John Holsgrove	Palace 1964-65	Wednesday 1971-75
Jeff Johnson	Palace 1973-76	Wednesday 1976-81
Kevin Taylor	Wednesday 1978-84	Palace 1984-88
Andy McCulloch	Wednesday 1979-83	Palace 1983-84
Garry Thompson	Wednesday 1985-86	Palace 1989-91
Paul Warhurst	Wednesday 1990-93	Palace 1997-99
Paul Williams	Wednesday 1990-93	Palace 1992-95
Mark Bright	Palace 1986-93	Wednesday 1992-97
Matt Clarke	Wednesday 1996-98	Palace 2001-04
Lee Bradbury	Palace 1998-2000	Wednesday 2002-03

Brian Joicey hit a hat-trick as Sheffield Wednesday beat Palace 3-2 in an FA Cup Fourth Round replay at Villa Park in February 1973.

v. Darlington

Season	League		Home Date	Result	Wed'day	Darl'ton	Away Date	Result	Wed'day	Darl'ton	Final Positions Wed'day	Darl'ton
1925-26	Division 2		14 November	Won	4	0	27 March	Lost	1	5	1stP	15th

FA Cup — *Division*

Season	Round		Home Date	Result	Wed'day	Darl'ton	Away Date	Result	Wed'day	Darl'ton	Wed'day	Darl'ton
1919-20	Round 1	19 January	Lost	0	2		14 January	Drew	0	0	Div 1	Non L
1976-77	Round 2						15 December	Lost	0	1	Div 3	Div 4

League Cup

Season	Round		Home Date	Result	Wed'day	Darl'ton	Away Date	Result	Wed'day	Darl'ton	Wed'day	Darl'ton
1975-76	Round 1	27 August	Lost	0	2		19 August	Won	2	0	Div 3	Div 4
		3 September	Drew	0	0		(replay) (lost 3-5 pens)				Div 2	Div 4
1983-84	Round 2	4 October	Won	3	0		25 October	Won	4	2		

Summary	P	W	D	L	F	A	
Wednesday's home league record:	1	1	0	0	4	0	
Wednesday's away league record:	1	0	0	1	1	5	
Wednesday's cup record:	8	3	2	3	9	7	
TOTAL:	**10**	**4**	**2**	**4**	**14**	**12**	(+one penalty shoot-out defeat)

FACT FILE

- Darlington were the opposition for Wednesday's first-ever penalty shoot-out.

Wednesday's top scorers vs Darlington
Jimmy Trotter 4
Gary Bannister 3

Wednesday hat-tricks vs Darlington
14 Nov 1925 Jimmy Trotter

Played for both clubs

Bert Burridge	Darlington 1921-26	Wednesday 1926-30
Mark Hooper	Darlington 1923-27	Wednesday 1926-38
Bob Gregg	Darlington 1926-28	Wednesday 1928-31
Charlie Luke	Darlington 1928-29	Wednesday 1935-38
John Logan	Darlington 1935-37	Wednesday 1946-47
Tommy Ward	Wednesday 1946-48	Darlington 1948-54
Doug Fletcher	Wednesday 1948-50	Darlington 1958-59
Harold Clark	Darlington 1950-57	Wednesday 1957-58
Ronnie Ferguson	Wednesday 1974-75	Darlington 1975-80
Graeme Hedley	Wednesday 1977-78	Darlington 1978-79
Gary Bannister	Wednesday 1981-84	Darlington 1995-96
David Mills	Wednesday 1982-83	Darlington 1986-87
Lawrie Madden	Wednesday 1983-91	Darlington 1993-94
Carl Shutt	Wednesday 1985-88	Darlington 1996-99
Colin Walker	Wednesday 1986-87	Darlington 1986-87
David Lucas	Darlington 1995-97	Wednesday 2003-04

v. Darwen

			Home				Away		Final Positions	
Season	League	Date	Result	Wed'day Darwen	Date	Result	Wed'day Darwen		Wed'day	Darwen
1893-94	Division 1	15 January	Won	**5 0**	11 December	Lost	**1 2**		12th	15thR

FA Cup

					Date	Result				
1880-81	Round 4				5 February	Lost	**2 5**			

Summary	P	W	D	L	F	A
Wednesday's home league record:	1	1	0	0	5	0
Wednesday's away league record:	1	0	0	1	1	2
Wednesday's cup record:	1	0	0	1	2	5
TOTAL:	**3**	**1**	**0**	**2**	**8**	**7**

Wednesday's top scorers vs Darwen
John Webster 3

Played for both clubs
W. Dunlop   Wednesday 1892-93   Darwen 1893-94

Ambrose Langley was
in his first season at
Wednesday when he
played in the 5-0 win
over Darwen in
January 1894. Langley
went on to make 317
appearances in 11
seasons.

v. Derby County

		Home					Away			Final Positions	
Season	League	Date	Result	Wed'day	Derby	Date	Result	Wed'day	Derby	Wed'day	Derby
1892-93	Division 1	10 December	Drew	3	3	25 March	Drew	2	2	12th	13th
1893-94	Division 1	14 October	Won	4	0	21 October	Drew	3	3	12th	3rd
1894-95	Division 1	27 December	Drew	1	1	15 September	Won	2	1	8th	15th
1895-96	Division 1	28 December	Lost	0	4	28 September	Lost	1	3	7th	2nd
1896-97	Division 1	28 November	Won	2	0	9 January	Lost	1	2	6th	3rd
1897-98	Division 1	15 January	Won	3	1	19 February	Won	2	1	5th	10th
1898-99	Division 1	24 September	Won	3	1	21 January	Lost	0	9	18thR	9th
1900-01	Division 1	22 December	Won	2	1	27 April	Lost	1	3	8th	12th
1901-02	Division 1	17 March	Won	2	0	26 April	Drew	2	2	9th	6th
1902-03	Division 1	13 December	Lost	0	1	11 April	Lost	0	1	1st	9th
1903-04	Division 1	21 November	Won	1	0	30 April	Won	2	0	1st	14th
1904-05	Division 1	3 April	Drew	1	1	5 November	Lost	0	1	9th	11th
1905-06	Division 1	23 December	Won	1	0	28 April	Lost	1	2	3rd	15th
1906-07	Division 1	25 December	Drew	1	1	1 April	Lost	0	1	13th	19thR
1912-13	Division 1	1 January	Drew	3	3	24 March	Won	4	1	3rd	7th
1913-14	Division 1	1 November	Lost	1	3	11 March	Drew	1	1	18th	20thR
1919-20	Division 1	15 November	Won	2	0	8 November	Lost	1	2	22ndR	18th
1921-22	Division 2	5 September	Drew	1	1	29 August	Won	1	0	10th	12th
1922-23	Division 2	9 September	Drew	0	0	16 September	Drew	1	1	8th	14th
1923-24	Division 2	5 January	Won	1	0	29 December	Drew	1	1	8th	3rd
1924-25	Division 2	1 September	Lost	0	1	8 September	Lost	1	2	14th	3rd
1925-26	Division 2	17 October	Lost	1	4	27 February	Lost	1	4	1stP	2ndP
1926-27	Division 1	30 October	Won	2	1	19 March	Lost	0	8	16th	12th
1927-28	Division 1	7 April	Drew	2	2	26 November	Won	6	4	14th	4th
1928-29	Division 1	18 February	Won	5	0	15 September	Lost	0	6	1st	6th
1929-30	Division 1	22 April	Won	6	3	21 April	Lost	1	4	1st	2nd
1930-31	Division 1	20 April	Won	3	2	25 October	Won	3	2	3rd	6th
1931-32	Division 1	24 October	Won	3	1	5 March	Won	1	0	3rd	15th
1932-33	Division 1	7 January	Drew	0	0	3 September	Lost	0	2	3rd	7th
1933-34	Division 1	14 October	Drew	1	1	24 February	Drew	1	1	11th	4th
1934-35	Division 1	3 November	Won	1	0	20 March	Lost	0	4	3rd	6th
1935-36	Division 1	12 October	Won	1	0	19 February	Lost	1	3	20th	2nd
1936-37	Division 1	12 September	Lost	2	3	9 January	Lost	2	3	22ndR	4th
1950-51	Division 1	18 April	Won	4	3	21 October	Lost	1	4	21stR	11th
1952-53	Division 1	18 October	Won	2	0	7 March	Lost	1	2	18th	22ndR
1958-59	Division 2	31 January	Drew	1	1	13 September	Won	4	1	1stP	7th
1969-70	Division 1	27 September	Won	1	0	17 January	Lost	0	1	22ndR	4th
1980-81	Division 2	7 March	Drew	0	0	4 October	Lost	1	3	10th	6th
1981-82	Division 2	19 September	Drew	1	1	30 January	Lost	1	3	4th	16th
1982-83	Division 2	6 November	Won	2	0	19 March	Drew	0	0	6th	13th
1983-84	Division 2	10 April	Won	3	1	29 August	Drew	1	1	2ndP	20thR
1987-88	Division 1	28 December	Won	2	1	19 September	Drew	2	2	11th	15th
1988-89	Division 1	3 December	Drew	1	1	22 April	Lost	0	1	15th	5th
1989-90	Division 1	3 March	Won	1	0	18 November	Lost	0	2	18thR	16th

				Home				Away		Final Positions	
Season	League	Date	Result	Wed'day	Derby	Date	Result	Wed'day	Derby	Wed'day	Derby
1996-97	Premiership	21 September	Drew	0	0	19 February	Drew	2	2	7th	12th
1997-98	Premiership	24 September	Lost	2	5	28 February	Lost	0	3	16th	9th
1998-99	Premiership	30 January	Lost	0	1	9 September	Lost	0	1	12th	8th
1999-00	Premiership	25 August	Lost	0	2	5 February	Drew	3	3	19thR	16th
2002-03	Division 1	2 November	Lost	1	3	15 February	Drew	2	2	22ndR	18th

FA Cup

										Division	
1890-91	Round 2					31 January	Won	3	2	Non L	Div 1
1892-93	Round 1	2 February	Won	4	2					Div 1	Div 1
1922-23	Round 3					24 February	Lost	0	1	Div 2	Div 2
1985-86	Round 5	5 March	Won	2	0	26 February	Drew	1	1	Div 1	Div 3
1986-87	Round 3	26 January	Won	1	0					Div 1	Div 2
1992-93	Q'ter final	17 March	Won	1	0	8 March	Drew	3	3	Prem	Div 1

League Cup

1989-90	Round 3					25 October	Lost	1	2	Div 1	Div 1
1990-91	Round 4	28 November	Drew	1	1	12 December	Won	2	1	Div 2	Div 1

Summary

	P	W	D	L	F	A
Wednesday's home league record:	49	24	15	10	80	58
Wednesday's away league record:	49	9	13	27	61	111
Wednesday's cup record:	11	6	3	2	19	13
TOTAL:	**109**	**39**	**31**	**39**	**160**	**182**

Wednesday's top scorers vs Derby
Fred Spiksley 8
Ted Harper, Mark Hooper 6
Gary Bannister, Alec Brady, David McLean,
Ellis Rimmer 4

Wednesday hat-tricks vs Derby
14 Oct 1893 Alec Brady
26 Nov 1927 Ted Harper
18 Feb 1929 Ted Harper
22 Apr 1930 Jack Allen

John Harkes scored a 40-
yard wonder goal at Derby
for the Owls in 1990. Later
he joined the Rams for a
couple of seasons.

FACT FILE

- Between 1926 and 1996, Wednesday lost just once in 27 home games against Derby.
- Wednesday have won once in their last 21 league matches in Derby.
- Wednesday have not won in their last 10 matches in the series.
- The 1893 FA Cup tie was high on controversy. Wednesday originally won 3-2 at home (with a Spiksley hat-trick) on 21 January. However, following Derby protests, the FA ordered the match to be replayed in Derby seven days later. This time Derby won 1-0, but now it was Wednesday's turn to protest. Again a replay was ordered, back in Sheffield this time, and Wednesday came through 4-2.
- On New Year's Day 1913, Derby led 3-0 with just 20 minutes left, but Wednesday produced a stirring comeback to draw 3-3 and go temporarily top of the league.

Played for both clubs

Bruce Chalmers	Derby 1890-91	Wednesday 1892-94
Samuel Bosworth	Derby 1898-99	Wednesday 1898-99
Fred Richards	Derby 1898-99	Wednesday 1898-99
Reginald Hounsfield	Wednesday 1902-03	Derby 1904-06
Jimmy Gill	Wednesday 1913-20	Derby 1925-28
Alec Cruickshank	Derby 1924-25	Wednesday 1926-27
Jack Whitehouse	Derby 1923-29	Wednesday 1928-30
Tommy Davison	Derby 1925-31	Wednesday 1930-32
George Stephenson	Derby 1927-31	Wednesday 1930-33
Gavin Malloch	Derby 1927-32	Wednesday 1931-36
Charlie Napier	Derby 1935-38	Wednesday 1937-40
Dennis Woodhead	Wednesday 1946-55	Derby 1955-59
Tony Conwell	Wednesday 1953-55	Derby 1959-62
David Cargill	Wednesday 1956-58	Derby 1958-61
Terry Curran	Derby 1977-78	Wednesday 1978-82
Kevin Taylor	Wednesday 1978-84	Derby 1984-85
Jeff King	Derby 1975-78	Wednesday 1979-82
John Harkes	Wednesday 1990-93	Derby 1993-96
Simon Coleman	Derby 1991-94	Wednesday 1993-95
Ian Taylor	Wednesday 1994-95	Derby 2003-04
Mark Pembridge	Derby 1992-95	Wednesday 1995-98
Benito Carbone	Wednesday 1996-2000	Derby 2001-02
Con Blatsis	Wednesday 2000-01	Derby 2000-01
Tommy Johnson	Derby 1991-95	Wednesday 2001-02
Darryl Powell	Derby 1995-2002	Wednesday 2002-03
Lee Bradbury	Wednesday 2002-03	Derby 2003-04

v. Doncaster Rovers

Season	League	Date	Result	Wed'day	Donc'ter	Date	Result	Wed'day	Donc'ter	Wed'day	Donc'ter
			Home					**Away**		*Final Positions*	
1947-48	Division 2	5 April	Won	2	0	4 October	Won	1	0	4th	21stR
1951-52	Division 2	18 August	Won	3	1	15 December	Drew	1	1	1stP	16th
1955-56	Division 2	14 January	Won	5	2	10 September	Drew	2	2	1stP	17th

League Cup — *Division*

			Result	Wed'day	Donc'ter		Result	Wed'day	Donc'ter		
1977-78	Round 1	13 August	Won	5	2	16 August	Won	3	0	Div 3	Div 4
1978-79	Round 1	15 August	Lost	0	1	12 August	Won	1	0	Div 3	Div 4
		(replay)				22 August	Won	1	0		

Summary	P	W	D	L	F	A
Wednesday's home league record:	3	3	0	0	10	3
Wednesday's away league record:	3	1	2	0	4	3
Wednesday's cup record:	5	4	0	1	10	3
TOTAL:	**11**	**8**	**2**	**1**	**24**	**9**

FACT FILE

- Wednesday were unbeaten in their first nine matches against Doncaster.
- Doncaster have not won a home match in the series.

Wednesday's top scorers vs Doncaster
Rodger Wylde 4
Roy Shiner 3

Wednesday hat-tricks vs Doncaster
13 Aug 1977 Rodger Wylde (cup)

Played for both clubs

Frank Foxall	Doncaster 1902-03	Wednesday 1906-10
Matt Moralee	Wednesday 1901-04	Doncaster 1904-05
Billy Taylor	Wednesday 1919-22	Doncaster 1925-26
Len Hargreaves	Doncaster 1925-27/32-33	Wednesday 1928-29
Jack Thompson	Wednesday 1933-46	Doncaster 1946-48
Arnold Lowes	Wednesday 1938-48	Doncaster 1947-51
Alex Wands	Wednesday 1946-47	Doncaster 1947-48
Clarrie Jordan	Doncaster 1946-48	Wednesday 1947-55
Dave McIntosh	Wednesday 1947-58	Doncaster 1957-59
Norman Curtis	Wednesday 1950-60	Doncaster 1960-61
Alan Finney	Wednesday 1950-66	Doncaster 1965-67
Tony Conwell	Wednesday 1953-55	Doncaster 1962-64
Albert Broadbent	Wednesday 1955-58	Doncaster 1959-66
John Ballagher	Wednesday 1958-59	Doncaster 1960-62
Bobby Lodge	Wednesday 1960-61	Doncaster 1961-62
John Meredith	Doncaster 1958-61	Wednesday 1960-61
Brian Usher	Wednesday 1965-68	Doncaster 1968-73

Played for both clubs cont.

Ian Branfoot	Wednesday 1965-70	Doncaster 1969-73
Archie Irvine	Wednesday 1968-70	Doncaster 1969-75
Alan Warboys	Doncaster 1966-68/79-82	Wednesday 1968-71
Tony Coleman	Doncaster 1965-67	Wednesday 1969-70
Harold Wilcockson	Doncaster 1967-70/71-73	Wednesday 1969-71
Hugh Dowd	Wednesday 1974-79	Doncaster 1979-83
Dave Cusack	Wednesday 1975-78	Doncaster 1985-88/89-90
Ian Nimmo	Wednesday 1975-79	Doncaster 1979-82
David Rushbury	Wednesday 1976-79	Doncaster 1985-87
Tommy Tynan	Wednesday 1976-79	Doncaster 1991-92
Gordon Owen	Wednesday 1977-83	Doncaster 1982-83
Terry Curran	Doncaster 1973-76	Wednesday 1978-82
Ian Bailey	Doncaster 1976-77	Wednesday 1982-83
Tony Cunningham	Wednesday 1983-84	Doncaster 1993-94
Glynn Snodin	Doncaster 1976-85	Wednesday 1985-87
Colin Walker	Doncaster 1982-83/85-86	Wednesday 1986-87
Kenny Brannigan	Wednesday 1986-87	Doncaster 1987-88
O'Neill Donaldson	Doncaster 1994-95	Wednesday 1994-98

v. Everton

Season	League	Date	Result	Home Wed'day	Everton	Date	Result	Away Wed'day	Everton	Final Positions Wed'day	Everton
1892-93	Division 1	13 February	Lost	0	2	26 November	Won	5	3	12th	3rd
1893-94	Division 1	4 November	Drew	1	1	23 December	Lost	1	8	12th	6th
1894-95	Division 1	1 January	Won	3	0	1 September	Lost	1	3	8th	2nd
1895-96	Division 1	18 February	Won	3	1	2 September	Drew	2	2	7th	3rd
1896-97	Division 1	24 October	Won	4	1	5 September	Lost	1	2	6th	7th
1897-98	Division 1	5 February	Won	2	1	8 January	Lost	0	1	5th	4th
1898-99	Division 1	4 March	Lost	1	2	5 November	Lost	0	2	18thR	4th
1900-01	Division 1	30 March	Won	3	1	24 November	Drew	1	1	8th	7th
1901-02	Division 1	5 April	Drew	1	1	7 December	Lost	0	5	9th	2nd
1902-03	Division 1	6 December	Won	4	1	4 April	Drew	1	1	1st	12th
1903-04	Division 1	7 November	Won	1	0	4 April	Lost	0	2	1st	3rd
1904-05	Division 1	12 November	Drew	5	5	11 March	Lost	2	5	9th	2nd
1905-06	Division 1	23 April	Won	3	1	16 December	Lost	0	2	3rd	11th
1906-07	Division 1	27 April	Drew	1	1	22 December	Lost	0	2	13th	3rd
1907-08	Division 1	28 December	Lost	1	2	25 April	Drew	0	0	5th	11th
1908-09	Division 1	17 April	Won	2	0	12 December	Lost	0	1	5th	2nd
1909-10	Division 1	20 September	Lost	1	3	1 September	Drew	1	1	11th	10th
1910-11	Division 1	17 December	Lost	0	2	22 April	Drew	1	1	6th	4th
1911-12	Division 1	20 April	Lost	1	3	16 December	Lost	0	1	5th	2nd
1912-13	Division 1	21 December	Lost	1	2	26 April	Lost	1	3	3rd	11th
1913-14	Division 1	11 April	Drew	2	2	6 December	Drew	1	1	18th	15th
1914-15	Division 1	28 November	Lost	1	4	3 April	Won	1	0	7th	1st
1919-20	Division 1	17 January	Won	1	0	3 January	Drew	1	1	22ndR	16th
1926-27	Division 1	11 September	Won	4	0	2 March	Lost	1	2	16th	20th
1927-28	Division 1	31 December	Lost	1	2	27 August	Lost	0	4	14th	1st
1928-29	Division 1	3 September	Won	1	0	29 August	Drew	0	0	1st	18th
1929-30	Division 1	26 December	Won	4	0	25 December	Won	4	1	1st	22ndR
1931-32	Division 1	27 February	Lost	1	3	17 October	Lost	3	9	3rd	1st
1932-33	Division 1	5 September	Won	3	1	31 August	Lost	1	2	3rd	11th
1933-34	Division 1	20 January	Drew	0	0	9 September	Won	3	2	11th	14th
1934-35	Division 1	15 December	Drew	0	0	1 May	Drew	2	2	3rd	8th
1935-36	Division 1	3 February	Drew	3	3	26 December	Lost	3	4	20th	16th
1936-37	Division 1	10 September	Won	6	4	2 September	Lost	1	3	22ndR	17th
1950-51	Division 1	5 May	Won	6	0	26 March	Drew	0	0	21stR	22ndR
1951-52	Division 2	22 December	Won	4	0	25 August	Drew	3	3	1stP	7th
1954-55	Division 1	5 March	Drew	2	2	11 December	Lost	1	3	22ndR	11th
1956-57	Division 1	6 April	Drew	2	2	24 November	Lost	0	1	14th	15th
1957-58	Division 1	12 April	Won	2	1	30 November	Drew	1	1	22ndR	16th
1959-60	Division 1	6 February	Drew	2	2	19 September	Lost	1	2	5th	15th
1960-61	Division 1	22 April	Lost	1	2	3 December	Lost	2	4	2nd	5th
1961-62	Division 1	13 January	Won	3	1	2 September	Won	4	0	6th	4th
1962-63	Division 1	22 December	Drew	2	2	25 August	Lost	1	4	6th	1st
1963-64	Division 1	1 February	Lost	0	3	21 September	Lost	2	3	6th	3rd
1964-65	Division 1	20 February	Lost	0	1	10 October	Drew	1	1	8th	4th

| | | **Home** | | | | | **Away** | | | *Final Positions* | |
Season	League	Date	Result	Wed'day	Everton	Date	Result	Wed'day	Everton	Wed'day	Everton
1965-66	Division 1	25 August	Won	3	1	31 August	Lost	1	5	17th	11th
1966-67	Division 1	5 November	Lost	1	2	15 October	Lost	1	2	11th	6th
1967-68	Division 1	16 April	Drew	0	0	15 April	Lost	0	1	19th	5th
1968-69	Division 1	19 April	Drew	2	2	14 September	Lost	0	3	15th	3rd
1969-70	Division 1	4 April	Lost	0	1	26 August	Lost	1	2	22ndR	1st
1984-85	Division 1	4 May	Lost	0	1	1 December	Drew	1	1	8th	1st
1985-86	Division 1	3 September	Lost	1	5	28 December	Lost	1	3	5th	2nd
1986-87	Division 1	25 August	Drew	2	2	17 January	Lost	0	2	13th	1st
1987-88	Division 1	1 January	Won	1	0	29 August	Lost	0	4	11th	4th
1988-89	Division 1	5 November	Drew	1	1	11 March	Lost	0	1	15th	8th
1989-90	Division 1	30 August	Drew	1	1	20 January	Lost	0	2	18thR	6th
1991-92	Division 1	28 August	Won	2	1	26 December	Won	1	0	3rd	12th
1992-93	Premiership	6 February	Won	3	1	15 August	Drew	1	1	7th	13th
1993-94	Premiership	2 April	Won	5	1	27 December	Won	2	0	7th	17th
1994-95	Premiership	17 April	Drew	0	0	26 December	Won	4	1	13th	15th
1995-96	Premiership	27 April	Lost	2	5	25 November	Drew	2	2	15th	6th
1996-97	Premiership	11 January	Won	2	1	28 September	Lost	0	2	7th	15th
1997-98	Premiership	4 October	Won	3	1	25 April	Won	3	1	16th	17th
1998-99	Premiership	24 October	Drew	0	0	5 April	Won	2	1	12th	14th
1999-00	Premiership	11 September	Lost	0	2	4 March	Drew	1	1	19thR	13th

FA Cup

										Division	
1892-93	Q'ter final					18 February	Lost	0	3	Div 1	Div 1
1894-95	Q'ter final	2 March	Won	2	0					Div 1	Div 1
1895-96	Q'ter final	29 February	Won	4	0					Div 1	Div 1
1905-06	Q'ter final					10 March	Lost	3	4	Div 1	Div 1
1906-07	Final	20 April	Crystal Palace				Won	2	1	Div 1	Div 1
1920-21	Round 2	3 February	Lost	0	1	29 January	Drew	1	1	Div 2	Div 1
1936-37	Round 4					30 January	Lost	0	3	Div 1	Div 1
1946-47	Round 4	25 January	Won	2	1					Div 2	Div 1
1953-54	Round 5	20 February	Won	3	1					Div 1	Div 2
1964-65	Round 3	13 January	Lost	0	3	9 January	Drew	2	2	Div 1	Div 1
1965-66	Final	14 May	Wembley				Lost	2	3	Div 1	Div 1
1985-86	Semi-Final	5 April	Villa Park				Lost*	1	2	Div 1	Div 1
1987-88	Round 3	9 January	Drew	1	1	13 January	Drew*	1	1	Div 1	Div 1
		(2nd replay)				25 January	Drew*	1	1		
		27 January	Lost	0	5	(3rd replay)					
1989-90	Round 4	28 January	Lost	1	2					Div 1	Div 1

League Cup

										Div 3	Div 1
1977-78	Round 4	29 November	Lost	1	3					Div 3	Div 1
1986-87	Round 3					28 October	Lost	0	4	Div 1	Div 1

Summary	P	W	D	L	F	A
Wednesday's home league record:	64	26	19	19	118	93
Wednesday's away league record:	64	10	18	36	75	134
Wednesday's cup record:	21	5	5	11	27	42
TOTAL:	**149**	**41**	**42**	**66**	**220**	**269**

FACT FILE

- No team has played more matches against Wednesday than Everton. Not only is this series of matches long, but it is packed with drama and records as well.
- The sides have twice met in FA Cup finals, and both have proved dramatic. In 1907 Everton, who would finish 10 places higher than Wednesday in the league, were expected to win, but George Simpson scored the winning goal for Wednesday in the 89th minute.
- In 1966, the Owls took the lead in the fourth minute, and then, early in the second half, went 2-0 up. Everton, however, came back to win 3-2. It was the last time a team came from two goals down to win an FA Cup final.
- It was Wednesday who made a great comeback in a league game in 1904. Trailing 5-0 at one point, they came back to draw 5-5. It is Wednesday's highest ever scoring draw, and is thought to be the only time in league history that any team has recovered from five goals down to draw.
- Wednesday's highest scoring league game of all time was against Everton in 1931, when the Toffees won 9-3. Five years later, Wednesday won a match against Everton 6-4.
- On the final day of the 1950-51 season, Wednesday beat Everton 6-0, but it still wasn't enough to avoid relegation on goal average. Everton were also relegated on goal average, while Chelsea (who beat Bolton 4-0 on the final day) survived.
- In 1988, Everton became the first team since 1890 to beat Wednesday by a five-goal margin in the FA Cup. The margin of victory was particularly surprising given that the sides had already drawn three matches in that cup tie.
- From 1932 to 1960, Wednesday were unbeaten in 13 home games in the series.
- Wednesday won once in 32 matches against Everton away from Hillsborough between 1935 and 1990.

Wednesday's top scorers vs Everton
Harry Davis 8
Ellis Rimmer 7
Mark Bright, Mark Hooper, Jackie Sewell,
Fred Spiksley, Andrew Wilson 6
Laurie Bell, John Fantham, David Hirst 5

Wednesday hat-tricks vs Everton
6 Dec 1902 Andrew Wilson
11 Sep 1926 Jimmy Trotter
25 Dec 1929 Mark Hooper
3 Feb 1936 Ellis Rimmer
10 Sep 1936 Neil Dewar
22 Dec 1951 Derek Dooley (4)

Played for both clubs

Alec Brady	Everton 1889-91	Wednesday 1892-99
Jack Earp	Everton 1891-92	Wednesday 1893-1900
James Jamieson	Everton 1892-93	Wednesday 1893-99
Laurie Bell	Wednesday 1895-97	Everton 1897-99
Frank Bradshaw	Wednesday 1905-10	Everton 1911-14
Walter Holbern	Wednesday 1906-11	Everton 1911-13
Joe Peacock	Everton 1919-27	Wednesday 1930-31
Tom Robson	Everton 1929-30	Wednesday 1930-32
Jimmy McCambridge	Everton 1930-31	Wednesday 1936-37
Tony Kay	Wednesday 1954-63	Everton 1962-64
George Kirby	Everton 1955-58	Wednesday 1959-60
Dave Clements	Wednesday 1971-74	Everton 1973-76
Colin Harvey	Everton 1963-75	Wednesday 1974-76
Terry Curran	Wednesday 1978-82	Everton 1982-85
Gary Megson	Everton 1979-81	Wednesday 1981-84/85-89
Pat Heard	Everton 1978-80	Wednesday 1982-85
Mick Lyons	Everton 1970-82	Wednesday 1982-86
Imre Varadi	Everton 1979-81	Wednesday 1983-85/88-90
Martin Hodge	Everton 1979-81	Wednesday 1983-88
Alan Harper	Everton 1983-88/91-93	Wednesday 1988-90
Mark Pembridge	Wednesday 1995-98	Everton 1999-2004
Niclas Alexandersson	Wednesday 1997-2000	Everton 2000-03
Andy Hinchcliffe	Everton 1990-98	Wednesday 1997-2002
Earl Barrett	Everton 1994-98	Wednesday 1997-99
Barry Horne	Everton 1992-96	Wednesday 1999-2000
Tommy Johnson	Everton 1999-2000	Wednesday 2001-02
David Burrows	Everton 1994-95	Wednesday 2001-03

Sheffield Wednesday lead 2-0 in the 1966 FA Cup final at Wembley against Everton. Here David Ford scores the Owls' second after West had parried John Fantham's shot. Alas, Everton came back to win 3-2.

v. Exeter City

				Home				Away		Final Positions	
Season	League	Date	Result	Wed'day	Exeter	Date	Result	Wed'day	Exeter	Wed'day	Exeter
1977-78	Division 3	17 January	Won	2	1	12 October	Lost	1	2	14th	17th
1978-79	Division 3	24 October	Won	2	1	24 March	Drew	2	2	14th	9th
1979-80	Division 3	8 December	Lost	0	1	26 April	Lost	0	1	3rdP	8th

League Cup *Division*

Season	Round					Date	Result	Wed'day	Exeter		
1968-69	Round 2					4 September	Lost	1	3	Div 1	Div 4

Summary	P	W	D	L	F	A
Wednesday's home league record:	3	2	0	1	4	3
Wednesday's away league record:	3	0	1	2	3	5
Wednesday's cup record:	1	0	0	1	1	3
TOTAL:	**7**	**2**	**1**	**4**	**8**	**11**

Wednesday's top scorers vs Exeter
Brian Hornsby, Rodger Wylde 2

Played for both clubs

John Edmondson	Wednesday 1919-20	Exeter 1923-24
Fred Dent	Wednesday 1920-21	Exeter 1926-28
George Shelton	Wednesday 1919-22	Exeter 1922-26
Jimmy McCambridge	Exeter 1935-36	Wednesday 1936-37
Harry Hanford	Wednesday 1935-40	Exeter 1946-47
Jim Fallon	Wednesday 1937-40	Exeter 1947-48
Jimmy Dailey	Wednesday 1946-49	Exeter 1952-54
Keith Thomas	Wednesday 1950-52	Exeter 1955-57
Peter Fox	Wednesday 1972-77	Exeter 1993-97
Gordon Owen	Wednesday 1977-83	Exeter 1990-91
Mark Chamberlain	Wednesday 1985-88	Exeter 1995-97
Phil King	Exeter 1984-86	Wednesday 1989-94
Lee Bradbury	Exeter 1995-96	Wednesday 2002-03

v. Fulham

		Home				Away				Final Positions	
Season	League	Date	Result	Wed'day	Fulham	Date	Result	Wed'day	Fulham	Wed'day	Fulham
1920-21	Division 2	20 November	Won	3	0	27 November	Lost	0	2	10th	9th
1921-22	Division 2	5 November	Lost	1	4	12 November	Lost	1	3	10th	7th
1922-23	Division 2	7 October	Won	1	0	14 October	Lost	0	1	8th	10th
1923-24	Division 2	22 September	Won	2	1	29 September	Lost	1	4	8th	20th
1924-25	Division 2	11 April	Won	3	1	6 December	Lost	1	2	14th	12th
1925-26	Division 2	29 August	Won	3	0	2 January	Lost	0	3	1stP	19th
1937-38	Division 2	2 September	Won	2	1	6 September	Drew	0	0	17th	8th
1938-39	Division 2	27 December	Won	5	1	17 April	Drew	2	2	3rd	12th
1946-47	Division 2	16 September	Drew	1	1	7 April	Won	2	1	20th	15th
1947-48	Division 2	15 November	Won	2	0	3 April	Won	2	0	4th	11th
1948-49	Division 2	30 October	Lost	1	2	26 March	Drew	1	1	8th	1stP
1950-51	Division 1	7 April	Drew	2	2	18 November	Lost	2	4	21stR	18th
1955-56	Division 2	14 April	Lost	2	3	3 December	Won	2	1	1stP	9th
1958-59	Division 2	30 March	Drew	2	2	27 March	Lost	2	6	1stP	2ndP
1959-60	Division 1	26 December	Drew	1	1	28 December	Won	2	1	5th	10th
1960-61	Division 1	10 September	Won	2	0	21 January	Won	6	1	2nd	17th
1961-62	Division 1	9 September	Drew	1	1	20 January	Won	2	0	6th	20th
1962-63	Division 1	12 September	Won	1	0	19 September	Lost	1	4	6th	16th
1963-64	Division 1	4 September	Won	3	0	28 August	Lost	0	2	6th	15th
1964-65	Division 1	14 November	Drew	1	1	27 March	Lost	0	2	8th	20th
1965-66	Division 1	20 November	Won	1	0	16 April	Lost	2	4	17th	20th
1966-67	Division 1	22 October	Drew	1	1	18 March	Won	2	1	11th	18th
1967-68	Division 1	6 September	Won	4	2	28 February	Lost	0	2	19th	22ndR
1971-72	Division 2	2 October	Won	4	0	28 March	Lost	0	4	14th	20th
1972-73	Division 2	12 August	Won	3	0	17 February	Lost	0	1	10th	9th
1973-74	Division 2	15 December	Lost	0	3	2 February	Lost	1	4	19th	13th
1974-75	Division 2	23 November	Won	1	0	25 February	Lost	1	2	22ndR	9th
1982-83	Division 2	30 April	Won	2	1	27 November	Lost	0	1	6th	4th
1983-84	Division 2	7 March	Drew	1	1	11 November	Drew	1	1	2ndP	11th
2000-01	Division 1	28 October	Drew	3	3	16 April	Drew	1	1	17th	1stP

FA Cup

										Division	
1950-51	Round 3					6 January	Lost	0	1	Div 1	Div 1
1972-73	Round 3	13 January	Won	2	0					Div 2	Div 2
1984-85	Round 3					5 January	Won	3	2	Div 1	Div 2

League Cup

1984-85	Round 3	30 October	Won	3	2					Div 1	Div 2

Summary	P	W	D	L	F	A
Wednesday's home league record:	30	17	9	4	59	32
Wednesday's away league record:	30	7	5	18	35	61
Wednesday's cup record:	4	3	0	1	8	5
TOTAL:	64	27	14	23	102	98

FACT FILE

- Between 1959 and 1973, Wednesday were unbeaten in 13 home matches against Fulham.
- Wednesday have won one of their last 13 league games at Craven Cottage.
- Between 1921 and 1937, the series produced 10 successive home wins.

Wednesday's top scorers vs Fulham
John Fantham 8
Alan Finney, Sam Powell, Roy Shiner 4

Wednesday hat-tricks vs Fulham
11 Apr 1924 Sam Powell

Played for both clubs

Ted Worrall	Wednesday 1910-15	Fulham 1919-23
Johnny McIntyre	Fulham 1919-20	Wednesday 1919-22
Sid Binks	Wednesday 1922-25	Fulham 1928-30
Mark Pearson	Wednesday 1963-65	Fulham 1965-68
Alan Warboys	Wednesday 1968-71	Fulham 1976-78
Simon Stewart	Wednesday 1992-93	Fulham 1996-97
Mark Pembridge	Wednesday 1995-98	Fulham 2003-04
Wayne Collins	Wednesday 1996-98	Fulham 1997-2001

On 12 August 1972 Sheffield Wednesday were at home to Fulham. It was the first Football League appearance by ex-England centre-half Peter Swan since 8 April 1964. Swan had been banned for life for his involvement in the Soccer Bribes case. The Owls won the game 3-0.

v. Gainsborough Trinity

Season	League	Date	Home Result	Wed'day	Gainsb'gh	Date	Away Result	Wed'day	Gainsb'gh	Final Positions Wed'day	Gainsb'gh
1899-00	Division 2	6 January	Won	5	1	9 September	Won	2	0	1stP	13th

Summary	P	W	D	L	F	A
Wednesday's home league record:	1	1	0	0	5	1
Wednesday's away league record:	1	1	0	0	2	0
TOTAL:	2	2	0	0	7	1

Wednesday's top scorers vs Gainsborough
Harry Millar 5

Wednesday hat-tricks vs Gainsborough
6 Jan 1900 Harry Millar (4)

Played for both clubs
John Webster	Wednesday 1893-95	Gainsborough 1896-99
Fred Thackeray	Wednesday 1900-03	Gainsborough 1904-05
Frank Foxall	Gainsborough 1903-07	Wednesday 1906-10
Ollie Tummon	Wednesday 1905-10	Gainsborough 1910-12

Harry Millar hit four goals as a new century dawned. He is also the leading Wednesday scorer against the Lincolnshire club.

v. Gillingham

		Home				Away		Final Positions	
Season	League	Date	Result	Wed'day Gill'ham	Date	Result	Wed'day Gill'ham	Wed'day	Gill'ham
1975-76	Division 3	5 November	Won	1 0	7 February	Drew	0 0	20th	15th
1976-77	Division 3	9 October	Won	2 0	19 March	Lost	0 1	8th	12th
1977-78	Division 3	19 November	Drew	0 0	15 April	Lost	1 2	14th	7th
1978-79	Division 3	6 March	Won	2 1	12 September	Drew	0 0	14th	4th
1979-80	Division 3	7 April	Won	1 0	18 March	Drew	1 1	3rdP	16th
2000-01	Division 1	3 March	Won	2 1	30 September	Lost	0 2	17th	13th
2001-02	Division 1	9 March	Drew	0 0	15 December	Lost	1 2	20th	12th
2002-03	Division 1	14 December	Lost	0 2	16 November	Drew	1 1	22ndR	11th

FA Cup								Division	
1994-95	Round 3				7 January	Won	2 1	Prem	Div 3
1999-00	Round 5				29 January	Lost	1 3	Prem	Div 2
2002-03	Round 3				7 January	Lost	1 4	Div 1	Div 1

Summary	P	W	D	L	F	A
Wednesday's home league record:	8	5	2	1	8	4
Wednesday's away league record:	8	0	4	4	4	9
Wednesday's cup record:	3	1	0	2	4	8
TOTAL:	19	6	6	7	16	21

FACT FILE

- Wednesday have only won once in 11 visits to Priestfield, but then Gillingham have only won once in eight visits to Hillsborough.

Wednesday's top scorers vs Gillingham
Gerald Sibon 3
Rodger Wylde 2

Played for both clubs

Harry Anstiss	Wednesday 1926-27	Gillingham 1934-35
Fred Lester	Gillingham 1930-38	Wednesday 1937-39
Cyril Walker	Gillingham 1937-38	Wednesday 1937-38
John Ballagher	Wednesday 1958-59	Gillingham 1962-64
John Meredith	Wednesday 1960-61	Gillingham 1963-69
Kevin Johnson	Wednesday 1971-72	Gillingham 1973-74
Michael Kent	Gillingham 1970-71	Wednesday 1973-74
Neil O'Donnell	Gillingham 1974-76	Wednesday 1975-77
Peter Feely	Gillingham 1974-76	Wednesday 1975-77
John Davis	Gillingham 1975-76	Wednesday 1976-77
Donald Rushbury	Wednesday 1976-79	Gillingham 1984-85
Jeff Johnson	Wednesday 1976-81	Gillingham 1982-85
Martin Hodge	Gillingham 1982-83	Wednesday 1983-88
Tommy Johnson	Wednesday 2001-02	Gillingham 2002-04
Craig Armstrong	Gillingham 1996-97	Wednesday 2001-04

v. Glossop

FA Cup	Date	Result	Home Wed'day Glossop						Division Wed'day Glossop
1908-09 Round 3	20 February	Lost	0 1						Div 1 Div 2

Summary	P	W	D	L	F	A
Wednesday's cup record:	1	0	0	1	0	1
TOTAL:	1	0	0	1	0	1

FACT FILE

- Of Wednesday's 123 domestic opponents, Glossop are the only ones against whom they have never scored. Glossop are also the only ones Wednesday have never beaten.

Played for both clubs

| Fred Spiksley | Wednesday 1892-1903 | Glossop 1904-05 |
| Jack Pryce | Glossop 1898-99 | Wednesday 1898-1901 |

Jack Pryce arrived at
Sheffield from Glossop in
1899.

v. Grimsby Town

Season	League	Date (Home)	Result	Wed'day	Grimsby	Date (Away)	Result	Wed'day	Grimsby	Wed'day	Grimsby
1899-00	Division 2	1 January	Won	2	1	13 April	Won	2	1	1stP	6th
1901-02	Division 1	7 September	Won	3	1	4 January	Lost	1	3	9th	15th
1902-03	Division 1	14 February	Drew	1	1	18 October	Won	1	0	1st	17thR
1929-30	Division 1	26 April	Won	1	0	5 February	Won	5	0	1st	18th
1930-31	Division 1	17 January	Won	4	1	13 September	Won	3	2	3rd	13th
1931-32	Division 1	31 August	Won	4	1	7 May	Lost	1	3	3rd	21stR
1934-35	Division 1	4 May	Won	1	0	22 December	Lost	1	3	3rd	5th
1935-36	Division 1	16 November	Won	3	0	24 March	Lost	0	4	20th	17th
1936-37	Division 1	7 November	Won	2	1	13 March	Lost	1	5	22ndR	12th
1948-49	Division 2	16 October	Won	4	1	12 March	Lost	0	2	8th	11th
1949-50	Division 2	26 April	Won	4	0	8 October	Lost	1	4	2ndP	11th
1958-59	Division 2	18 October	Won	6	0	7 March	Won	2	0	1stP	21stR
1975-76	Division 3	20 September	Won	4	0	17 January	Drew	1	1	20th	18th
1976-77	Division 3	9 April	Won	1	0	28 December	Drew	1	1	8th	23rdR
1979-80	Division 3	23 October	Won	2	0	6 November	Lost	1	3	3rdP	1stP
1980-81	Division 2	28 April	Lost	1	2	21 October	Drew	0	0	10th	7th
1981-82	Division 2	20 February	Drew	1	1	26 September	Won	1	0	4th	17th
1982-83	Division 2	23 October	Won	2	0	5 March	Drew	1	1	6th	19th
1983-84	Division 2	21 April	Won	1	0	26 December	Lost	0	1	2ndP	5th
2000-01	Division 1	1 January	Won	1	0	26 August	Won	1	0	17th	18th
2001-02	Division 1	10 November	Drew	0	0	1 April	Drew	0	0	20th	19th
2002-03	Division 1	19 April	Drew	0	0	21 December	Lost	0	2	22ndR	24thR
2003-04	Division 2	27 September	Drew	0	0	3 April	Lost	0	2	16th	21stR

FA Cup

Season	Round	Date	Result	Wed'day	Grimsby			Division	
1912-13	Round 1	16 January	Won	5	1			Div 1	Div 2
1996-97	Round 3	4 January	Won	7	1			Prem	Div 1

League Cup

Season	Round	Date	Result	Wed'day	Grimsby	Date	Result	Wed'day	Grimsby	Division	
1976-77	Round 1	18 August	Drew	0	0	14 August	Won	3	0	Div 3	Div 3
1997-98	Round 2	1 October	Won	3	2	17 September	Lost	0	2	Prem	Div 2

Once on the books at Grimsby, much-travelled winger Terry Curran played 125 games for the Owls and scored 35 goals before moving to Southampton.

Summary	P	W	D	L	F	A
Wednesday's home league record:	23	17	5	1	48	10
Wednesday's away league record:	23	7	5	11	24	38
Wednesday's cup record:	6	4	1	1	18	6
TOTAL:	52	28	11	13	90	54

FACT FILE

- Wednesday won 15 and drew two of their first 17 home games against Grimsby.
- Overall, Grimsby have won at Hillsborough just once in 27 attempts. They have not scored there in their last six league matches, and have scored more than once in a match just twice.
- From 1932 to 1949, Wednesday lost six successive away games in the series.

Wednesday's top scorers vs Grimsby
Ellis Rimmer 7
Rodger Wylde 5
Jack Ball, Redfern Froggatt, David McLean 4

Wednesday hat-tricks vs Grimsby
16 Jan 1913 David McLean (4) (cup)
26 Apr 1950 Walter Rickett

Played for both clubs

Bill Hemingfield	Wednesday 1898-99/1903-07	Grimsby 1899-1903
Jack Reynolds	Grimsby 1904-05	Wednesday 1905-07
Christopher Crapper	Wednesday 1905-06	Grimsby 1907-08
Martin Bradley	Grimsby 1907-09	Wednesday 1910-11
Ted Gleenon	Grimsby 1907-09	Wednesday 1910-15
Jack Burkinshaw	Grimsby 1907-09	Wednesday 1913-20
Joe Cooper	Wednesday 1920-21	Grimsby 1924-32
Ernie Thompson	Wednesday 1921-22	Grimsby 1924-25
Billy Felton	Grimsby 1921-23	Wednesday 1922-29
Billy Powell	Wednesday 1924-25	Grimsby 1927-30
Charlie Wilson	Wednesday 1927-32	Grimsby 1931-33
Jim Wright	Grimsby 1932-35	Wednesday 1934-36
Laurie MacKenzie	Wednesday 1946-48	Grimsby 1949-51
Brian Slater	Wednesday 1952-53	Grimsby 1954-55
Roy Coyle	Wednesday 1972-74	Grimsby 1974-75
Terry Curran	Wednesday 1978-82	Grimsby 1987-88
Mick Lyons	Wednesday 1982-86	Grimsby 1985-87
Ian Knight	Wednesday 1985-89	Grimsby 1989-92
Des Hazel	Grimsby 1986-87	Wednesday 1987-88
Craig Shakespeare	Wednesday 1989-90	Grimsby 1993-97
Paul Warhurst	Wednesday 1990-93	Grimsby 2003-04
Nigel Jemson	Wednesday 1991-94	Grimsby 1993-94
Terry Cooke	Wednesday 2000-01/03-04	Grimsby 2001-03
Tony Crane	Wednesday 2000-03	Grimsby 2003-04
Marlon Broomes	Wednesday 2001-02	Grimsby 2001-02
Craig Armstrong	Wednesday 2001-04	Grimsby 2003-04
Mickael Antoine-Curier	Grimsby 2003-04	Wednesday 2003-04

v. Halifax Town

Season	League	Date	Result	Home Wed'day	Halifax	Date	Result	Away Wed'day	Halifax	Final Positions Wed'day	Halifax
1975-76	Division 3	20 April	Won	1	0	2 March	Drew	0	0	20th	24thR

Summary	P	W	D	L	F	A
Wednesday's home league record:	1	1	0	0	1	0
Wednesday's away league record:	1	0	1	0	0	0
TOTAL:	2	1	1	0	1	0

FACT FILE

- Phil Henson scored Wednesday's one goal against Halifax.

Played for both clubs

Laurie Burkinshaw	Wednesday 1911-14	Halifax 1922-23
John Whalley	Wednesday 1919-20	Halifax 1921-26
Fred Dent	Wednesday 1920-21	Halifax 1921-23
Sam Taylor	Wednesday 1920-25	Halifax 1928-29
Sedley Cooper	Halifax 1928-31	Wednesday 1933-36
Frank Westlake	Wednesday 1937-50	Halifax 1950-51
Edgar Packard	Wednesday 1946-52	Halifax 1952-54
Doug Fletcher	Wednesday 1948-50	Halifax 1959-60
Gerald Henry	Wednesday 1949-52	Halifax 1951-53
Walter Rickett	Wednesday 1949-53	Halifax 1953-54
Bill Shadbolt	Wednesday 1952-53	Halifax 1953-54
Walter Bingley	Wednesday 1955-57	Halifax 1963-65
John Quinn	Wednesday 1959-68	Halifax 1972-75
Mark Pearson	Wednesday 1963-65	Halifax 1968-69
Andy Burgin	Wednesday 1964-65	Halifax 1968-75
David Ford	Wednesday 1965-70	Halifax 1973-76
Kenny Burton	Wednesday 1968-72	Halifax 1980-81
Mick Prendergast	Wednesday 1968-78	Halifax 1978-79
Steve Downes	Wednesday 1969-72	Halifax 1974-76
Kevin Johnson	Wednesday 1971-72	Halifax 1978-81
Derek Bell	Wednesday 1975-76	Halifax 1975-79
John Collins	Halifax 1974-76	Wednesday 1976-77
Tony Gregory	Wednesday 1985-89	Halifax 1990-92
Mike Williams	Halifax 1992-93/99-2000	Wednesday 1992-97
Grant Holt	Halifax 1999-2001	Wednesday 2002-04

v. Halliwell

FA Cup		Date	Result	Home Wed'day	Halliwell					Division Wed'day	Halliwell
1890-91	Round 1	17 January	Won	12	0					Non L	Non L

Summary	P	W	D	L	F	A
Wednesday's cup record:	1	1	0	0	12	0
TOTAL:	1	1	0	0	12	0

FACT FILE

- This is Wednesday's biggest-ever win in the FA Cup, and the last occasion on which they reached double figures.
- Halliwell were based in Bolton.

Wednesday's top scorers vs Halliwell
Harry Woolhouse 5
Tom Brandon, T.E. Cawley 2

Wednesday hat-tricks vs Halliwell
17 Jan 1891 Harry Woolhouse (5) (cup)

v. Hartlepool United

Season	League	Date	Result	Home Wed'day	Hartlep'l	Date	Result	Away Wed'day	Hartlep'l	Final Positions Wed'day	Hartlep'l
2003-04	Division 2	14 February	Won	1	0	10 October	Drew	1	1	16th	6th

League Cup		Date	Result	Home Wed'day	Hartlep'l	Date	Result	Away Wed'day	Hartlep'l	Division Wed'day	Hartlep'l
1992-93	Round 2	23 September	Won	3	0	6 October	Drew	2	2	Prem	Div 2
2003-04	Round 1	13 August	Drew*	2	2	(lost 4-5 penalties)				Div 2	Div 2

Summary	P	W	D	L	F	A	
Wednesday's home league record:	1	1	0	0	1	0	
Wednesday's away league record:	1	0	1	0	1	1	
Wednesday's cup record:	3	1	2	0	7	4	
TOTAL:	5	2	3	0	9	5	(+one penalty shoot-out defeat)

FACT FILE

- **No side has played Wednesday so often without winning at least once.**

Wednesday's top scorers vs Hartlepool
Mark Bright 2

Played for both clubs

George Kell	Wednesday 1920-21	Hartlepool 1925-28
Tom Mackey	Hartlepool 1928-30	Wednesday 1929-32
Jim Wright	Wednesday 1934-36	Hartlepool 1938-40
Jack Brown	Wednesday 1922-37	Hartlepool 1937-38
Jimmy McCambridge	Wednesday 1936-37	Hartlepool 1936-37
Peter Howells	Wednesday 1954-56	Hartlepool 1956-57
Albert Broadbent	Wednesday 1955-58	Hartlepool 1966-68
Harold Clark	Wednesday 1957-58	Hartlepool 1958-61
Kevin Johnson	Wednesday 1971-72	Hartlepool 1974-77/80-84
Eddie Prudham	Wednesday 1970-75	Hartlepool 1976-77
Eric McMordie	Wednesday 1974-75	Hartlepool 1976-78
Barry Watling	Hartlepool 1972-76	Wednesday 1975-76
Malcolm Darling	Wednesday 1977-78	Hartlepool 1977-78
Brian Cox	Wednesday 1978-81	Hartlepool 1990-91
Martin Hodge	Wednesday 1983-88	Hartlepool 1991-93
Mark Proctor	Wednesday 1987-89	Hartlepool 1996-97
Gordon Watson	Wednesday 1990-95	Hartlepool 2001-03
David Johnson	Wednesday 1991-92	Hartlepool 1991-93
Richie Humphreys	Wednesday 1995-2001	Hartlepool 2001-04
Brian Barry-Murphy	Wednesday 2002-03	Hartlepool 2002-03
Graeme Lee	Hartlepool 1995-2003	Wednesday 2003-04
Paul Smith	Hartlepool 2001-03	Wednesday 2003-04

v. Hastings United

FA Cup	Date	Result	Home Wed'day Hastings		Division Wed'day Hastings
1954-55 Round 3	8 January	Won	2 1		Div 1 Non L

Summary	P	W	D	L	F	A
Wednesday's cup record:	1	1	0	0	2	1
TOTAL:	1	1	0	0	2	1

FACT FILE

● Goals from Shaw and Greensmith settled this surprisingly close tie.

Goalkeeper Dave McIntosh, who kept for the Owls in the cup-tie against Hastings.

v. Hereford United

Season	League	Date	Result	Wed'day	Hereford	Date	Result	Wed'day	Hereford	Wed'day	Hereford
			Home					**Away**		*Final Positions*	
1975-76	Division 3	10 January	Lost	**1**	**2**	30 August	Lost	**1**	**3**	20th	1stP
1977-78	Division 3	31 December	Won	**1**	**0**	1 April	Won	**1**	**0**	14th	23rdR

FA Cup

		Date	Result			*Division*
1957-58	Round 3	4 January	Won	**3**	**0**	Div 1 Non L

Summary	P	W	D	L	F	A
Wednesday's home league record:	2	1	0	1	2	2
Wednesday's away league record:	2	1	0	1	2	3
Wednesday's cup record:	1	1	0	0	3	0
TOTAL:	5	3	0	2	7	5

Wednesday's top scorers vs Hereford
Redfern Froggatt, Rodger Wylde 2

Played for both clubs

David Layne	Wednesday 1962-64	Hereford 1972-73
Paul Taylor	Wednesday 1971-73	Hereford 1973-74
Andy Proudlove	Wednesday 1975-76	Hereford 1977-78
Derek Jefferson	Wednesday 1976-77	Hereford 1976-78
Jimmy Hinch	Hereford 1973-74	Wednesday 1977-78
Trevor Matthewson	Wednesday 1980-83	Hereford 1996-97
Dean Smith	Hereford 1994-97	Wednesday 2002-04

Sheffield United when they won the Second Division, featuring Redfern Froggatt, who scored twice in the 1958 FA Cup win at Edgar Street, front row, second from left.

v. Huddersfield Town

Season	League	Date	Result	Home Wed'day	Home Hudd'fd	Date	Result	Away Wed'day	Away Hudd'fd	Final Wed'day	Final Hudd'fd
1926-27	Division 1	25 September	Drew	1	1	12 February	Lost	3	4	16th	2nd
1927-28	Division 1	27 December	Lost	0	5	26 December	Lost	0	1	14th	2nd
1928-29	Division 1	1 January	Drew	1	1	2 April	Drew	0	0	1st	16th
1929-30	Division 1	19 October	Won	3	1	22 February	Lost	1	4	1st	10th
1930-31	Division 1	1 January	Won	2	1	7 April	Drew	1	1	3rd	5th
1931-32	Division 1	19 September	Won	4	1	30 January	Lost	1	6	3rd	4th
1932-33	Division 1	26 November	Won	2	1	8 April	Lost	0	4	3rd	6th
1933-34	Division 1	24 March	Lost	1	2	11 November	Lost	2	3	11th	2nd
1934-35	Division 1	9 March	Drew	1	1	27 October	Lost	0	4	3rd	16th
1935-36	Division 1	16 September	Lost	1	2	2 May	Lost	0	1	20th	3rd
1936-37	Division 1	17 September	Drew	2	2	1 May	Lost	0	1	22ndR	15th
1950-51	Division 1	3 February	Won	3	2	23 September	Won	4	3	21stR	19th
1953-54	Division 1	3 April	Lost	1	4	14 November	Lost	0	2	19th	3rd
1954-55	Division 1	6 September	Won	4	1	13 September	Lost	0	3	22ndR	12th
1958-59	Division 2	29 November	Won	4	1	18 April	Won	2	1	1stP	14th
1972-73	Division 2	27 September	Won	3	2	4 November	Lost	0	1	10th	21stR
1983-84	Division 2	29 October	Drew	0	0	1 May	Won	1	0	2ndP	12th
2000-01	Division 1	19 August	Lost	2	3	30 December	Drew	0	0	17th	22ndR

FA Cup

										Division	
1929-30	Semi-Final	22 March		Old Trafford			Lost	1	2	Div 1	Div 1
1965-66	Round 5					5 March	Won	2	1	Div 1	Div 2

League Cup

1984-85	Round 2	25 September	Won	3	0	9 October	Lost	1	2	Div 1	Div 2

Summary	P	W	D	L	F	A
Wednesday's home league record:	18	8	5	5	35	31
Wednesday's away league record:	18	3	3	12	15	39
Wednesday's cup record:	4	2	0	2	7	5
TOTAL:	40	13	8	19	57	75

FACT FILE

- The 1930 FA Cup semi-final defeat was probably the most agonising defeat in Wednesday's history. Wednesday were 1-0 up, then Huddersfield equalised with a definite handball in the build-up and took the lead against the run of play. Wednesday then seemed to be about to equalise, only for the referee to blow the final whistle as the ball was heading for goal. Some say that the final whistle went after 43 minutes of play in the second half.
- Wednesday failed to win in their first 12 games in the series outside of Sheffield.

Wednesday's top scorers vs Huddersfield
Ellis Rimmer 8
Redfern Froggatt 5
Harry Burgess, Alan Finney 3

Played for both clubs

William Bartlett	Wednesday 1903-10	Huddersfield 1910-12
Henry Hamilton	Wednesday 1909-10	Huddersfield 1910-11
Jimmy Campbell	Wednesday 1910-20	Huddersfield 1920-21
Colin McKay	Wednesday 1919-20	Huddersfield 1920-22
Stanley Pearson	Wednesday 1919-20	Huddersfield 1921-22
Sam Taylor	Huddersfield 1919-21	Wednesday 1920-25
Fred Lunn	Huddersfield 1920-21	Wednesday 1921-22
Sid Binks	Wednesday 1922-25	Huddersfield 1924-26
Ted Richardson	Huddersfield 1923-25	Wednesday 1924-25
Norman Smith	Huddersfield 1924-28	Wednesday 1927-28
Jack Ball	Wednesday 1930-34	Huddersfield 1934-35
Charlie Luke	Huddersfield 1931-36	Wednesday 1935-38
Sedley Cooper	Wednesday 1933-36	Huddersfield 1936-37
Jack Marriott	Wednesday 1946-55	Huddersfield 1955-57
Tony Conwell	Wednesday 1953-55	Huddersfield 1955-59
Don McEvoy	Huddersfield 1949-55	Wednesday 1954-58
Ron Staniforth	Huddersfield 1952-55	Wednesday 1955-59
Roy Shiner	Huddersfield 1951-55	Wednesday 1955-60
Colin Dobson	Wednesday 1961-66	Huddersfield 1966-71
Graham Pugh	Wednesday 1965-72	Huddersfield 1972-75
Kevin Johnson	Wednesday 1971-72	Huddersfield 1976-78
Mark Smith	Wednesday 1977-87	Huddersfield 1992-93
Brian Cox	Wednesday 1978-81	Huddersfield 1981-88
Terry Curran	Wednesday 1978-82	Huddersfield 1985-86
Julian Watts	Wednesday 1992-96	Huddersfield 1997-98
Mike Williams	Wednesday 1992-97	Huddersfield 1996-97
Andy Booth	Huddersfield 1991-96/2000-04	Wednesday 1996-2001
Barry Horne	Huddersfield 1997-2000	Wednesday 1999-2000
Steve Harkness	Huddersfield 1993-94	Wednesday 2000-01
Kevin Gallacher	Wednesday 2001-02	Huddersfield 2002-03
Craig Armstrong	Huddersfield 1998-2001	Wednesday 2001-04
Leon Knight	Huddersfield 2001-02	Wednesday 2002-03

v. Hull City

Season	League	Date	Result	Home Wed'day	Hull	Date	Result	Away Wed'day	Hull	Final Positions Wed'day	Hull
1920-21	Division 2	21 March	Won	3	0	26 February	Drew	1	1	10th	13th
1921-22	Division 2	17 April	Drew	0	0	14 April	Drew	0	0	10th	5th
1922-23	Division 2	25 November	Won	1	0	18 November	Drew	0	0	8th	12th
1923-24	Division 2	17 November	Won	1	0	24 November	Drew	1	1	8th	17th
1924-25	Division 2	25 April	Won	5	0	20 December	Lost	2	4	14th	10th
1925-26	Division 2	3 April	Won	2	0	21 November	Won	1	0	1stP	13th
1949-50	Division 2	24 September	Won	6	2	4 February	Drew	1	1	2ndP	7th
1951-52	Division 2	1 March	Won	6	0	13 October	Won	1	0	1stP	18th
1955-56	Division 2	11 February	Won	4	1	1 October	Drew	2	2	1stP	22ndR
1970-71	Division 2	10 April	Drew	1	1	26 December	Drew	4	4	15th	5th
1971-72	Division 2	4 December	Won	2	1	22 April	Lost	0	1	14th	12th
1972-73	Division 2	26 August	Won	4	2	6 January	Drew	1	1	10th	13th
1973-74	Division 2	26 December	Drew	1	1	2 March	Lost	1	2	19th	9th
1974-75	Division 2	19 October	Won	2	1	26 April	Lost	0	1	22ndR	8th
1978-79	Division 3	19 May	Lost	2	3	13 April	Drew	1	1	14th	8th
1979-80	Division 3	21 August	Drew	0	0	9 October	Drew	1	1	3rdP	20th
1990-91	Division 2	1 September	Won	5	1	12 January	Won	1	0	3rdP	24thR

FA Cup

										Division	
1957-58	Round 4	29 January	Won	4	3					Div 1	Div 3N

League Cup

| 1979-80 | Round 1 | 11 August | Drew | 1 | 1 | 14 August | Won | 2 | 1 | Div 3 | Div 3 |

Summary	P	W	D	L	F	A
Wednesday's home league record:	17	12	4	1	45	13
Wednesday's away league record:	17	3	10	4	18	20
Wednesday's cup record:	3	2	1	0	7	5
TOTAL:	**37**	**17**	**15**	**5**	**70**	**38**

Tough-tackling Ken
Knighton served Sheffield
Wednesday and Hull City.

FACT FILE

- **Wednesday were unbeaten in their first 15 home matches against Hull.**
- **Wednesday lost once in their first 22 games in the series.**

Wednesday's top scorers vs Hull
Derek Dooley, Redfern Froggatt, Clarrie Jordan 4
Terry Curran, Brian Joicey, Johnny McIntyre,
Roy Shiner, Jimmy Trotter 3

Wednesday hat-tricks vs Hull
24 Sep 1949 Clarrie Jordan (4)
1 Mar 1952 Derek Dooley (4)
1 Sep 1990 David Hirst

Played for both clubs

Ambrose Langley	Wednesday 1893-1904	Hull 1905-06
Harry Chapman	Wednesday 1900-11	Hull 1910-12
Pat O'Connell	Wednesday 1908-12	Hull 1912-14
Joe Harron	Hull 1920-21	Wednesday 1922-25
Ernie Blenkinsop	Hull 1921-23	Wednesday 1922-34
Arthur Prince	Wednesday 1924-28	Hull 1928-29
Jack Wilkinson	Wednesday 1925-30	Hull 1936-37
Ronnie Starling	Hull 1927-30	Wednesday 1932-37
Bill Gowdy	Hull 1929-32	Wednesday 1931-32
Jackie Sewell	Wednesday 1950-56	Hull 1959-61
Ron Capewell	Wednesday 1952-54	Hull 1954-55
Roy Shiner	Wednesday 1955-60	Hull 1959-60
John Hickton	Wednesday 1963-66	Hull 1976-77
Alan Warboys	Wednesday 1968-71	Hull 1977-79
Dave Sunley	Wednesday 1970-76	Hull 1975-78
Ken Knighton	Hull 1970-73	Wednesday 1973-76
Gordon Owen	Wednesday 1977-83	Hull 1987-88
Terry Curran	Wednesday 1978-82	Hull 1986-87
John Pearson	Wednesday 1980-85	Hull 1991-92
Pat Heard	Wednesday 1982-85	Hull 1985-88/92-93
Brian Marwood	Hull 1979-84	Wednesday 1984-88
Wayne Jacobs	Wednesday 1987-88	Hull 1987-92
Owen Morrison	Wednesday 1998-2003	Hull 2002-03
Dean Windass	Hull 1991-96	Wednesday 2001-02
Michael Reddy	Hull 2001-02	Wednesday 2002-04

Ken Knighton

v. Ipswich Town

			Home				Away			Final Positions	
Season	League	Date	Result	Wed'day	Ipswich	Date	Result	Wed'day	Ipswich	Wed'day	Ipswich
1958-59	Division 2	3 January	Won	3	1	30 August	Won	2	0	1stP	16th
1961-62	Division 1	30 September	Lost	1	4	9 March	Lost	1	2	6th	1st
1962-63	Division 1	20 April	Lost	0	3	1 December	Lost	0	2	6th	17th
1963-64	Division 1	7 September	Won	3	1	11 January	Won	4	1	6th	22ndR
1968-69	Division 1	7 September	Won	2	1	25 April	Lost	0	2	15th	12th
1969-70	Division 1	31 January	Drew	2	2	4 October	Lost	0	1	22ndR	18th
1984-85	Division 1	22 September	Drew	2	2	13 April	Won	2	1	8th	17th
1985-86	Division 1	3 May	Won	1	0	30 November	Lost	1	2	5th	20thR
1990-91	Division 2	15 December	Drew	2	2	25 August	Won	2	0	3rdP	14th
1992-93	Premiership	21 November	Drew	1	1	10 March	Won	1	0	7th	16th
1993-94	Premiership	23 April	Won	5	0	6 November	Won	4	1	7th	19th
1994-95	Premiership	14 May	Won	4	1	16 October	Won	2	1	13th	22ndR
2002-03	Division 1	15 March	Lost	0	1	12 October	Lost	1	2	22ndR	7th

FA Cup

										Division	
1984-85	Round 5					4 March	Lost	2	3	Div 1	Div 1

League Cup

1992-93	Q'ter final	3 February	Won	1	0	19 January	Drew	1	1	Prem	Prem

Summary

	P	W	D	L	F	A
Wednesday's home league record:	13	6	4	3	26	19
Wednesday's away league record:	13	7	0	6	20	15
Wednesday's cup record:	3	1	1	1	4	4
TOTAL:	**29**	**14**	**5**	**10**	**50**	**38**

Steve McCall had played for eight seasons at Ipswich before arriving at Hillsborough in 1987.

FACT FILE

- Only one of the 15 meetings at Portman Road has ended in a draw.
- There has never been a goalless draw between these sides.
- Wednesday were unbeaten in 11 games from 1986 to 1995.

Wednesday's top scorers vs Ipswich
Mark Bright, David Layne 4
Brian Marwood 3

Wednesday hat-tricks vs Ipswich
11 Jan 1964 David Layne

Played for both clubs

Ellis Rimmer	Wednesday 1927-38	Ipswich 1938-39
Jack Roy	Wednesday 1936-38	Ipswich 1946-47
Allenby Driver	Wednesday 1937-46	Ipswich 1949-52
Derek Jefferson	Ipswich 1967-73	Wednesday 1976-77
Lee Chapman	Wednesday 1984-88	Ipswich 1994-96
Ian Cranson	Ipswich 1983-88	Wednesday 1987-89
Steve McCall	Ipswich 1979-87	Wednesday 1987-91
Steve Whitton	Wednesday 1988-91	Ipswich 1990-94
Dalian Atkinson	Ipswich 1985-89	Wednesday 1989-90
Chris Bart-Williams	Wednesday 1991-95	Ipswich 2003-04
Jim Magilton	Wednesday 1997-99	Ipswich 1998-2004
Danny Sonner	Ipswich 1996-99	Wednesday 1998-2000
David Johnson	Ipswich 1997-2001	Wednesday 2001-02
Shefki Kuqi	Wednesday 2001-04	Ipswich 2003-04
Mark Burchill	Ipswich 2000-01	Wednesday 2003-04

v. Leeds United

			Home				Away		Final Positions	
Season	League	Date	Result	Wed'day	Leeds	Date	Result	Wed'day	Leeds	Wed'day	Leeds
1920-21	Division 2	9 October	Won	2	0	16 October	Lost	0	2	10th	14th
1921-22	Division 2	27 December	Won	2	1	26 December	Drew	1	1	10th	8th
1922-23	Division 2	19 March	Won	3	1	17 February	Drew	0	0	8th	7th
1923-24	Division 2	19 January	Drew	0	0	26 January	Lost	0	1	8th	1stP
1926-27	Division 1	7 May	Won	1	0	18 October	Lost	1	4	16th	21stR
1928-29	Division 1	30 March	Won	4	2	17 November	Won	2	0	1st	13th
1929-30	Division 1	21 September	Lost	1	2	9 April	Lost	0	3	1st	5th
1930-31	Division 1	14 March	Won	2	1	8 November	Won	3	2	3rd	21stR
1932-33	Division 1	8 February	Won	2	0	17 September	Lost	2	3	3rd	8th
1933-34	Division 1	26 February	Lost	0	2	7 October	Lost	1	2	11th	9th
1934-35	Division 1	23 February	Won	1	0	13 October	Drew	0	0	3rd	18th
1935-36	Division 1	29 February	Won	3	0	9 November	Lost	2	7	20th	11th
1936-37	Division 1	21 November	Lost	1	2	27 March	Drew	1	1	22ndR	19th
1947-48	Division 2	27 March	Won	3	1	8 November	Drew	2	2	4th	18th
1948-49	Division 2	11 September	Won	3	1	22 January	Drew	1	1	8th	15th
1949-50	Division 2	25 March	Won	5	2	5 November	Drew	1	1	2ndP	5th
1951-52	Division 2	19 January	Lost	1	2	15 September	Lost	2	3	1stP	6th
1955-56	Division 2	15 October	Won	4	0	25 February	Lost	1	2	1stP	2ndP
1956-57	Division 1	26 March	Lost	2	3	10 November	Lost	1	3	14th	8th
1957-58	Division 1	9 November	Won	3	2	5 April	Drew	2	2	22ndR	17th
1959-60	Division 1	9 April	Won	1	0	21 November	Won	3	1	5th	21stR
1964-65	Division 1	19 April	Won	3	0	20 April	Lost	0	2	8th	2nd
1965-66	Division 1	9 October	Drew	0	0	1 January	Lost	0	3	17th	2nd
1966-67	Division 1	3 December	Drew	0	0	15 May	Lost	0	1	11th	4th
1967-68	Division 1	26 December	Lost	0	1	30 December	Lost	2	3	19th	4th
1968-69	Division 1	1 April	Drew	0	0	7 December	Lost	0	2	15th	1st
1969-70	Division 1	13 September	Lost	1	2	13 December	Lost	0	2	22ndR	2nd
1982-83	Division 2	11 September	Lost	2	3	27 April	Won	2	1	6th	8th
1983-84	Division 2	8 October	Won	3	1	31 March	Drew	1	1	2ndP	10th
1991-92	Division 1	12 January	Lost	1	6	24 August	Drew	1	1	3rd	1st
1992-93	Premiership	4 May	Drew	1	1	12 December	Lost	1	3	7th	17th
1993-94	Premiership	30 October	Drew	3	3	3 May	Drew	2	2	7th	5th
1994-95	Premiership	26 September	Drew	1	1	4 March	Won	1	0	13th	5th
1995-96	Premiership	16 December	Won	6	2	30 September	Lost	0	2	15th	13th
1996-97	Premiership	22 March	Drew	2	2	20 August	Won	2	0	7th	11th
1997-98	Premiership	13 August	Lost	1	3	17 January	Won	2	1	16th	5th
1998-99	Premiership	13 March	Lost	0	2	8 November	Lost	1	2	12th	4th
1999-00	Premiership	30 April	Lost	0	3	16 October	Lost	0	2	19thR	3rd

FA Cup	Date	Home Result	Wed'day	Leeds	Date	Away Result	Wed'day	Leeds	Division Wed'day	Leeds
1960-61	Round 3	7 January	Won	2	0					Div 1	Div 2
1968-69	Round 3	4 January	Drew	1	1	8 January	Won	3	1	Div 1	Div 1

Summary	P	W	D	L	F	A
Wednesday's home league record:	38	18	8	12	68	52
Wednesday's away league record:	38	7	11	20	41	69
Wednesday's cup record:	3	2	1	0	6	2
TOTAL:	79	27	20	32	115	123

FACT FILE

- In December 1995 against Leeds, Wednesday scored six in a Premiership match for the first and, so far, only time.
- That was Wednesday's only home win in their last nine attempts against Leeds.
- From 1965 to 1982, Wednesday failed to win in 12 league games against Leeds.
- Between 1932 and 1958, Leeds were unbeaten in 12 home games in the series.

Wednesday's top scorers vs Leeds
Ellis Rimmer 7
David Hirst, Eddie Quigley 5
Jack Ball, Andy Booth 4

Wednesday hat-tricks vs Leeds
30 Mar 1929 Ellis Rimmer

Played for both clubs

Len Armitage	Wednesday 1919-20	Leeds 1920-23
Jack Allen	Leeds 1923-24	Wednesday 1926-31
Sam Powell	Leeds 1920-25	Wednesday 1924-28
Gerald Henry	Leeds 1938-48	Wednesday 1949-52
Chris Turner	Wednesday 1976-79/88-91	Leeds 1989-90
Mel Sterland	Wednesday 1978-89	Leeds 1989-93
John Pearson	Wednesday 1980-85	Leeds 1986-91
Imre Varadi	Wednesday 1983-85/88-90	Leeds 1989-93
Nigel Worthington	Wednesday 1983-94	Leeds 1994-96
Lee Chapman	Wednesday 1984-88	Leeds 1989-93/95-96
Glynn Snodin	Wednesday 1985-87	Leeds 1987-91
Paul Hart	Leeds 1977-83	Wednesday 1985-87
Carl Shutt	Wednesday 1985-88	Leeds 1988-93
Carlton Palmer	Wednesday 1988-94/2000-02	Leeds 1994-97
Jon Newsome	Wednesday 1989-91/95-2000	Leeds 1991-94
John Sheridan	Leeds 1982-89	Wednesday 1989-97
Simon Grayson	Leeds 1987-88	Wednesday 2000-01

v. Leicester City

Season	League	Home Date	Result	Wed'day	Leicester	Away Date	Result	Wed'day	Leicester	Final Positions Wed'day	Leicester
1899-00	Division 2	31 March	Won	2	0	25 November	Drew	0	0	1stP	5th
1908-09	Division 1	1 January	Won	3	1	1 September	Drew	1	1	5th	20thR
1920-21	Division 2	18 December	Drew	0	0	1 January	Lost	1	2	10th	12th
1921-22	Division 2	6 May	Won	1	0	29 April	Drew	1	1	10th	9th
1922-23	Division 2	9 December	Won	2	1	2 December	Lost	1	3	8th	3rd
1923-24	Division 2	11 February	Won	2	1	9 February	Lost	1	2	8th	12th
1924-25	Division 2	4 October	Lost	1	4	7 February	Lost	1	6	14th	1stP
1926-27	Division 1	22 January	Drew	2	2	4 September	Lost	3	5	16th	7th
1927-28	Division 1	19 November	Lost	1	2	31 March	Drew	2	2	14th	3rd
1928-29	Division 1	16 March	Won	1	0	3 November	Drew	1	1	1st	2nd
1929-30	Division 1	2 November	Won	4	0	8 March	Lost	1	2	1st	8th
1930-31	Division 1	28 March	Won	4	0	22 November	Won	5	2	3rd	16th
1931-32	Division 1	20 February	Won	3	1	10 October	Lost	2	3	3rd	19th
1932-33	Division 1	18 March	Won	4	1	5 November	Drew	0	0	3rd	19th
1933-34	Division 1	2 December	Drew	1	1	14 April	Lost	0	2	11th	17th
1934-35	Division 1	20 April	Drew	1	1	8 December	Won	1	0	3rd	21stR
1946-47	Division 2	18 January	Lost	1	3	14 September	Won	5	3	20th	9th
1947-48	Division 2	1 November	Drew	1	1	20 March	Won	3	2	4th	9th
1948-49	Division 2	11 April	Lost	0	1	4 September	Drew	2	2	8th	19th
1949-50	Division 2	20 August	Won	3	1	17 December	Drew	2	2	2ndP	15th
1951-52	Division 2	27 August	Won	1	0	20 August	Lost	1	3	1stP	5th
1954-55	Division 1	16 April	Won	1	0	27 November	Lost	3	4	22ndR	21stR
1955-56	Division 2	12 September	Drew	1	1	2 April	Won	2	1	1stP	5th
1957-58	Division 1	11 September	Won	2	1	18 September	Lost	1	4	22ndR	18th
1959-60	Division 1	6 April	Drew	2	2	7 November	Lost	0	2	5th	12th
1960-61	Division 1	8 April	Drew	2	2	19 November	Lost	1	2	2nd	6th
1961-62	Division 1	10 February	Lost	1	2	23 September	Lost	0	1	6th	14th
1962-63	Division 1	29 August	Lost	0	3	22 August	Drew	3	3	6th	4th
1963-64	Division 1	2 October	Lost	1	2	11 September	Lost	0	2	6th	11th
1964-65	Division 1	28 December	Drew	0	0	26 December	Drew	2	2	8th	18th
1965-66	Division 1	8 January	Lost	1	2	11 December	Lost	1	4	17th	7th
1966-67	Division 1	3 September	Drew	1	1	7 January	Won	1	0	11th	8th
1967-68	Division 1	23 August	Won	2	1	30 August	Lost	0	3	19th	13th
1968-69	Division 1	14 April	Lost	1	3	23 November	Drew	1	1	15th	21stR
1970-71	Division 2	24 October	Lost	0	3	10 March	Lost	0	1	15th	1stP
1981-82	Division 2	20 March	Won	2	0	31 October	Drew	0	0	4th	8th
1982-83	Division 2	22 March	Drew	2	2	30 October	Won	2	0	6th	3rdP
1984-85	Division 1	20 October	Won	5	0	9 March	Lost	1	3	8th	15th
1985-86	Division 1	18 March	Won	1	0	19 October	Won	3	2	5th	19th
1986-87	Division 1	13 September	Drew	2	2	3 January	Lost	1	6	13th	20thR
1990-91	Division 2	24 April	Drew	0	0	22 September	Won	4	2	3rdP	22nd
1994-95	Premiership	8 April	Won	1	0	31 December	Won	1	0	13th	21stR
1996-97	Premiership	2 September	Won	2	1	7 May	Lost	0	1	7th	9th
1997-98	Premiership	30 August	Won	1	0	28 December	Drew	1	1	16th	10th

Season	League	Date	Result	Wed'day	Leicester	Date	Result	Wed'day	Leicester	Wed'day	Leicester
1998-99	Premiership	26 December	Lost	0	1	6 February	Won	2	0	12th	10th
1999-00	Premiership	14 May	Won	4	0	30 October	Lost	0	3	19thR	8th
2002-03	Division 1	21 September	Drew	0	0	8 March	Drew	1	1	22ndR	2ndP

FA Cup   *Division*

										Wed'day	Leicester
1923-24	Round 1	12 January	Won	4	1					Div 2	Div 2
1947-48	Round 4					24 January	Lost	1	2	Div 2	Div 2

League Cup

										Wed'day	Leicester
1992-93	Round 3	27 October	Won	7	1					Prem	Div 1
2002-03	Round 2	2 October	Lost*	1	2					Div 1	Div 1

Summary	P	W	D	L	F	A
Wednesday's home league record:	47	22	14	11	73	50
Wednesday's away league record:	47	11	14	22	65	93
Wednesday's cup record:	4	2	0	2	13	6
TOTAL:	98	35	28	35	151	149

FACT FILE

- Wednesday have lost one of their last 12 home league matches against Leicester.
- Wednesday failed to win in their first 11 visits to Leicester.
- Wednesday won five home games in succession from 1929 to 1933.

Wednesday's top scorers vs Leicester

Jack Ball 11

Redfern Froggatt 7

Jack Allen, Harry Burgess, Eddie Quigley,
Jimmy Trotter 5

Wednesday hat-tricks vs Leicester

2 Nov 1929 Jack Allen

22 Nov 1930 Jack Ball

18 Mar 1933 Jack Ball

20 Oct 1984 Imre Varadi

Played for both clubs

Alec Gillies	Wednesday 1896-97	Leicester 1897-98
Archie Brash	Wednesday 1894-98/99-1900	Leicester 1900-01
Frank Rollinson	Wednesday 1906-11	Leicester 1911-12
Jacki Sinclair	Leicester 1965-68	Wednesday 1969-73
Peter Rodrigues	Leicester 1965-71	Wednesday 1970-75
Martin Hodge	Wednesday 1983-88	Leicester 1988-91
Lawrie Madden	Wednesday 1983-91	Leicester 1990-91
Larry May	Leicester 1976-83	Wednesday 1986-88
Franz Carr	Wednesday 1989-90	Leicester 1994-95
Julian Watts	Wednesday 1992-96	Leicester 1995-98
Mark Bright	Leicester 1984-87	Wednesday 1992-97
Scott Oakes	Leicester 1989-92	Wednesday 1996-99
Richard Cresswell	Wednesday 1998-2001	Leicester 2000-01
Simon Grayson	Leicester 1991-97	Wednesday 2000-01
Mark Robins	Leicester 1994-97	Wednesday 2003-04

v. Leyton Orient

				Home				Away		Final Positions	
Season	League	Date	Result	Wed'day	Leyton O	Date	Result	Wed'day	Leyton O	Wed'day	Leyton O
1920-21	Division 2	9 April	Drew	1	1	16 April	Lost	0	1	10th	7th
1921-22	Division 2	3 December	Drew	0	0	10 December	Drew	1	1	10th	15th
1922-23	Division 2	28 October	Won	4	1	21 October	Drew	2	2	8th	19th
1923-24	Division 2	16 February	Won	1	0	23 February	Drew	0	0	8th	10th
1924-25	Division 2	2 May	Drew	0	0	2 October	Lost	0	1	14th	11th
1925-26	Division 2	17 April	Won	3	0	5 December	Drew	0	0	1stP	20th
1958-59	Division 2	20 September	Won	2	0	7 February	Won	2	0	1stP	17th
1962-63	Division 1	4 May	Won	3	1	22 September	Won	4	2	6th	22ndR
1970-71	Division 2	16 January	Won	2	1	19 October	Drew	1	1	15th	17th
1971-72	Division 2	17 April	Won	3	1	27 November	Won	3	0	14th	17th
1972-73	Division 2	31 March	Won	2	0	25 November	Lost	2	3	10th	15th
1973-74	Division 2	10 November	Lost	1	2	23 March	Won	1	0	19th	4th
1974-75	Division 2	15 March	Lost	0	1	28 September	Lost	0	1	22ndR	12th
1980-81	Division 2	25 October	Drew	2	2	28 March	Lost	0	2	10th	17th
1981-82	Division 2	27 March	Won	2	0	7 November	Lost	0	3	4th	22ndR

FA Cup

										Division	
1960-61	Round 5					18 February	Won	2	0	Div 1	Div 2
1985-86	Round 4	25 January	Won	5	0					Div 1	Div 4

League Cup

1991-92	Round 2	9 October	Won	4	1	24 September	Drew	0	0	Div 1	Div 3

Summary	P	W	D	L	F	A
Wednesday's home league record:	15	9	4	2	26	10
Wednesday's away league record:	15	4	5	6	16	1?
Wednesday's cup record:	4	3	1	0	11	1
TOTAL:	**34**	**16**	**10**	**8**	**53**	**28**

Mike Pinner, the amateur goalkeeper, turned out every now and then for various League clubs. He appeared for seven in all including Sheffield Wednesday and Leyton Orient.

FACT FILE

> ● Wednesday were unbeaten in their first 11 home games in the series.

Wednesday's top scorers vs Orient
Brian Joicey 7
Sam Taylor 4

Wednesday hat-tricks vs Orient
28 Oct 1922 Sam Taylor
17 Apr 1972 Brian Joicey

Played for both clubs

Joe Peacock	Wednesday 1930-31	Orient 1931-33
Doug Hunt	Wednesday 1937-40	Orient 1946-48
Don Gibson	Wednesday 1955-60	Orient 1960-61
Mike Pinner	Wednesday 1957-59	Orient 1962-65
Chris Turner	Wednesday 1976-79/88-91	Orient 1991-95
Colin West	Wednesday 1987-89	Orient 1993-98
Greg Fee	Wednesday 1987-90	Orient 1990-91
Chris Bart-Williams	Orient 1990-92	Wednesday 1991-95
Scott Oakes	Wednesday 1996-99	Orient 2001-02
Ian Hendon	Orient 1991-92/93-97	Wednesday 2000-03
Paul Heald	Orient 1988-95	Wednesday 2001-02
Dean Smith	Orient 1997-2003	Wednesday 2002-04

v. Lincoln City

Season	League	Date	Result	Home Wed'day	Lincoln	Date	Result	Away Wed'day	Lincoln	Final Positions Wed'day	Lincoln
1899-00	Division 2	17 April	Won	1	0	14 October	Won	2	1	1stP	9th
1948-49	Division 2	2 October	Drew	2	2	26 February	Lost	1	3	8th	22ndR
1955-56	Division 2	28 April	Won	5	3	7 September	Drew	2	2	1stP	8th
1958-59	Division 2	26 December	Won	7	0	27 December	Won	1	0	1stP	19th
1976-77	Division 3	12 March	Drew	1	1	2 October	Drew	1	1	8th	9th
1977-78	Division 3	22 October	Won	2	0	18 March	Lost	1	3	14th	16th
1978-79	Division 3	11 November	Drew	0	0	2 September	Won	2	1	14th	24thR

FA Cup										Division	
1979-80	Round 1	24 November	Won	3	0					Div 3	Div 4

Summary	P	W	D	L	F	A
Wednesday's home league record:	7	4	3	0	18	6
Wednesday's away league record:	7	3	2	2	10	11
Wednesday's cup record:	1	1	0	0	3	0
TOTAL:	**15**	**8**	**5**	**2**	**31**	**17**

FACT FILE

- Lincoln have never won in their eight away matches against Wednesday.

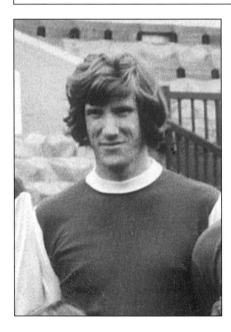

Sam Ellis, six years an Owl and four an Imp.

Wednesday's top scorers vs Lincoln
Roy Shiner 6
Alan Finney, Redfern Froggatt 3

Wednesday hat-tricks vs Lincoln
28 Apr 1956 Roy Shiner

Played for both clubs

Henry Hibbert	Wednesday 1907-08	Lincoln 1909-10
Walter Miller	Wednesday 1907-08	Lincoln 1912-14
Michael Dowling	Wednesday 1910-11	Lincoln 1914-20
Joe Cooper	Wednesday 1920-21	Lincoln 1932-33
Harold Armitage	Wednesday 1920-22	Lincoln 1926-27
Jack Wilkinson	Wednesday 1925-30	Lincoln 1932-35
George Nevin	Wednesday 1932-33	Lincoln 1937-39
Tony Leach	Wednesday 1926-34	Lincoln 1938-39
Jackie Robinson	Wednesday 1934-47	Lincoln 1949-50
Derek Dooley	Lincoln 1946-47	Wednesday 1949-53
Donald Watson	Wednesday 1954-57	Lincoln 1956-58
Don McEvoy	Wednesday 1954-58	Lincoln 1958-60
Keith Ellis	Wednesday 1954-64	Lincoln 1965-66
Albert Broadbent	Wednesday 1955-58	Lincoln 1961-63
David Cargill	Wednesday 1956-58	Lincoln 1960-61
Jim McCalliog	Wednesday 1965-69	Lincoln 1978-79
Sam Ellis	Wednesday 1965-71	Lincoln 1973-77
Ian Branfoot	Wednesday 1965-70	Lincoln 1973-78
Colin Symm	Wednesday 1966-69	Lincoln 1972-75
Dave Sunley	Wednesday 1970-76	Lincoln 1978-80
Derek Bell	Wednesday 1975-76	Lincoln 1979-83
Gordon Simmonite	Wednesday 1976-77	Lincoln 1982-85
Tommy Tynan	Wednesday 1976-79	Lincoln 1978-79
Chris Turner	Wednesday 1976-79/88-91	Lincoln 1978-79
Mark Smith	Wednesday 1977-87	Lincoln 1993-94
Charles Williamson	Wednesday 1979-84	Lincoln 1983-84
Trevor Matthewson	Wednesday 1980-83	Lincoln 1988-89
Tony Simmons	Wednesday 1981-83	Lincoln 1986-87
Gary Bannister	Wednesday 1981-84	Lincoln 1994-95
Gary Megson	Wednesday 1981-84/85-89	Lincoln 1995-96
Tony Cunningham	Lincoln 1979-83	Wednesday 1983-84
David Johnson	Wednesday 1991-92	Lincoln 1993-96
Julian Watts	Wednesday 1992-96	Lincoln 1998-99
Manuel Agogo	Wednesday 1997-99	Lincoln 1999-2000
Aaron Lescott	Lincoln 1999-2000	Wednesday 2000-02

v. Liverpool

		Home				Away				Final Positions	
Season	League	Date	Result	Wed'day	Liverpool	Date	Result	Wed'day	Liverpool	Wed'day	Liverpool
1894-95	Division 1	5 January	Won	5	0	30 March	Lost	2	4	8th	16thR
1896-97	Division 1	1 September	Lost	1	2	3 April	Drew	2	2	6th	5th
1897-98	Division 1	18 September	Won	4	2	11 April	Lost	0	4	5th	9th
1898-99	Division 1	31 December	Lost	0	3	3 September	Lost	0	4	18thR	2nd
1900-01	Division 1	17 November	Won	3	2	23 March	Drew	1	1	8th	1st
1901-02	Division 1	1 April	Drew	1	1	12 October	Won	2	1	9th	11th
1902-03	Division 1	31 January	Won	3	1	4 October	Lost	2	4	1st	5th
1903-04	Division 1	9 January	Won	2	1	12 September	Won	3	1	1st	17thR
1905-06	Division 1	14 October	Won	3	2	17 February	Lost	1	2	3rd	1st
1906-07	Division 1	16 February	Lost	2	3	13 October	Won	2	1	13th	15th
1907-08	Division 1	9 March	Lost	1	2	26 October	Lost	0	3	5th	8th
1908-09	Division 1	5 December	Lost	2	3	10 April	Won	2	1	5th	16th
1909-10	Division 1	5 March	Won	3	0	23 October	Lost	1	3	11th	2nd
1910-11	Division 1	8 October	Won	1	0	11 February	Lost	0	3	6th	13th
1911-12	Division 1	14 October	Drew	2	2	17 February	Drew	1	1	5th	17th
1912-13	Division 1	12 October	Won	1	0	15 February	Lost	1	2	3rd	12th
1913-14	Division 1	4 October	Won	4	1	7 February	Won	2	1	18th	16th
1914-15	Division 1	23 January	Won	2	1	19 September	Lost	1	2	7th	13th
1919-20	Division 1	13 March	Drew	2	2	10 March	Lost	0	1	22ndR	4th
1926-27	Division 1	16 October	Won	3	2	5 March	Lost	0	3	16th	9th
1927-28	Division 1	24 March	Won	4	0	12 November	Lost	2	5	14th	16th
1928-29	Division 1	24 November	Won	3	2	6 April	Lost	2	3	1st	5th
1929-30	Division 1	30 November	Won	2	1	5 April	Won	3	1	1st	12th
1930-31	Division 1	14 February	Lost	3	5	11 October	Won	2	1	3rd	9th
1931-32	Division 1	26 December	Drew	1	1	25 December	Lost	1	3	3rd	10th
1932-33	Division 1	24 December	Won	3	0	6 May	Lost	1	4	3rd	14th
1933-34	Division 1	21 April	Lost	1	2	9 December	Won	3	1	11th	18th
1934-35	Division 1	6 October	Won	4	1	20 February	Won	2	1	3rd	7th
1935-36	Division 1	25 April	Drew	0	0	21 December	Lost	0	1	20th	19th
1936-37	Division 1	20 March	Lost	1	2	14 November	Drew	2	2	22ndR	18th
1950-51	Division 1	28 October	Won	4	1	17 March	Lost	1	2	21stR	9th
1952-53	Division 1	3 September	Lost	0	2	27 August	Lost	0	1	18th	17th
1953-54	Division 1	24 February	Drew	1	1	3 October	Drew	2	2	19th	22ndR
1955-56	Division 2	31 August	Drew	1	1	24 August	Won	3	0	1stP	3rd
1958-59	Division 2	14 April	Won	1	0	25 October	Lost	2	3	1stP	4th
1962-63	Division 1	8 December	Lost	0	2	29 April	Won	2	0	6th	8th
1963-64	Division 1	4 March	Drew	2	2	9 October	Lost	1	3	6th	1st
1964-65	Division 1	12 September	Won	1	0	16 January	Lost	2	4	8th	7th
1965-66	Division 1	6 November	Lost	0	2	6 April	Lost	0	1	17th	1st
1966-67	Division 1	14 January	Lost	0	1	10 September	Drew	1	1	11th	5th
1967-68	Division 1	23 March	Lost	1	2	28 October	Lost	0	1	19th	3rd
1968-69	Division 1	16 November	Lost	1	2	1 February	Lost	0	1	15th	2nd
1969-70	Division 1	30 August	Drew	1	1	16 March	Lost	0	3	22ndR	5th
1984-85	Division 1	2 February	Drew	1	1	29 September	Won	2	0	8th	2nd

			Home				Away			Final Positions	
Season	League	Date	Result	Wed'day	Liverpool	Date	Result	Wed'day	Liverpool	Wed'day	Liverpool
1985-86	Division 1	29 March	Drew	0	0	1 January	Drew	2	2	5th	1st
1986-87	Division 1	27 December	Lost	0	1	16 November	Drew	1	1	13th	2nd
1987-88	Division 1	7 May	Lost	1	5	19 December	Lost	0	1	11th	1st
1988-89	Division 1	14 January	Drew	2	2	8 April	Lost	1	5	15th	2nd
1989-90	Division 1	29 November	Won	2	0	26 December	Lost	1	2	18thR	1st
1991-92	Division 1	2 May	Drew	0	0	28 September	Drew	1	1	3rd	6th
1992-93	Premiership	27 February	Drew	1	1	3 October	Lost	0	1	7th	6th
1993-94	Premiership	4 December	Won	3	1	14 August	Lost	0	2	7th	8th
1994-95	Premiership	25 February	Lost	1	2	1 October	Lost	1	4	13th	4th
1995-96	Premiership	13 January	Drew	1	1	19 August	Lost	0	1	15th	3rd
1996-97	Premiership	11 May	Drew	1	1	7 December	Won	1	0	7th	4th
1997-98	Premiership	14 February	Drew	3	3	13 September	Lost	1	2	16th	3rd
1998-99	Premiership	8 May	Won	1	0	19 December	Lost	0	2	12th	7th
1999-00	Premiership	7 August	Lost	1	2	5 December	Lost	1	4	19thR	4th

FA Cup

										Division	
1906-07	Q'ter final	9 March	Won	1	0					Div 1	Div 1

League Cup

1983-84	Q'ter final	17 January	Drew	2	2	25 January	Lost	0	3	Div 2	Div 1

Summary		P	W	D	L	F	A
Wednesday's home league record:		58	23	17	18	98	81
Wednesday's away league record:		58	13	9	36	67	116
Wednesday's cup record:		3	1	1	1	3	5
TOTAL:		**119**	**37**	**27**	**55**	**168**	**202**

Striker Jack Whitham
always got goals but
suffered with injuries
both at Hillsborough
and Anfield.

FACT FILE

- From 1986 to 1995, Wednesday failed to win in 10 trips to Anfield. This is their longest such run, and is quite short compared to most other clubs' sequences of failure at Anfield.
- Between 1910 and 1929, Wednesday were undefeated in 11 home games against Liverpool.
- Strangely for two clubs so prominent in 20th-century English football, they have not met in the FA Cup since 1907.
- Wednesday failed to win in 11 home games in the series from 1965 to 1989.

Wednesday's top scorers vs Liverpool
Andrew Wilson 10
Mark Hooper 8
Harry Chapman, Redfern Froggatt 6
Harry Burgess, Harry Davis, Ellis Rimmer 5

Wednesday hat-tricks vs Liverpool
28 Oct 1950 Redfern Froggatt

Played for both clubs

Vic Wright	Wednesday 1931-32	Liverpool 1933-37
Ernie Blenkinsop	Wednesday 1922-34	Liverpool 1933-38
Jack Whitham	Wednesday 1966-70	Liverpool 1970-72
David Hodgson	Liverpool 1982-84	Wednesday 1988-89
Steve Nicol	Liverpool 1982-95	Wednesday 1995-98
Steve Harkness	Liverpool 1991-99	Wednesday 2000-01
David Burrows	Liverpool 1988-94	Wednesday 2001-03

Ellis Rimmer

v. Lockwood Bros

Home

FA Cup		Date	Result	Wed'day	Lockw'd
1882-83	Round 2	2 December	Won	6	0

Summary	P	W	D	L	F	A
Wednesday's cup record:	1	1	0	0	6	0
TOTAL:	**1**	**1**	**0**	**0**	**6**	**0**

FACT FILE

- This team was made up of workers from the Lockwood Brothers factory in Sheffield.

Wednesday's top scorers vs Lockwood Bros
R. Gregory 2

Billy Mosforth scored
as the factory team
were beaten.

v. Long Eaton Rangers

FA Cup		Home Date	Result	Wed'day	Hastings	Away Date	Result	Wed'day	Hastings
1884-85	Round 1	8 November	Won	1	0				
1885-86	Round 1					31 October	Lost	0	2
1887-88	Round 2					5 November	Won*	2	1

Summary	P	W	D	L	F	A
Wednesday's cup record:	3	2	0	1	3	3
TOTAL:	3	2	0	1	3	3

Jim Smith, back row fourth right, kept goal for Wednesday in all three encounters with Long Eaton from 1884 to 1887.

v. Loughborough Town

				Home					Away		Final Positions	
Season	League	Date	Result	Wed'day	Loughb'h	Date	Result	Wed'day	Loughb'h		Wed'day	Loughb'h
1899-00	Division 2	20 January	Won	5	0	23 September	Drew	0	0		1stP	18thF

Summary

	P	W	D	L	F	A
Wednesday's home league record:	1	1	0	0	5	0
Wednesday's away league record:	1	0	1	0	0	0
TOTAL:	2	1	1	0	5	0

Wednesday's top scorers vs Loughborough
Jocky Wright 3

Wednesday hat-tricks vs Loughborough
20 Jan 1900 Jocky Wright

Played for both clubs

Albert Mumford	Wednesday 1892-94	Loughborough 1896-1900
Billy Mellor	Wednesday 1893-94	Loughborough 1895-96
Samuel Bosworth	Loughborough 1898-99	Wednesday 1898-99
Frank Stubbs	Loughborough 1899-1900	Wednesday 1900-03

v. Luton Town

Season	League	Home Date	Result	Wed'day	Luton	Away Date	Result	Wed'day	Luton	Final Positions Wed'day	Luton
1899-00	Division 2	2 December	Won	6	0	7 April	Won	1	0	1stP	17thF
1937-38	Division 2	13 November	Won	4	0	26 March	Drew	2	2	17th	12th
1938-39	Division 2	1 April	Won	4	1	26 November	Won	5	1	3rd	7th
1939-40	Division 2					26 August	Lost	0	3		
1946-47	Division 2	28 December	Drew	1	1	31 August	Lost	1	4	20th	13th
1947-48	Division 2	18 October	Won	1	0	6 March	Drew	1	1	4th	13th
1948-49	Division 2	30 April	Drew	0	0	4 December	Lost	1	2	8th	10th
1949-50	Division 2	26 November	Drew	1	1	1 April	Drew	0	0	2ndP	17th
1951-52	Division 2	2 April	Won	4	0	10 November	Lost	3	5	1stP	8th
1956-57	Division 1	20 April	Won	3	0	13 October	Lost	0	2	14th	16th
1957-58	Division 1	1 March	Won	2	1	19 October	Lost	0	2	22ndR	8th
1959-60	Division 1	26 September	Won	2	0	13 February	Won	1	0	5th	22ndR
1970-71	Division 2	10 October	Lost	1	5	17 April	Drew	2	2	15th	6th
1971-72	Division 2	27 December	Drew	2	2	1 April	Lost	1	3	14th	13th
1972-73	Division 2	23 September	Won	4	0	26 December	Drew	0	0	10th	12th
1973-74	Division 2	13 April	Drew	2	2	17 November	Lost	1	2	19th	2ndP
1980-81	Division 2	4 April	Won	3	1	1 November	Lost	0	3	10th	5th
1981-82	Division 2	6 February	Drew	3	3	12 September	Won	3	0	4th	1stP
1984-85	Division 1	16 March	Drew	1	1	13 October	Won	2	1	8th	13th
1985-86	Division 1	28 September	Won	3	2	1 March	Lost	0	1	5th	9th
1986-87	Division 1	22 November	Won	1	0	25 April	Drew	0	0	13th	7th
1987-88	Division 1	14 November	Lost	0	2	5 April	Drew	2	2	11th	9th
1988-89	Division 1	27 August	Won	1	0	18 March	Won	1	0	15th	16th
1989-90	Division 1	9 December	Drew	1	1	22 August	Lost	0	2	18thR	17th
1991-92	Division 1	1 February	Won	3	2	19 October	Drew	2	2	3rd	20thR
2003-04	Division 2	22 November	Drew	0	0	1 May	Lost	2	3	16th	10th

League Cup

Season	Round	Date	Result							Division	
1984-85	Round 4	20 November	Won	4	2					Div 1	Div 1

Summary

	P	W	D	L	F	A
Wednesday's home league record:	25	14	9	2	53	25
Wednesday's away league record:	26	6	8	12	31	43
Wednesday's cup record:	1	1	0	0	4	0
TOTAL:	52	21	17	14	88	70

FACT FILE

- Wednesday were unbeaten in their first 11 games of the series. They conceded just four goals in the process.
- From 1939 to 1980, Wednesday won once in 14 visits to Kenilworth Road.

Wednesday's top scorers vs Luton

Derek Dooley, Doug Hunt, Jackie Robinson 4
Andy Blair, Lee Chapman, Jim Fallon,
David Hirst, Brian Joicey, Brian Marwood,
Fred Spiksley 3

Wednesday hat-tricks vs Luton

2 Dec 1899 Fred Spiksley
26 Nov 1938 Doug Hunt
20 Nov 1984 Andy Blair (3 pens)

Played for both clubs

John Lamb	Wednesday 1913-20	Luton 1920-21
Fred Dent	Wednesday 1920-21	Luton 1930-31
Lewis Bedford	Wednesday 1925-26	Luton 1928-30
Dan Kirkwood	Wednesday 1926-28	Luton 1933-34
Fred Kean	Wednesday 1920-29	Luton 1931-35
Tom Mackey	Wednesday 1929-32	Luton 1932-38
Jack Ball	Wednesday 1930-34	Luton 1934-36
Allenby Driver	Wednesday 1937-46	Luton 1946-48
Hugh McJarrow	Wednesday 1949-52	Luton 1951-54
Imre Varadi	Wednesday 1983-85/88-90	Luton 1991-92
Alan Harper	Wednesday 1988-90	Luton 1993-94
Danny Wilson	Luton 1987-90	Wednesday 1990-93
Julian Watts	Wednesday 1992-96	Luton 1999-2001
Mark Pembridge	Luton 1990-92	Wednesday 1995-98
Scott Oakes	Luton 1991-96	Wednesday 1996-99
Marlon Beresford	Wednesday 2000-01	Luton 2003-04
Paul McLaren	Luton 1993-2001	Wednesday 2001-04

v. Macclesfield Town

		Home						Division

FA Cup	Date	Result	Wed'day Macclesf'd					Wed'day Macclesf'd
1975-76 Round 1	22 November	Won	**3**	**1**				Div 3 Non L

Summary	P	W	D	L	F	A
Wednesday's cup record:	1	1	0	0	3	1

Played for both clubs

John Beswetherick   Wednesday 2002-04   Macclesfield 2003-04

In 1975 Wednesday played in the First Round of the FA Cup against then non-League Macclesfield Town. Mick Prendergast scored in the 3-1 Owls win.

v. Manchester City

Season	League	Home Date	Result	Wed'day	Man City	Away Date	Result	Wed'day	Man City	Final Positions Wed'day	Man City
1900-01	Division 1	29 December	Won	4	1	1 September	Drew	2	2	8th	11th
1901-02	Division 1	26 December	Won	2	1	28 March	Won	3	0	9th	18thR
1903-04	Division 1	26 March	Won	1	0	28 November	Drew	1	1	1st	2nd
1904-05	Division 1	26 November	Won	2	1	15 April	Drew	1	1	9th	3rd
1905-06	Division 1	2 September	Won	1	0	30 December	Lost	1	2	3rd	5th
1906-07	Division 1	8 September	Won	3	1	5 January	Won	1	0	13th	17th
1907-08	Division 1	25 January	Won	5	1	28 September	Lost	2	3	5th	3rd
1908-09	Division 1	21 November	Won	3	1	27 March	Lost	0	4	5th	19thR
1910-11	Division 1	15 April	Won	4	1	10 December	Won	2	1	6th	17th
1911-12	Division 1	9 December	Won	3	0	13 April	Lost	0	4	5th	15th
1912-13	Division 1	7 December	Won	1	0	12 April	Drew	2	2	3rd	6th
1913-14	Division 1	14 March	Drew	2	2	8 November	Won	2	1	18th	13th
1914-15	Division 1	14 November	Won	2	1	20 March	Lost	0	4	7th	5th
1919-20	Division 1	1 November	Drew	0	0	25 October	Lost	2	4	22ndR	7th
1928-29	Division 1	25 December	Won	4	0	26 December	Drew	2	2	1st	8th
1929-30	Division 1	3 May	Won	5	1	1 January	Drew	3	3	1st	3rd
1930-31	Division 1	18 October	Drew	1	1	21 February	Lost	0	2	3rd	8th
1931-32	Division 1	19 December	Drew	1	1	30 April	Won	2	1	3rd	14th
1932-33	Division 1	27 December	Won	2	1	26 December	Drew	2	2	3rd	16th
1933-34	Division 1	30 December	Drew	1	1	26 August	Won	3	2	11th	5th
1934-35	Division 1	5 January	Won	1	0	1 September	Lost	1	4	3rd	4th
1935-36	Division 1	28 March	Won	1	0	23 November	Lost	0	3	20th	9th
1936-37	Division 1	19 December	Won	5	1	24 April	Lost	1	4	22ndR	1st
1938-39	Division 2	8 October	Won	3	1	26 April	Drew	1	1	3rd	5th
1946-47	Division 2	26 May	Won	1	0	12 October	Lost	1	2	20th	1stP
1952-53	Division 1	6 April	Drew	1	1	3 April	Lost	1	3	18th	20th
1953-54	Division 1	19 August	Won	2	0	12 December	Lost	2	3	19th	17th
1954-55	Division 1	6 November	Lost	2	4	30 March	Drew	2	2	22ndR	7th
1956-57	Division 1	23 February	Drew	2	2	27 December	Lost	2	4	14th	18th
1957-58	Division 1	21 December	Lost	4	5	9 October	Lost	0	2	22ndR	5th
1959-60	Division 1	29 August	Won	1	0	2 January	Lost	1	4	5th	16th
1960-61	Division 1	14 September	Won	3	1	7 September	Drew	1	1	2nd	13th
1961-62	Division 1	23 April	Won	1	0	20 April	Lost	1	3	6th	12th
1962-63	Division 1	9 March	Won	4	1	20 October	Lost	2	3	6th	21stR
1966-67	Division 1	27 December	Won	1	0	2 January	Drew	0	0	11th	15th
1967-68	Division 1	2 December	Drew	1	1	25 April	Lost	0	1	19th	1st
1968-69	Division 1	18 January	Drew	1	1	9 November	Won	1	0	15th	13th
1969-70	Division 1	22 April	Lost	1	2	9 August	Lost	1	4	22ndR	10th
1983-84	Division 2	7 May	Drew	0	0	10 December	Won	2	1	2ndP	4th
1985-86	Division 1	21 December	Won	3	2	24 August	Won	3	1	5th	15th
1986-87	Division 1	20 April	Won	2	1	26 December	Lost	0	1	13th	21stR
1989-90	Division 1	1 January	Won	2	0	14 April	Lost	1	2	18thR	14th
1991-92	Division 1	11 April	Won	2	0	14 September	Won	1	0	3rd	5th
1992-93	Premiership	5 September	Lost	0	3	23 February	Won	2	1	7th	9th

			Home				Away			Final Positions	
Season	League	Date	Result	Wed'day	Man City	Date	Result	Wed'day	Man City	Wed'day	Man City
1993-94	Premiership	7 May	Drew	1	1	27 November	Won	3	1	7th	16th
1994-95	Premiership	17 September	Drew	1	1	18 March	Lost	2	3	13th	17th
1995-96	Premiership	18 November	Drew	1	1	13 April	Lost	0	1	15th	18thR
2001-02	Division 1	22 September	Lost	2	6	27 February	Lost	0	4	20th	1stP

										Division	
FA Cup											
1903-04	Semi-Final	19 March	Goodison Park				Lost	0	3	Div 1	Div 1
1933-34	Round 5	17 February	Drew	2	2	21 February	Lost	0	2	Div 1	Div 1

League Cup											
1979-80	Round 2	28 August	Drew	1	1	4 September	Lost	1	2	Div 3	Div 1

Summary	P	W	D	L	F	A
Wednesday's home league record:	48	30	13	5	96	50
Wednesday's away league record:	48	12	11	25	63	100
Wednesday's cup record:	5	0	2	3	4	10
TOTAL:	**101**	**42**	**26**	**33**	**163**	**160**

FACT FILE

- Wednesday were undefeated in their first 28 home matches against Man City. Wednesday won all of the first 11 matches in this sequence. City finally got their first away win in 1954, over half a century after their first visit.
- Between 1934 and 1968, Wednesday failed to win in 17 visits to Maine Road.
- Only 17 of the 100 matches between the sides (excluding the match on neutral territory) have resulted in away wins.
- Wednesday have not won in their last seven matches against City.
- The 1934 FA Cup tie produced Hillsborough's highest-ever attendance of 72,841.
- The 1904 FA Cup semi-final defeat ended Wednesday's hopes of the double. They did win the league title, though, by way of consolation.

The sky blue half of Manchester had the services of Earl Barrett for over a decade before the defender joined Wednesday.

Wednesday's top scorers vs City

Harry Chapman, Andrew Wilson 8
Jack Allen, Jack Ball, Mark Hooper,
Jimmy Stewart 6
Ellis Rimmer 5

Wednesday hat-tricks vs City

21 Nov 1908 Harry Chapman
3 May 1930 Mark Hooper
9 Mar 1963 David Layne

Played for both clubs

Sandy Rowan	Wednesday 1892-94	Man City 1894-96
Alec Gillies	Man City 1895-96	Wednesday 1896-97
Jack Reynolds	Man City 1902-03	Wednesday 1905-07
Jack Lyall	Wednesday 1901-09	Man City 1909-11
Matt Barrass	Wednesday 1924-26	Man City 1926-33
Billy Felton	Wednesday 1922-29	Man City 1928-32
Ernie Toseland	Man City 1928-39	Wednesday 1938-40
Tony Coleman	Man City 1966-70	Wednesday 1969-70
Phil Henson	Man City 1971-75	Wednesday 1974-77
Jeff Johnson	Man City 1970-72	Wednesday 1976-81
Dennis Leman	Man City 1973-76	Wednesday 1976-82
Ian Mellor	Man City 1970-73	Wednesday 1979-82
Gary Megson	Wednesday 1981-84/85-89	Man City 1988-92
Tony Cunningham	Wednesday 1983-84	Man City 1984-85
Imre Varadi	Wednesday 1983-85/88-90	Man City 1986-89
Carl Shutt	Wednesday 1985-88	Man City 1993-94
Carl Bradshaw	Wednesday 1986-89	Man City 1988-89
Gary Owen	Man City 1975-79	Wednesday 1987-88
Dave Bennett	Man City 1978-81	Wednesday 1988-90
Alan Harper	Wednesday 1988-90	Man City 1989-91
Dalian Atkinson	Wednesday 1988-90	Man City 1996-97
Trevor Francis	Man City 1981-82	Wednesday 1989-94
Steve McKenzie	Man City 1979-81	Wednesday 1990-92
Lee Briscoe	Wednesday 1993-2000	Man City 1997-98
Andy Hinchcliffe	Man City 1987-90	Wednesday 1997-2002
Earl Barrett	Man City 1985-87	Wednesday 1997-99
Terry Cooke	Man City 1998-2000	Wednesday 2000-01/03-04
Lee Bradbury	Man City 1997-99	Wednesday 2002-03
Eric Nixon	Man City 1983-88	Wednesday 2003-04
Mark Robins	Man City 1998-99	Wednesday 2003-04

v. Manchester United

Season	League	Home Date	Result	Wed'day	Man Utd	Away Date	Result	Wed'day	Man Utd	Final Positions Wed'day	Man Utd
1892-93	Division 1	22 October	Won	1	0	24 December	Won	5	1	12th	16th
1893-94	Division 1	16 September	Lost	0	1	13 January	Won	2	1	12th	16thR
1899-00	Division 2	30 September	Won	2	1	3 February	Lost	0	1	1stP	4th
1906-07	Division 1	17 November	Won	5	2	10 April	Lost	0	5	13th	8th
1907-08	Division 1	30 November	Won	2	0	28 March	Lost	1	4	5th	1st
1908-09	Division 1	3 April	Won	2	0	28 November	Lost	1	3	5th	13th
1909-10	Division 1	27 December	Won	4	1	25 December	Won	3	0	11th	5th
1910-11	Division 1	17 April	Drew	0	0	1 October	Lost	2	3	6th	1st
1911-12	Division 1	10 February	Won	3	0	7 October	Lost	1	3	5th	13th
1912-13	Division 1	28 September	Drew	3	3	25 January	Lost	0	2	3rd	4th
1913-14	Division 1	6 September	Lost	1	3	27 December	Lost	1	2	18th	14th
1914-15	Division 1	10 October	Won	1	0	13 February	Lost	0	2	7th	18th
1919-20	Division 1	8 September	Lost	1	3	1 September	Drew	0	0	22ndR	12th
1922-23	Division 2	28 August	Won	1	0	4 September	Lost	0	1	8th	4th
1923-24	Division 2	3 May	Won	2	0	26 April	Lost	0	2	8th	14th
1924-25	Division 2	23 February	Drew	1	1	27 September	Lost	0	2	14th	2ndP
1926-27	Division 1	26 March	Won	2	0	6 November	Drew	0	0	16th	15th
1927-28	Division 1	29 August	Lost	0	2	7 September	Drew	1	1	14th	18th
1928-29	Division 1	10 November	Won	2	1	23 March	Lost	1	2	1st	12th
1929-30	Division 1	16 November	Won	7	2	14 April	Drew	2	2	1st	17th
1930-31	Division 1	20 September	Won	3	0	28 January	Lost	1	4	3rd	22ndR
1936-37	Division 1	23 January	Won	1	0	19 September	Drew	1	1	22ndR	21stR
1937-38	Division 2	5 March	Lost	1	3	23 October	Lost	0	1	17th	2ndP
1950-51	Division 1	26 February	Lost	0	4	7 October	Lost	1	3	21stR	2nd
1952-53	Division 1	28 March	Drew	0	0	8 November	Drew	1	1	18th	8th
1953-54	Division 1	26 December	Lost	0	1	25 December	Lost	2	5	19th	4th
1954-55	Division 1	23 August	Lost	2	4	1 September	Lost	0	2	22ndR	5th
1956-57	Division 1	19 January	Won	2	1	15 September	Lost	1	4	14th	1st
1957-58	Division 1	29 March	Won	1	0	16 November	Lost	1	2	22ndR	9th
1959-60	Division 1	30 March	Won	4	2	24 October	Lost	1	3	5th	7th
1960-61	Division 1	25 March	Won	5	1	5 November	Drew	0	0	2nd	7th
1961-62	Division 1	4 November	Won	3	1	24 March	Drew	1	1	6th	15th
1962-63	Division 1	29 September	Won	1	0	1 May	Won	3	1	6th	19th
1963-64	Division 1	24 August	Drew	3	3	14 December	Lost	1	3	6th	2nd
1964-65	Division 1	20 March	Won	1	0	7 November	Lost	0	1	8th	1st
1965-66	Division 1	29 January	Drew	0	0	21 August	Lost	0	1	17th	4th
1966-67	Division 1	10 April	Drew	2	2	12 November	Lost	0	2	11th	1st
1967-68	Division 1	16 September	Drew	1	1	20 January	Lost	2	4	19th	2nd
1968-69	Division 1	31 August	Won	5	4	22 March	Lost	0	1	15th	11th
1969-70	Division 1	17 September	Lost	1	3	15 April	Drew	2	2	22ndR	8th
1974-75	Division 2	7 December	Drew	4	4	11 January	Lost	0	2	22ndR	1stP
1984-85	Division 1	9 April	Won	1	0	1 January	Won	2	1	8th	4th
1985-86	Division 1	9 November	Won	1	0	13 April	Won	2	0	5th	4th
1986-87	Division 1	21 March	Won	1	0	11 October	Lost	1	3	13th	11th

				Home				Away		Final Positions	
Season	League	Date	Result	Wed'day	Man Utd	Date	Result	Wed'day	Man Utd	Wed'day	Man Utd
1987-88	Division 1	10 October	Lost	2	4	12 March	Lost	1	4	11th	2nd
1988-89	Division 1	11 February	Lost	0	2	23 November	Drew	1	1	15th	11th
1989-90	Division 1	21 March	Won	1	0	14 October	Drew	0	0	18thR	13th
1991-92	Division 1	26 October	Won	3	2	8 February	Drew	1	1	3rd	6th
1992-93	Premiership	26 December	Drew	3	3	10 April	Lost	1	2	7th	1st
1993-94	Premiership	2 October	Lost	2	3	16 March	Lost	0	5	7th	1st
1994-95	Premiership	8 October	Won	1	0	7 May	Lost	0	1	13th	2nd
1995-96	Premiership	23 September	Drew	0	0	9 December	Drew	2	2	15th	1st
1996-97	Premiership	18 December	Drew	1	1	17 March	Lost	0	2	7th	1st
1997-98	Premiership	7 March	Won	2	0	1 November	Lost	1	6	16th	2nd
1998-99	Premiership	21 November	Won	3	1	17 April	Lost	0	3	12th	1st
1999-00	Premiership	2 February	Lost	0	1	11 August	Lost	0	4	19thR	1st

FA Cup

				Home				Away		Division	
1903-04	Round 2	20 February	Won	6	0					Div 1	Div 2
1914-15	Round 1	9 January	Won	1	0					Div 1	Div 1
1924-25	Round 1	10 January	Won	2	0					Div 2	Div 2
1957-58	Round 5					19 February	Lost	0	3	Div 1	Div 1
1959-60	Round 5	20 February	Won	1	0					Div 1	Div 1
1960-61	Round 4	28 January	Drew	1	1	1 February	Won	7	2	Div 1	Div 1
1961-62	Round 5	21 February	Lost	0	2	17 February	Drew	0	0	Div 1	Div 1

League Cup

										Division	
1990-91	Final	21 April		Wembley			Won	1	0	Div 2	Div 1
1993-94	Semi-Final	2 March	Lost	1	4	13 February	Lost	0	1	Prem	Prem

Summary

	P	W	D	L	F	A
Wednesday's home league record:	56	31	12	13	101	71
Wednesday's away league record:	56	6	13	37	50	116
Wednesday's cup record:	12	6	2	4	20	13
TOTAL:	124	43	27	54	171	200

Albert Quixall cost Manchester
United a record £45,000 when he
left Hillsborough in 1958.

FACT FILE

- Even the most successful Man United squads have not liked coming to Hillsborough. Between 1957 and 1968, they failed to win in 12 league matches there, yet finished in the league's top two six times in that period.
- The all-conquering United of the 1990s also failed to win in five matches at Hillsborough from 1994 to 1998.
- Wednesday's most recent trophy came in 1991 when, as a second division side, they upset the odds to beat United at Wembley with John Sheridan's goal.
- United are unbeaten in their last 13 home games against Wednesday.
- Between 1910 and 1962, Wednesday failed to win in 25 away matches against United. Nonetheless, Wednesday won a cup tie 7-2 there in 1961!

Wednesday's top scorers vs United
Andrew Wilson 8
John Fantham, David Hirst 7
Jack Allen, Jack Whitham 6
Frank Bradshaw 5
Keith Ellis, Alan Finney 4

Wednesday hat-tricks vs United
20 Feb 1904 Vivien Simpson (cup)
16 Nov 1929 Jack Allen (4)
1 Feb 1961 Keith Ellis (cup)
25 Mar 1961 Gerry Young
31 Aug 1968 Jack Whitham

Played for both clubs

Pat O'Connell	Wednesday 1908-12	Man United 1914-15
Alf Capper	Man United 1911-12	Wednesday 1914-21
Billy Chapman	Wednesday 1923-25	Man United 1926-28
Bill Inglis	Wednesday 1924-25	Man United 1925-29
Rees Williams	Wednesday 1922-28	Man United 1927-29
Jack Ball	Man United 1929-30/33-35	Wednesday 1930-34
George Nevin	Wednesday 1932-33	Man United 1933-34
Tommy Jones	Wednesday 1929-34	Man United 1934-35
Jack Breedon	Wednesday 1930-34	Man United 1935-40
Neil Dewar	Man United 1932-34	Wednesday 1933-37
Albert Quixall	Wednesday 1950-59	Man United 1958-64
Don Gibson	Man United 1950-55	Wednesday 1955-60
Mike Pinner	Wednesday 1957-59	Man United 1960-61
Mark Pearson	Man United 1957-63	Wednesday 1963-65
Jim McCalliog	Wednesday 1965-69	Man United 1973-75
Chris Turner	Wednesday 1976-79/88-91	Man United 1985-88
Viv Anderson	Man United 1987-91	Wednesday 1990-93
Terry Cooke	Man United 1995-96	Wednesday 2000-01/03-04
Bojan Djordjic	Man United 2000-01	Wednesday 2001-02
Mark Robins	Man United 1989-92	Wednesday 2003-04
Mark Wilson	Man United 1999-2000	Wednesday 2003-04

v. Mansfield Town

Season	League	Date	Result	Wed'day	Mansf'd	Date	Result	Wed'day	Mansf'd	Wed'day	Mansf'd
			Home					**Away**		**Final Positions**	
1975-76	Division 3	27 December	Drew	0	0	19 April	Lost	0	3	20th	11th
1976-77	Division 3	30 October	Lost	0	2	11 January	Lost	0	1	8th	1stP
1978-79	Division 3	3 April	Lost	1	2	16 September	Drew	1	1	14th	18th
1979-80	Division 3	6 October	Drew	0	0	15 March	Drew	1	1	3rdP	23rdR

FA Cup

Season	Round	Date	Result	Wed'day	Mansf'd	Date	Result	Wed'day	Mansf'd	Division	
1945-46	Round 3	9 January	Won	5	0	5 January	Drew	0	0	Div 2	Div 3S
1966-67	Round 4	18 February	Won	4	0					Div 1	Div 3
1990-91	Round 3					5 January	Won	2	0	Div 2	Div 3

Summary	P	W	D	L	F	A
Wednesday's home league record:	4	0	2	2	1	4
Wednesday's away league record:	4	0	2	2	2	6
Wednesday's cup record:	4	3	1	0	11	0
TOTAL:	12	3	5	4	14	10

FACT FILE

● It's three wins out of four for Wednesday in cup matches (without a single goal conceded), but they have not managed a single win in the league against Mansfield.

Wednesday's top scorers vs Mansfield
John Ritchie 2

Played for both clubs

Harold Hill	Wednesday 1924-29	Mansfield 1933-34
Albert Ashley	Mansfield 1933-36	Wednesday 1935-40
Jack Roy	Mansfield 1936-37	Wednesday 1936-38
Jimmy McCarter	Wednesday 1946-47	Mansfield 1948-50
Oscar Fox	Wednesday 1946-50	Mansfield 1950-57
Wilf Ibbotson	Wednesday 1947-48	Mansfield 1948-49
Sam Ellis	Wednesday 1965-71	Mansfield 1971-73
Sammy Todd	Wednesday 1970-73	Mansfield 1973-74
Gordon Owen	Wednesday 1977-83	Mansfield 1987-89
Brian Cox	Wednesday 1978-81	Mansfield 1988-90
Ray Blackhall	Wednesday 1978-82	Mansfield 1982-83
John Pearson	Wednesday 1980-85	Mansfield 1994-95
Imre Varadi	Wednesday 1983-85/88-90	Mansfield 1995-96
Lawrie Madden	Mansfield 1974-76	Wednesday 1983-91
John Ryan	Wednesday 1984-85	Mansfield 1987-89
Greg Fee	Wednesday 1987-90	Mansfield 1990-93
Simon Coleman	Mansfield 1986-90	Wednesday 1993-95
O'Neill Donaldson	Mansfield 1994-95	Wednesday 1994-98
Richard Cresswell	Mansfield 1996-97	Wednesday 1998-2001
Leigh Bromby	Mansfield 1999-2000	Wednesday 2000-04

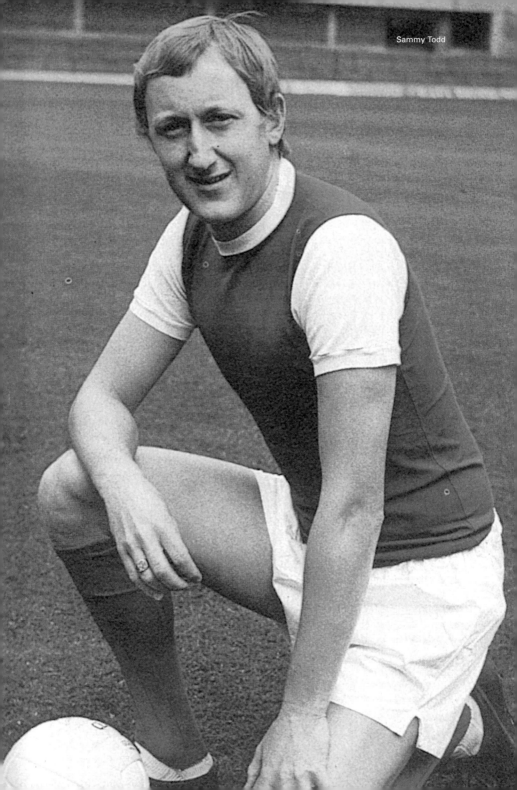
Sammy Todd

v. Middlesbrough

Season	League		Home Date	Result	Wed'day	Middb'h	Away Date	Result	Wed'day	Middb'h	Final Positions Wed'day	Middb'h
1899-00	Division 2	28 April	Won	3	0	23 December	Won	2	1	1stP	14th
1902-03	Division 1	13 September	Won	2	0	10 January	Lost	1	2	1st	13th
1903-04	Division 1	5 September	Won	4	1	2 January	Won	1	0	1st	10th
1904-05	Division 1	31 December	Won	5	0	3 September	Won	3	1	9th	15th
1905-06	Division 1	16 September	Won	3	0	20 January	Drew	2	2	3rd	18th
1906-07	Division 1	19 January	Lost	0	2	15 September	Won	3	1	13th	11th
1907-08	Division 1	2 November	Won	3	2	8 April	Lost	1	6	5th	6th
1908-09	Division 1	7 November	Won	3	2	13 March	Lost	1	2	5th	9th
1909-10	Division 1	4 September	Lost	1	5	8 January	Lost	0	4	11th	17th
1910-11	Division 1	10 September	Drew	1	1	7 January	Won	1	0	6th	16th
1911-12	Division 1	16 September	Lost	0	2	20 January	Drew	1	1	5th	7th
1912-13	Division 1	14 September	Won	3	1	4 January	Won	2	0	3rd	16th
1913-14	Division 1	18 October	Won	2	0	18 March	Lost	2	5	18th	3rd
1914-15	Division 1	1 September	Won	3	1	5 April	Lost	1	3	7th	12th
1919-20	Division 1	30 August	Lost	0	1	6 September	Lost	0	3	22ndR	13th
1924-25	Division 2	15 November	Won	2	0	21 March	Lost	0	2	14th	13th
1925-26	Division 2	22 February	Won	2	0	19 September	Lost	0	3	1stP	10th
1927-28	Division 1	11 February	Lost	2	3	1 October	Drew	3	3	14th	22ndR
1929-30	Division 1	12 April	Won	1	0	7 December	Lost	1	4	1st	16th
1930-31	Division 1	29 December	Won	3	2	26 December	Lost	0	2	3rd	7th
1931-32	Division 1	25 January	Drew	1	1	12 September	Lost	0	4	3rd	18th
1932-33	Division 1	10 December	Won	2	1	22 April	Drew	1	1	3rd	17th
1933-34	Division 1	16 September	Won	3	0	7 February	Won	3	2	11th	16th
1934-35	Division 1	8 September	Drew	3	3	19 January	Lost	3	5	3rd	20th
1935-36	Division 1	14 April	Drew	0	0	13 April	Lost	0	5	20th	14th
1936-37	Division 1	5 December	Won	1	0	10 April	Lost	0	2	22ndR	7th
1950-51	Division 1	16 September	Lost	0	1	20 January	Lost	1	2	21stR	6th
1952-53	Division 1	17 September	Won	2	0	1 January	Drew	2	2	18th	13th
1953-54	Division 1	6 February	Won	4	2	19 September	Lost	1	4	19th	21stR
1955-56	Division 2	12 November	Won	3	1	24 March	Drew	2	2	1stP	14th
1958-59	Division 2	13 December	Won	2	0	22 April	Drew	2	2	1stP	13th
1970-71	Division 2	21 November	Won	3	2	20 February	Lost	0	1	15th	7th
1971-72	Division 2	26 April	Won	1	0	31 August	Lost	1	2	14th	9th
1972-73	Division 2	18 November	Won	2	1	21 April	Lost	0	3	10th	4th
1973-74	Division 2	8 December	Drew	2	2	20 April	Lost	0	8	19th	1stP
1982-83	Division 2	28 August	Won	3	1	15 January	Drew	1	1	6th	16th
1983-84	Division 2	27 December	Lost	0	2	25 April	Lost	0	2	2ndP	17th
1988-89	Division 1	13 May	Won	1	0	26 November	Won	1	0	15th	18thR
1990-91	Division 2	13 April	Won	2	0	1 January	Won	2	0	3rdP	7th
1992-93	Premiership	1 May	Lost	2	3	24 October	Drew	1	1	7th	21stR
1995-96	Premiership	15 October	Lost	0	1	5 April	Lost	1	3	15th	12th
1996-97	Premiership	1 March	Won	3	1	18 January	Lost	2	4	7th	19thR
1998-99	Premiership	27 February	Won	3	1	3 October	Lost	0	4	12th	9th
1999-00	Premiership	26 December	Won	1	0	25 March	Lost	0	1	19thR	12th

FA Cup		Date	Result	Home Wed'day	Home Middb'h	Date	Result	Away Wed'day	Away Middb'h	Division Wed'day	Division Middb'h
1894-95	Round 2	16 February	Won	6	1					Div 1	Non L
1911-12	Round 1	25 January	Lost	1	2	13 January	Drew	0	0	Div 1	Div 1
1959-60	Round 3	9 January	Won	2	1					Div 1	Div 2
1991-92	Round 4	4 February	Lost	1	2					Div 1	Div 2

League Cup											
1993-94	Round 3	10 November	Won*	2	1	27 October	Drew	1	1	Prem	Div 1

Summary	P	W	D	L	F	A
Wednesday's home league record:	44	30	5	9	87	46
Wednesday's away league record:	44	9	9	26	49	106
Wednesday's cup record:	7	3	2	2	13	8
TOTAL:	95	42	16	37	149	160

FACT FILE

- Between 1930 and 1982, Wednesday lost once in 19 home matches against Boro.
- Wednesday won once in 25 visits to Teesside from 1914 to 1984.

Wednesday's top scorers vs Middlesbrough
Andrew Wilson 14
Harry Chapman 10
Harry Davis, Mark Hooper 9
David McLean, Ellis Rimmer 5
Jack Ball, Mark Pembridge, Jimmy Stewart 4

Wednesday hat-tricks vs Middlesbrough
16 Feb 1895 Harry Davis (3)

Played for both clubs

Joe Peacock	Middlesbrough 1927-30	Wednesday 1930-31
Jack Surtees	Middlesbrough 1931-32	Wednesday 1934-37
Bobby Bruce	Middlesbrough 1927-35	Wednesday 1935-36
Derrick Goodfellow	Wednesday 1936-47	Middlesbrough 1947-48
Eddie Holliday	Middlesbrough 1957-62/65-66	Wednesday 1961-64
John Hickton	Wednesday 1963-66	Middlesbrough 1968-78
Eric McMordie	Middlesbrough 1965-74	Wednesday 1974-75
Graeme Hedley	Middlesbrough 1976-82	Wednesday 1977-78
Ian Bailey	Middlesbrough 1975-82	Wednesday 1982-83
David Mills	Middlesbrough 1968-79/84-85	Wednesday 1982-83
Pat Heard	Wednesday 1982-85	Middlesbrough 1985-86
Brian Marwood	Wednesday 1984-88	Middlesbrough 1991-92
Mark Proctor	Middlesbrough 1978-81/88-93	Wednesday 1987-89
Nigel Pearson	Wednesday 1987-94	Middlesbrough 1994-98
David Hodgson	Middlesbrough 1978-82/86-87	Wednesday 1988-89
Darren Wood	Middlesbrough 1981-85	Wednesday 1988-90
Viv Anderson	Wednesday 1990-93	Middlesbrough 1994-95
Simon Coleman	Middlesbrough 1989-91	Wednesday 1993-95
Benito Carbone	Wednesday 1996-2000	Middlesbrough 2001-02
Stuart Ripley	Middlesbrough 1984-92	Wednesday 2000-01
Robbie Stockdale	Middlesbrough 1997-2004	Wednesday 2000-01
Marlon Beresford	Middlesbrough 1997-2002	Wednesday 2000-01
Dean Windass	Middlesbrough 2000-03	Wednesday 2001-02
Allan Johnston	Middlesbrough 2001-02	Wednesday 2002-03
Robbie Mustoe	Middlesbrough 1990-2002	Wednesday 2003-04
Mark Wilson	Middlesbrough 2001-03	Wednesday 2003-04

v. Millwall

Season	League	Date	Result	Wed'day	Millwall	Date	Result	Wed'day	Millwall	Wed'day	Millwall
			Home					**Away**		*Final Positions*	
1938-39	Division 2	10 April	Won	3	1	7 April	Lost	0	2	3rd	13th
1946-47	Division 2	1 February	Won	3	0	28 September	Drew	2	2	20th	18th
1947-48	Division 2	23 August	Won	3	2	20 December	Drew	0	0	4th	22ndR
1970-71	Division 2	7 November	Won	1	0	20 March	Lost	0	1	15th	8th
1971-72	Division 2	22 January	Drew	1	1	27 September	Drew	1	1	14th	3rd
1972-73	Division 2	2 December	Drew	2	2	7 April	Lost	1	2	10th	11th
1973-74	Division 2	3 October	Won	3	2	17 September	Lost	0	1	19th	12th
1974-75	Division 2	29 March	Lost	0	1	21 December	Lost	1	2	22ndR	20thR
1975-76	Division 3	11 October	Won	4	1	13 March	Lost	0	1	20th	3rdP
1979-80	Division 3	2 October	Won	2	0	18 September	Drew	3	3	3rdP	14th
1988-89	Division 1	1 April	Won	3	0	17 December	Lost	0	1	15th	10th
1989-90	Division 1	3 February	Drew	1	1	23 September	Lost	0	2	18thR	20thR
1990-91	Division 2	4 May	Won	2	1	27 October	Lost	2	4	3rdP	5th
2001-02	Division 1	8 December	Drew	1	1	16 March	Won	2	1	20th	4th
2002-03	Division 1	30 October	Lost	0	1	22 March	Lost	0	3	22ndR	9th

FA Cup

Season	Round	Date	Result	Wed'day	Millwall	Date	Result	Wed'day	Millwall	Division	
1905-06	Round 2	3 February	Drew	1	1	8 February	Won	3	0	Div 1	Non L
1990-91	Round 4	30 January	Won	2	0	26 January	Drew	4	4	Div 2	Div 2

League Cup

Season	Round	Date	Result	Wed'day	Millwall	Date	Result	Wed'day	Millwall	Division	
1976-77	Round 4					27 October	Lost	0	3	Div 3	Div 2
1995-96	Round 3					25 October	Won	2	0	Prem	Div 1

Reliable defender Lawrie Madden never let Wednesday down. He had previously appeared around 50 times for Millwall.

Summary	P	W	D	L	F	A
Wednesday's home league record:	15	9	4	2	29	14
Wednesday's away league record:	15	1	4	10	12	26
Wednesday's cup record:	6	3	2	1	12	8
TOTAL:	**36**	**13**	**10**	**13**	**53**	**48**

FACT FILE

- **Wednesday failed to win in 15 visits to Millwall from 1939 to 1991.**
- **Wednesday only lost one of their first 16 home games against Millwall.**

Wednesday's top scorers vs Millwall
David Hirst 7
Tommy Craig, Eric Potts 3

Played for both clubs
Harry Anstiss	Millwall 1922-23	Wednesday 1926-27
Tom Brolly	Wednesday 1933-34	Millwall 1935-50
Sydney Chedgzoy	Millwall 1934-35	Wednesday 1937-38
Gavin Malloch	Wednesday 1931-36	Millwall 1936-37
Wilf Smith	Wednesday 1964-71	Millwall 1974-75
Dave Cusack	Wednesday 1975-78	Millwall 1982-85
Lawrie Madden	Millwall 1981-83	Wednesday 1983-91
Mark Bright	Wednesday 1992-97	Millwall 1996-97
Ryan Green	Millwall 2001-02	Wednesday 2002-03

v. Nelson

Season	League	Date	Result (Home)	Wed'day	Nelson	Date	Result (Away)	Wed'day	Nelson	Final Positions Wed'day	Nelson
1923-24	Division 2	27 October	Won	5	0	20 October	Drew	1	1	8th	21stR

Summary	P	W	D	L	F	A
Wednesday's home league record:	1	1	0	0	5	0
Wednesday's away league record:	1	0	1	0	1	1
TOTAL:	2	1	1	0	6	1

Wednesday's top scorers vs Nelson
Charlie Petrie, Sam Taylor, Billy Walker 2

Played for both clubs
George Wilson	Wednesday 1919-25	Nelson 1925-30
Lewis Bedford	Wednesday 1925-26	Nelson 1926-28

Nelson were a Football League team when Wednesday played them. This picture features many players from 1923-24, being the previous season's Third Division North Championship-winning side.

v. New Brighton

FA Cup		Date	Result	Wed'day	N B'ton	Date	Result	Wed'day	N B'ton	Wed'day	N B'ton
				Home				**Away**		*Division*	
1922-23	Round 1	13 January	Won	**3**	**0**					Div 2	Non L
1925-26	Round 3					9 January	Lost	**1**	**2**	Div 2	Div 3N

Summary	P	W	D	L	F	A
Wednesday's cup record:	2	1	0	1	4	2
TOTAL:	2	1	0	1	4	2

Wednesday's top scorers vs New Brighton
Sid Binks 2

Played for both clubs
Ted Worrall	Wednesday 1910-15	New Brighton 1925-27
George Shilton	Wednesday 1919-22	New Brighton 1926-27

New Brighton upset the Owls in this FA Cup tie in 1926. Harry Gee scored the Rakers' first goal from the penalty spot.

v. New Brighton Tower

			Home				Away		Final Positions	
Season	League	Date	Result	Wed'day	Tower	Date	Result	Wed'day Tower	Wed'day	Tower
1899-00	Division 2	3 March	Won	4	0	25 December	Drew	2 2	1stP	10th

Summary	P	W	D	L	F	A
Wednesday's home league record:	1	1	0	0	4	0
Wednesday's away league record:	1	0	1	0	2	2
TOTAL:	2	1	1	0	6	2

FACT FILE

This club is separate to New Brighton. It folded 20 years prior to New Brighton's formation.

Wednesday's top scorers vs NB Tower
Jocky Wright 3
Archie Brash 2

Played for both clubs
Bob Petrie   Wednesday 1894-97   NB Tower 1900-01

v. Newcastle United

Season	League	Date	Result	Wed'day	Newcastle	Date	Result	Wed'day	Newcastle	Wed'day	Newcastle
				Home				**Away**		**Final Positions**	
1898-99	Division 1	15 April	Lost	1	3	17 December	Drew	2	2	18thR	13th
1900-01	Division 1	1 December	Drew	2	2	6 April	Drew	0	0	8th	6th
1901-02	Division 1	19 October	Drew	0	0	15 February	Lost	1	2	9th	3rd
1902-03	Division 1	17 January	Won	3	0	20 September	Lost	0	3	1st	14th
1903-04	Division 1	19 December	Drew	1	1	16 April	Lost	0	4	1st	4th
1904-05	Division 1	26 April	Lost	1	3	17 December	Lost	2	6	9th	1st
1905-06	Division 1	30 September	Drew	1	1	13 September	Won	3	0	3rd	4th
1906-07	Division 1	3 September	Drew	2	2	29 September	Lost	1	5	13th	1st
1907-08	Division 1	7 September	Won	3	1	4 January	Lost	1	2	5th	4th
1908-09	Division 1	26 September	Won	2	0	30 January	Lost	0	1	5th	1st
1909-10	Division 1	16 October	Won	3	1	26 February	Lost	1	3	11th	4th
1910-11	Division 1	27 December	Lost	0	2	14 April	Won	2	0	6th	8th
1911-12	Division 1	28 October	Lost	1	2	2 March	Won	2	0	5th	3rd
1912-13	Division 1	14 April	Lost	1	2	2 November	Lost	0	1	3rd	14th
1913-14	Division 1	24 January	Drew	0	0	27 September	Lost	1	3	18th	11th
1914-15	Division 1	1 January	Won	2	1	9 September	Drew	0	0	7th	15th
1919-20	Division 1	22 March	Lost	0	1	3 April	Drew	1	1	22ndR	8th
1926-27	Division 1	11 December	Won	3	2	30 April	Lost	1	2	16th	1st
1927-28	Division 1	25 February	Drew	0	0	15 October	Lost	3	4	14th	9th
1928-29	Division 1	8 December	Won	3	1	20 April	Lost	1	2	1st	10th
1929-30	Division 1	15 March	Won	4	2	9 November	Won	3	1	1st	19th
1930-31	Division 1	30 August	Won	2	1	27 December	Won	2	1	3rd	17th
1931-32	Division 1	6 February	Won	2	0	26 September	Lost	1	4	3rd	11th
1932-33	Division 1	29 October	Won	2	0	11 March	Lost	1	3	3rd	5th
1933-34	Division 1	30 September	Won	3	1	10 February	Drew	0	0	11th	21stR
1937-38	Division 2	16 April	Won	3	0	4 October	Lost	0	1	17th	19th
1938-39	Division 2	5 November	Lost	0	2	11 March	Lost	1	2	3rd	9th
1946-47	Division 2	24 May	Drew	1	1	9 November	Lost	0	4	20th	5th
1947-48	Division 2	29 November	Won	1	0	17 April	Lost	2	4	4th	2ndP
1950-51	Division 1	30 September	Drew	0	0	17 February	Lost	0	2	21stR	4th
1952-53	Division 1	23 August	Drew	2	2	20 December	Won	5	1	18th	16th
1953-54	Division 1	23 September	Won	3	0	16 April	Lost	0	3	19th	15th
1954-55	Division 1	4 December	Lost	0	3	9 April	Lost	0	5	22ndR	8th
1956-57	Division 1	1 September	Won	4	0	29 December	Won	2	1	14th	17th
1957-58	Division 1	4 September	Won	1	0	25 September	Drew	0	0	22ndR	19th
1959-60	Division 1	18 April	Won	2	0	15 April	Drew	3	3	5th	8th
1960-61	Division 1	3 April	Drew	1	1	31 March	Won	1	0	2nd	21stR
1965-66	Division 1	28 August	Won	1	0	5 February	Lost	0	2	17th	15th
1966-67	Division 1	22 April	Drew	0	0	26 November	Lost	1	3	11th	20th
1967-68	Division 1	2 March	Drew	1	1	25 November	Lost	0	4	19th	10th
1968-69	Division 1	14 August	Drew	1	1	9 April	Lost	2	3	15th	9th
1969-70	Division 1	20 August	Won	1	0	13 August	Lost	1	3	22ndR	7th
1980-81	Division 2	16 August	Won	2	0	15 November	Lost	0	1	10th	11th
1981-82	Division 2	12 April	Won	2	1	24 February	Lost	0	1	4th	9th

				Home			Away		Final Positions	
Season	League	Date	Result	Wed'day	Newcastle	Date	Result	Wed'day	Newcastle	Wed'day	Newcastle
1982-83	Division 2	18 December	Drew	1	1	7 May	Lost	1	2	6th	5th
1983-84	Division 2	19 November	Won	4	2	14 April	Won	1	0	2ndP	3rdP
1984-85	Division 1	30 March	Won	4	2	27 August	Lost	1	2	8th	14th
1985-86	Division 1	26 December	Drew	2	2	31 March	Lost	1	4	5th	11th
1986-87	Division 1	21 December	Won	2	0	6 September	Won	3	2	13th	17th
1987-88	Division 1	22 August	Lost	0	1	2 January	Drew	2	2	11th	8th
1988-89	Division 1	26 December	Lost	1	2	27 March	Won	3	1	15th	20thR
1990-91	Division 2	18 September	Drew	2	2	17 April	Lost	0	1	3rdP	11th
1993-94	Premiership	5 March	Lost	0	1	13 September	Lost	2	4	7th	3rd
1994-95	Premiership	21 January	Drew	0	0	22 October	Lost	1	2	13th	6th
1995-96	Premiership	27 August	Lost	0	2	3 February	Lost	0	2	15th	2nd
1996-97	Premiership	13 April	Drew	1	1	24 August	Won	2	1	7th	2nd
1997-98	Premiership	10 January	Won	2	1	9 August	Lost	1	2	16th	13th
1998-99	Premiership	21 April	Drew	1	1	14 November	Drew	1	1	12th	13th
1999-00	Premiership	26 February	Lost	0	2	19 September	Lost	0	8	19thR	11th

FA Cup

										Division	
1904-05	Semi-Final	25 March		Hyde Road, Manchester			Lost	0	1	Div 1	Div 1
1914-15	Round 3	20 February	Lost	1	2					Div 1	Div 1
1935-36	Round 4	25 January	Drew	1	1	29 January	Lost	1	3	Div 1	Div 2
1955-56	Round 3	7 January	Lost	1	3					Div 2	Div 1
1965-66	Round 4					12 February	Won	2	1	Div 1	Div 1
1980-81	Round 3					3 January	Lost	1	2	Div 2	Div 2

Summary	P	W	D	L	F	A
Wednesday's home league record:	59	26	20	13	88	61
Wednesday's away league record:	59	12	9	38	66	127
Wednesday's cup record:	7	1	1	5	7	13
TOTAL:	**125**	**39**	**30**	**56**	**161**	**201**

FACT FILE

- Wednesday's most recent trip to St James' Park was an extremely unhappy one. They came away with their worst Premiership defeat, their joint worst league defeat since the war, and the second worst Premiership defeat suffered by any club.
- Between 1956 and 1986, Wednesday were unbeaten in 16 home games in the series.
- From 1966 to 1983, Wednesday lost eight successive matches at St James' Park.
- Wednesday won seven successive home league games from 1928 to 1938.

Wednesday's top scorers vs Newcastle

Jack Allen 7
Ellis Rimmer, Andrew Wilson 6
Lee Chapman 5
Jack Ball, Frank Bradshaw, Redfern Froggatt,
David McLean 4

Wednesday hat-tricks vs Newcastle

26 Oct 1909 Frank Rollinson

Played for both clubs

John Smith	Wednesday 1893-94	Newcastle 1894-95
Jimmy Stewart	Wednesday 1902-08	Newcastle 1908-13
Andy Smailes	Newcastle 1919-23	Wednesday 1922-24
Ted Richardson	Newcastle 1922-23	Wednesday 1924-25
Jack Wilkinson	Wednesday 1925-30	Newcastle 1930-31
George Nevin	Newcastle 1929-30	Wednesday 1932-33
Jack Allen	Wednesday 1926-31	Newcastle 1931-35
Ronnie Starling	Newcastle 1930-32	Wednesday 1932-37
Tony Leach	Wednesday 1926-34	Newcastle 1934-36
Harry Ware	Newcastle 1935-37	Wednesday 1937-38
David Ford	Wednesday 1965-70	Newcastle 1969-71
Tommy Craig	Wednesday 1968-75	Newcastle 1974-78
Jackie Sinclair	Newcastle 1967-70	Wednesday 1969-73
Ray Blackhall	Newcastle 1974-78	Wednesday 1978-82
Gary Megson	Wednesday 1981-84/85-89	Newcastle 1984-86
David Mills	Newcastle 1981-82/83-84	Wednesday 1982-83
Pat Heard	Wednesday 1982-85	Newcastle 1984-85
Tony Cunningham	Wednesday 1983-84	Newcastle 1984-87
Imre Varadi	Newcastle 1981-83	Wednesday 1983-85/88-90
John Ryan	Newcastle 1983-85	Wednesday 1984-85
Franz Carr	Wednesday 1989-90	Newcastle 1991-93
Chris Waddle	Newcastle 1980-85	Wednesday 1992-96
Pavel Srnicek	Newcastle 1990-98	Wednesday 1998-2000
Kevin Gallacher	Newcastle 1999-2001	Wednesday 2001-02

England international Chris
Waddle had successful
spells at both Newcastle
and Sheffield Wednesday.

v. Newport County

			Home				Away		Final Positions	
Season	League	Date	Result	Wed'day	Newport	Date	Result	Wed'day Newport	Wed'day	Newport
1946-47	Division 2	26 April	Won	2	1	21 October	Lost	3 4	20th	22ndR

	Home						Away			Division
FA Cup										
1963-64	Round 3					4 January	Lost	2 3	Div 1	Div 4

Summary	P	W	D	L	F	A
Wednesday's home league record:	1	1	0	0	2	1
Wednesday's away league record:	1	0	0	1	3	4
Wednesday's cup record:	1	0	0	1	2	3
TOTAL:	3	1	0	2	7	8

FACT FILE

- All three matches ended in home wins.

Wednesday's top scorers vs Newport
Tommy Ward 2

Played for both clubs

Idris Lewis	Wednesday 1938-40	Newport 1946-48
Doug Witcomb	Wednesday 1946-53	Newport 1953-54
Jimmy Mullen	Wednesday 1970-80	Newport 1986-87
Richard Walden	Wednesday 1975-78	Newport 1978-82
Tommy Tynan	Wednesday 1976-79	Newport 1978-83
Jeff Johnson	Wednesday 1976-81	Newport 1981-82
Trevor Matthewson	Wednesday 1980-83	Newport 1983-85

v. Northampton Town

Season	League	Date	Result		Home Wed'day North'ton	Date	Result		Away Wed'day North'ton	Final Positions Wed'day North'ton
1965-66	Division 1	19 March	Won	3 1		25 September	Drew	0 0		17th 21stR
1976-77	Division 3	25 August	Won	2 1		15 January	Won	2 0		8th 22ndR

FA Cup										Division
1909-10	Round 1	20 January	Lost	0 1		15 January	Drew	0 0		Div 1 Non L

Summary	P	W	D	L	F	A
Wednesday's home league record:	2	2	0	0	5	2
Wednesday's away league record:	2	1	1	0	2	0
Wednesday's cup record:	2	0	1	1	0	1
TOTAL:	6	3	2	1	7	3

FACT FILE

- Northampton have only scored three goals in six matches.

Wednesday's top scorers vs Northampton
Rodger Wylde 3
David Ford 2

Played for both clubs
Joe Harron	Northampton 1921-22	Wednesday 1922-25
Bill Inglis	Wednesday 1924-25	Northampton 1930-32
Paddy McIlvenny	Wednesday 1925-26	Northampton 1928-29
Tom Robson	Wednesday 1930-32	Northampton 1934-38
Steve Bryant	Wednesday 1976-77	Northampton 1976-79/81-82
Paul Shirtliff	Wednesday 1980-83	Northampton 1984-85
Andy Blair	Wednesday 1984-86	Northampton 1988-89
Garry Thompson	Wednesday 1985-86	Northampton 1994-97
Colin West	Wednesday 1987-89	Northampton 1997-98
Greg Fee	Wednesday 1987-90	Northampton 1990-91
Kevin Nicholson	Wednesday 2000-01	Northampton 2000-01
Marlon Beresford	Northampton 1990-92	Wednesday 2000-01
Ian Hendon	Northampton 1998-2001	Wednesday 2000-03
Ashley Westwood	Wednesday 2000-03	Northampton 2003-04

v. Norwich City

Season	League	Date	Result	Wed'day	Norwich	Date	Result	Wed'day	Norwich	Wed'day	Norwich
			Home				**Away**			*Final Positions*	
1937-38	Division 2	22 January	Won	1	0	11 September	Lost	1	3	17th	14th
1938-39	Division 2	19 November	Won	7	0	25 March	Drew	2	2	3rd	21stR
1970-71	Division 2	13 March	Won	2	1	14 November	Drew	0	0	15th	10th
1971-72	Division 2	20 November	Drew	1	1	8 April	Lost	0	1	14th	1stP
1974-75	Division 2	8 April	Lost	0	1	31 August	Drew	1	1	22ndR	3rdP
1981-82	Division 2	15 May	Won	2	1	3 February	Won	3	2	4th	3rdP
1984-85	Division 1	3 November	Lost	1	2	3 April	Drew	1	1	8th	20thR
1986-87	Division 1	1 January	Drew	1	1	18 April	Lost	0	1	13th	5th
1987-88	Division 1	24 October	Won	1	0	26 March	Won	3	0	11th	14th
1988-89	Division 1	17 May	Drew	2	2	12 November	Drew	1	1	15th	4th
1989-90	Division 1	19 August	Lost	0	2	2 December	Lost	1	2	18thR	10th
1991-92	Division 1	20 April	Won	2	0	18 September	Lost	0	1	3rd	18th
1992-93	Premiership	10 January	Won	1	0	19 September	Lost	0	1	7th	3rd
1993-94	Premiership	1 September	Drew	3	3	25 February	Drew	1	1	7th	12th
1994-95	Premiership	31 August	Drew	0	0	5 March	Drew	0	0	13th	20thR
2000-01	Division 1	11 November	Won	3	2	28 April	Lost	0	1	17th	15th
2001-02	Division 1	29 December	Lost	0	5	27 August	Lost	0	2	20th	6th
2002-03	Division 1	8 February	Drew	2	2	9 November	Lost	0	3	22ndR	8th

FA Cup

Season	Round	Date	Result	Wed'day	Norwich	Date	Result	Wed'day	Norwich	Division	
1907-08	Round 1					11 January	Lost	0	2	Div 1	Non L
1934-35	Round 5					16 February	Won	1	0	Div 1	Div 2
1966-67	Round 5					11 March	Won	3	1	Div 1	Div 2
1998-99	Round 3	3 January	Won	4	1					Prem	Div 1
2000-01	Round 3	6 January	Won	2	1					Div 1	Div 1

Summary	P	W	D	L	F	A
Wednesday's home league record:	18	8	6	4	29	23
Wednesday's away league record:	18	2	7	9	14	23
Wednesday's cup record:	5	4	0	1	10	5
TOTAL:	**41**	**14**	**13**	**14**	**53**	**51**

FACT FILE

- Wednesday have lost one of their last nine matches at home.
- Norwich are undefeated in their last nine matches at home.
- Wednesday have not scored in their last four trips to Carrow Road.
- Doug Hunt's six goals in a match in 1938 are an all time Wednesday record.

Wednesday's top scorers vs Norwich
Doug Hunt 6
Gary Bannister, Mel Sterland 3
Richie Humphreys, Mick Prendergast 2

Wednesday hat-tricks vs Norwich
19 Nov 1938 Doug Hunt (6)

Played for both clubs

Fred Dent	Wednesday 1920-21	Norwich 1928-29
George Gray	Norwich 1920-22	Wednesday 1921-23
Joe Armstrong	Wednesday 1921-22	Norwich 1921-22
Joseph Wilson	Wednesday 1923-24	Norwich 1924-26
Jack Roy	Norwich 1934-36	Wednesday 1936-38
Harry Ware	Wednesday 1937-38	Norwich 1937-46
Cyril Walker	Wednesday 1937-38	Norwich 1946-47
Allenby Driver	Wednesday 1937-46	Norwich 1947-50
Barry Butler	Wednesday 1953-55	Norwich 1957-66
Colin Prophett	Wednesday 1969-73	Norwich 1973-74
John Sissons	Wednesday 1970-74	Norwich 1973-74
Andy Proudlove	Wednesday 1975-76	Norwich 1976-77
Neil O'Donnell	Norwich 1967-74	Wednesday 1975-77
Malcolm Darling	Norwich 1970-72	Wednesday 1977-78
Mike Pickering	Wednesday 1978-83	Norwich 1983-84
Ian Mellor	Norwich 1972-74	Wednesday 1979-82
Gary Megson	Wednesday 1982-84/85-89	Norwich 1992-95
Carl Bradshaw	Wednesday 1986-89	Norwich 1994-98
David Hodgson	Norwich 1986-87	Wednesday 1988-89
Jon Newsome	Wednesday 1989-91/95-2000	Norwich 1994-96
Chris Woods	Norwich 1980-86	Wednesday 1991-96
Efan Ekoku	Norwich 1992-95	Wednesday 2000-02
Leigh Bromby	Wednesday 2000-04	Norwich 2002-03
Mark Robins	Norwich 1992-95	Wednesday 2003-04

Chris Woods, who won the
League Cup with Norwich in
1985 before moving to the Owls
in 1991.

v. Nottingham Forest

Season	League	Home Date	Result	Wed'day	Forest	Away Date	Result	Wed'day	Forest	Final Positions Wed'day	Forest
1892-93	Division 1	3 October	Drew	2	2	1 December	Lost	0	2	12th	10th
1893-94	Division 1	5 March	Won	1	0	28 October	Lost	0	1	12th	7th
1894-95	Division 1	15 December	Drew	0	0	19 January	Lost	1	2	8th	7th
1895-96	Division 1	30 November	Won	3	0	7 April	Lost	0	1	7th	13th
1896-97	Division 1	5 April	Won	3	0	31 October	Drew	2	2	6th	11th
1897-98	Division 1	1 January	Lost	3	6	22 January	Lost	0	1	5th	8th
1898-99	Division 1	10 September	Won	2	1	7 January	Drew	1	1	18thR	11th
1900-01	Division 1	9 April	Won	4	1	29 September	Lost	0	1	8th	4th
1901-02	Division 1	8 March	Lost	0	2	9 November	Drew	1	1	9th	5th
1902-03	Division 1	28 February	Won	1	0	1 November	Won	4	1	1st	10th
1903-04	Division 1	3 October	Won	2	1	30 January	Won	1	0	1st	9th
1904-05	Division 1	8 October	Won	2	0	26 December	Lost	1	2	9th	16th
1905-06	Division 1	27 December	Won	1	0	16 April	Won	4	3	3rd	19thR
1907-08	Division 1	21 March	Won	2	1	23 November	Drew	2	2	5th	9th
1908-09	Division 1	23 January	Won	3	0	19 September	Won	2	1	5th	14th
1909-10	Division 1	11 December	Won	4	3	23 April	Won	6	0	11th	14th
1910-11	Division 1	3 December	Won	5	2	8 April	Won	1	0	6th	20thR
1920-21	Division 2	30 August	Drew	0	0	7 October	Lost	2	4	10th	18th
1921-22	Division 2	4 February	Lost	0	4	11 February	Lost	0	2	10th	1stP
1925-26	Division 2	22 March	Won	2	0	24 October	Lost	0	2	1stP	17th
1937-38	Division 2	27 November	Lost	0	2	9 April	Won	1	0	17th	20th
1938-39	Division 2	15 April	Drew	1	1	10 December	Drew	3	3	3rd	20th
1946-47	Division 2	12 April	Won	2	0	7 December	Drew	2	2	20th	11th
1947-48	Division 2	27 September	Won	2	1	14 February	Drew	0	0	4th	19th
1948-49	Division 2	19 March	Won	2	1	23 October	Won	2	1	8th	21stR
1951-52	Division 2	25 December	Drew	1	1	26 December	Lost	1	2	1stP	4th
1955-56	Division 2	24 September	Lost	1	2	4 February	Won	1	0	1stP	7th
1957-58	Division 1	31 August	Lost	1	2	28 December	Lost	2	5	22ndR	10th
1959-60	Division 1	16 September	Lost	0	1	9 September	Lost	1	2	5th	20th
1960-61	Division 1	21 February	Won	1	0	1 October	Won	2	1	2nd	14th
1961-62	Division 1	2 December	Won	3	0	21 April	Lost	1	3	6th	19th
1962-63	Division 1	13 October	Drew	2	2	2 March	Won	3	0	6th	9th
1963-64	Division 1	9 November	Won	3	1	21 March	Lost	2	3	6th	13th
1964-65	Division 1	3 April	Drew	0	0	21 November	Drew	2	2	8th	5th
1965-66	Division 1	11 September	Won	3	1	7 May	Lost	0	1	17th	18th
1966-67	Division 1	25 March	Lost	0	2	10 December	Drew	1	1	11th	2nd
1967-68	Division 1	20 April	Drew	0	0	14 October	Drew	0	0	19th	11th
1968-69	Division 1	7 April	Lost	0	1	20 August	Drew	0	0	15th	18th
1969-70	Division 1	21 March	Won	2	1	6 December	Lost	1	2	22ndR	15th
1972-73	Division 2	28 October	Lost	1	2	24 March	Lost	0	3	10th	14th
1973-74	Division 2	29 December	Drew	1	1	8 September	Lost	1	2	19th	7th
1974-75	Division 2	21 September	Lost	2	3	1 April	Lost	0	1	22ndR	16th
1984-85	Division 1	25 August	Won	3	1	20 March	Drew	0	0	8th	9th
1985-86	Division 1	7 December	Won	2	1	21 August	Won	1	0	5th	8th

		Home				Away				Final Positions	
Season	League	Date	Result	Wed'day	Forest	Date	Result	Wed'day	Forest	Wed'day	Forest
1986-87	Division 1	14 April	Lost	2	3	1 November	Lost	2	3	13th	8th
1987-88	Division 1	5 March	Lost	0	1	17 October	Lost	0	3	11th	3rd
1988-89	Division 1	31 December	Lost	0	3	3 September	Drew	1	1	15th	3rd
1989-90	Division 1	5 May	Lost	0	3	4 November	Won	1	0	18thR	9th
1991-92	Division 1	7 September	Won	2	1	4 April	Won	2	0	3rd	8th
1992-93	Premiership	19 August	Won	2	0	12 September	Won	2	1	7th	22ndR
1994-95	Premiership	1 April	Lost	1	7	10 September	Lost	1	4	13th	3rd
1995-96	Premiership	3 March	Lost	1	3	26 December	Lost	0	1	15th	9th
1996-97	Premiership	18 November	Won	2	0	5 March	Won	3	0	7th	20thR
1998-99	Premiership	7 December	Won	3	2	1 May	Lost	0	2	12th	20thR
2000-01	Division 1	13 September	Lost	0	1	21 February	Won	1	0	17th	11th
2001-02	Division 1	6 April	Lost	0	2	31 October	Won	1	0	20th	16th
2002-03	Division 1	26 December	Won	2	0	17 August	Lost	0	4	22ndR	6th

FA Cup

										Division	
1882-83	Round 3	13 January	Won	3	2	6 January	Drew	2	2		
1884-85	Round 3	3 January	Lost	1	2						
1887-88	Round 5					7 January	Won	4	2		
1896-97	Round 1	30 January	Lost	0	1					Div 1	Div 1
1905-06	Round 3	24 February	Won	4	1					Div 1	Div 1
1929-30	Q'ter final	8 March	Won	3	1	1 March	Drew	2	2	Div 1	Div 2
1961-62	Round 4					27 January	Won	2	0	Div 1	Div 1
1993-94	Round 3	8 January	Drew	1	1	19 January	Won	2	0	Prem	Div 1

League Cup

1999-00	Round 3	13 October	Won	4	1					Prem	Div 1

Summary	P	W	D	L	F	A
Wednesday's home league record:	57	29	9	19	88	76
Wednesday's away league record:	57	18	13	26	69	82
Wednesday's cup record:	12	7	3	2	28	15
TOTAL:	**126**	**54**	**25**	**47**	**185**	**173**

Viv Anderson, later to spend a few years at Hillsborough, pictured earlier in his career at Nottingham Forest.

FACT FILE

- In April 1910, Wednesday produced their joint biggest-ever away win in the league, 6-0 over Forest; however...
- In April 1995, Wednesday suffered their biggest-ever home defeat in the league, 7-1 at the hands of Forest.
- Wednesday enjoyed nine straight home wins in the series between 1903 and 1910.
- None of the last 16 league meetings at Hillsborough have ended in draws.
- From 1966 to 1975, Wednesday won once in 15 games against Forest.

Wednesday's top scorers vs Forest
Andrew Wilson 17
Harry Chapman, Harry Davis 7
Benito Carbone, Colin Dobson, John Fantham,
Jimmy Stewart 5

Wednesday hat-tricks vs Forest
7 Jan 1888 W Ingram (cup)
16 Apr 1906 Jimmy Stewart

Played for both clubs

Jack Earp	Forest 1892-93	Wednesday 1893-1900
Joe Ryalls	Wednesday 1902-04	Forest 1909-10
Tom Marrison	Wednesday 1902-05	Forest 1906-11
Jack Surtees	Wednesday 1934-37	Forest 1936-40
Peter Grummitt	Forest 1960-70	Wednesday 1969-73
Dave Sunley	Wednesday 1970-76	Forest 1975-76
Terry Curran	Forest 1975-77	Wednesday 1978-82
Gary Bannister	Wednesday 1981-84	Forest 1992-93
Lee Chapman	Wednesday 1984-88	Forest 1988-90
Paul Hart	Forest 1983-85	Wednesday 1985-87
Mark Proctor	Forest 1981-83	Wednesday 1987-89
Carlton Palmer	Wednesday 1988-94/2000-02	Forest 1998-2000
Franz Carr	Forest 1985-91	Wednesday 1989-90
Trevor Francis	Forest 1978-82	Wednesday 1989-94
Viv Anderson	Forest 1974-84	Wednesday 1990-93
Danny Wilson	Forest 1982-83	Wednesday 1990-93
Nigel Jemson	Forest 1989-92	Wednesday 1991-94
Chris Bart-Williams	Wednesday 1991-95	Forest 1995-2002
Des Walker	Forest 1983-92/2002-04	Wednesday 1993-2001
Danny Sonner	Wednesday 1998-2000	Forest 2003-04
David Johnson	Forest 2000-04	Wednesday 2001-02
Craig Armstrong	Forest 1997-99	Wednesday 2001-04
Adam Proudlock	Forest 2001-02	Wednesday 2002-04

v. Notts County

Season	League	Date	Result			Date	Result				
			Home	Wed'day	Notts C		**Away**	Wed'day	Notts C	*Final Positions* Wed'day	Notts C
1892-93	Division 1	3 April	Won	3	2	3 September	Won	1	0	12th	14thR
1897-98	Division 1	2 October	Won	3	1	4 December	Drew	0	0	5th	13th
1898-99	Division 1	12 November	Drew	1	1	11 March	Lost	0	1	18thR	5th
1900-01	Division 1	22 September	Won	4	1	19 January	Lost	0	2	8th	3rd
1901-02	Division 1	11 January	Won	4	0	14 September	Lost	1	6	9th	13th
1902-03	Division 1	27 December	Won	2	0	3 October	Won	3	0	1st	15th
1903-04	Division 1	22 February	Won	2	0	2 April	Lost	0	1	1st	13th
1904-05	Division 1	1 April	Won	1	0	3 December	Drew	2	2	9th	18th
1905-06	Division 1	28 October	Won	3	1	3 March	Won	3	1	3rd	16th
1906-07	Division 1	2 March	Lost	1	3	27 October	Drew	2	2	13th	18th
1907-08	Division 1	21 September	Won	2	0	18 January	Won	2	1	5th	18th
1908-09	Division 1	12 September	Won	2	0	9 January	Lost	0	1	5th	15th
1909-10	Division 1	19 February	Drew	0	0	9 October	Drew	0	0	11th	9th
1910-11	Division 1	24 September	Lost	1	3	28 January	Lost	0	2	6th	11th
1911-12	Division 1	27 January	Won	3	0	23 September	Lost	0	1	5th	16th
1912-13	Division 1	18 January	Won	3	1	21 September	Won	2	1	3rd	19thR
1914-15	Division 1	6 March	Drew	0	0	31 October	Won	2	1	7th	16th
1919-20	Division 1	13 September	Drew	0	0	20 September	Lost	1	3	22ndR	21stR
1920-21	Division 2	25 December	Drew	1	1	27 December	Lost	0	3	10th	6th
1921-22	Division 2	17 September	Drew	0	0	10 September	Lost	0	2	10th	13th
1922-23	Division 2	23 September	Lost	0	1	30 September	Lost	0	1	8th	1stP
1951-52	Division 2	3 November	Won	6	0	22 March	Drew	2	2	1stP	15th
1955-56	Division 2	31 March	Won	1	0	8 October	Drew	1	1	1stP	20th
1973-74	Division 2	27 October	Drew	0	0	9 March	Won	5	1	19th	10th
1974-75	Division 2	22 February	Lost	0	1	16 November	Drew	3	3	22ndR	14th
1980-81	Division 2	31 January	Lost	1	2	23 August	Lost	0	2	10th	2ndP
1990-91	Division 2	1 December	Drew	2	2	2 March	Won	2	0	3rdP	4thP
1991-92	Division 1	21 March	Won	1	0	3 September	Lost	1	2	3rd	21stR
2003-04	Division 2	1 October	Won	2	1	12 April	Drew	0	0	16th	23rdR

FA Cup

										Division	
1882-83	Round 4	12 February	Lost	1	4						
1888-89	Round 2	16 February	Won	3	2					Non L	Div 1
1889-90	Q'ter final	3 March		Derby Racecourse Ground			Won	2	1	Non L	Div 1
1894-95	Round 1	2 February	Won	5	1					Div 1	Div 2
1913-14	Round 1	10 January	Won	3	2					Div 1	Div 2
1954-55	Round 4	29 January	Drew	1	1	3 February	Lost*	0	1	Div 1	Div 2

Summary	P	W	D	L	F	A
Wednesday's home league record:	29	16	8	5	49	21
Wednesday's away league record:	29	8	8	13	33	42
Wednesday's cup record:	7	4	1	2	15	12
TOTAL:	**65**	**28**	**17**	**20**	**97**	**75**

FACT FILE

- 3 September 1892 saw Wednesday's first-ever Football League match. Having been elected straight into Division One, they celebrated with a 1-0 win at Trent Bridge, Tom Brandon scoring the winner.
- In November 1951, Derek Dooley scored five goals in the 6-0 win over Notts County. This feat has not been equalled by a Wednesday player since.
- The 1890 FA Cup tie was full of controversy. On 15 February Wednesday beat Notts County 5-0 at home, and thought they were through to the semi-finals. However, the FA upheld a Notts County appeal, and the match was replayed in Nottingham seven days later. Notts County won 3-2, but Wednesday appealed and another rematch was ordered, this time in Derby. At the third time of asking, the tie was completed and Wednesday went through.
- Wednesday won 10 and drew one of their 11 home games from 1889 to 1905.

Wednesday's top scorers vs Notts County	*Wednesday hat-tricks vs Notts County*
Andrew Wilson 10	3 Oct 1902 Fred Spiksley
Derek Dooley, Fred Spiksley 7	3 Nov 1951 Derek Dooley (5)
David McLean 6	
Harry Davis, George Simpson 4	

Eddie Gannon, an attacking wing-half signed by Eric Taylor from Notts County in March 1949. He stayed with Wednesday until 1955.

Played for both clubs

George Streets	Wednesday 1913-14	Notts Co 1919-28
George Toone	Notts Co 1913-14	Wednesday 1924-25
Joe Cooper	Wednesday 1920-21	Notts Co 1922-24
Horace Henshall	Notts Co 1912-22	Wednesday 1922-23
Harold Hill	Notts Co 1919-25	Wednesday 1924-29
Frank Froggatt	Wednesday 1921-28	Notts Co 1927-31
Sedley Cooper	Wednesday 1933-36	Notts Co 1936-40
Jim Fallon	Notts Co 1933-38/46-47	Wednesday 1937-40
Jack Roy	Wednesday 1936-38	Notts Co 1937-39
Roy Smith	Wednesday 1936-48	Notts Co 1948-53
Eddie Gannon	Notts Co 1946-49	Wednesday 1948-55
Jackie Sewell	Notts Co 1946-51	Wednesday 1950-56
Albert Broadbent	Notts Co 1953-55	Wednesday 1955-58
Barry Watling	Notts Co 1969-72	Wednesday 1975-76
Mark Smith	Wednesday 1977-87	Notts Co 1992-93
Jeff King	Notts Co 1975-76	Wednesday 1979-82
Gary Shelton	Notts Co 1979-80	Wednesday 1981-87
Nigel Worthington	Notts Co 1981-84	Wednesday 1983-94
Paul Hart	Wednesday 1985-87	Notts Co 1987-88
David Reeves	Wednesday 1988-89	Notts Co 1992-94
Phil King	Wednesday 1989-94	Notts Co 1993-94
Nigel Jemson	Wednesday 1991-94	Notts Co 1994-96
Adem Poric	Wednesday 1993-98	Notts Co 1997-98
Steve Nicol	Notts Co 1994-96	Wednesday 1995-98
Kevin Nicholson	Wednesday 2000-01	Notts Co 2000-04
Simon Grayson	Wednesday 2000-01	Notts Co 2001-02
Ian Hendon	Notts Co 1996-99	Wednesday 2000-03
Tommy Johnson	Notts Co 1988-92	Wednesday 2001-02
Mickael Antoine-Curier	Notts Co 2003-04	Wednesday 2003-04

Fred Spiksley scored one of his many hat-tricks against Notts County in 1902.

v. Notts Rangers

FA Cup	Date	Result	Home Wed'day Notts R	Date	Result	Away Wed'day Notts R	Division Wed'day Notts R
1888-89 Round 1	9 February	Won	3 0	2 February	Drew	1 1	Non L Non L

Summary	P	W	D	L	F	A
Wednesday's cup record:	2	1	1	0	4	1
TOTAL:	2	1	1	0	4	1

Wednesday's top scorers vs Notts Rangers

J. Dungworth 2

v. Oldham Athletic

Season	League	Date	Result	Wed'day	Oldham	Date	Result	Wed'day	Oldham	Wed'day	Oldham
		Home					**Away**			*Final Positions*	
1910-11	Division 1	29 April	Won	2	0	24 December	Lost	0	1	6th	7th
1911-12	Division 1	11 November	Won	1	0	16 March	Lost	0	1	5th	18th
1912-13	Division 1	9 November	Won	5	0	15 March	Lost	0	2	3rd	9th
1913-14	Division 1	22 September	Lost	1	2	14 April	Lost	0	2	18th	4th
1914-15	Division 1	6 February	Drew	2	2	3 October	Lost	2	5	7th	2nd
1919-20	Division 1	1 May	Won	1	0	26 April	Lost	0	1	22ndR	17th
1923-24	Division 2	22 March	Lost	1	2	15 March	Lost	0	2	8th	7th
1924-25	Division 2	1 January	Won	1	0	10 April	Drew	1	1	14th	18th
1925-26	Division 2	28 December	Won	5	1	7 September	Drew	1	1	1stP	7th
1974-75	Division 2	14 December	Drew	1	1	17 August	Lost	1	2	22ndR	18th
1980-81	Division 2	14 February	Won	3	0	6 September	Lost	0	2	10th	15th
1981-82	Division 2	24 October	Won	2	1	13 March	Won	3	0	4th	11th
1982-83	Division 2	4 December	Drew	1	1	23 April	Drew	1	1	6th	7th
1983-84	Division 2	2 January	Won	3	0	24 September	Won	3	1	2ndP	19th
1990-91	Division 2	3 November	Drew	2	2	11 May	Lost	2	3	3rdP	1stP
1991-92	Division 1	1 January	Drew	1	1	28 March	Lost	0	3	3rd	17th
1992-93	Premiership	17 October	Won	2	1	7 April	Drew	1	1	7th	19th
1993-94	Premiership	24 November	Won	3	0	30 April	Drew	0	0	7th	21stR
2003-04	Division 2	16 August	Drew	2	2	17 January	Lost	10	1	16th	15th

FA Cup — *Division*

Season		Date	Result	Wed'day	Oldham	Date	Result	Wed'day	Oldham		
1929-30	Round 4					25 January	Won	4	3	Div 1	Div 2
1933-34	Round 4	31 January	Won	6	1	27 January	Drew	1	1	Div 1	Div 2
1934-35	Round 3	12 January	Won	3	1					Div 1	Div 2
1984-85	Round 4	26 January	Won	5	1					Div 1	Div 2

League Cup

Season		Date	Result	Wed'day	Oldham	Date	Result	Wed'day	Oldham		
2000-01	Round 2	27 September	Won	5	1	19 September	Won	3	1	Div 1	Div 2

Summary

	P	W	D	L	F	A
Wednesday's home league record:	19	11	6	2	39	16
Wednesday's away league record:	19	2	5	12	15	30
Wednesday's cup record:	7	6	1	0	27	9
TOTAL:	**45**	**19**	**12**	**13**	**81**	**55**

FACT FILE

- Oldham have not won in their last 16 visits to Hillsborough. Their last win there was in 1924.
- Wednesday lost their first seven away games in the series.
- There has only ever been one goalless draw between the sides.

Wednesday's top scorers vs Oldham

Gary Bannister, Imre Varadi 5
Neil Dewar, Harold Hill, Mark Hooper,
David McLean, Jimmy Trotter, Gordon Watson,
Andrew Wilson 3

Wednesday hat-tricks vs Oldham

31 Jan 1934 Neil Dewar (cup)
26 Jan 1985 Imre Varadi (cup)

Played for both clubs

Tom Marrison	Wednesday 1902-05	Oldham 1911-12
Ollie Tummon	Wednesday 1905-10	Oldham 1912-15
Bert Burridge	Wednesday 1926-30	Oldham 1930-31
Bill Pickering	Wednesday 1938-46	Oldham 1948-50
Norman Jackson	Wednesday 1949-53	Oldham 1956-57
Albert Quixall	Wednesday 1950-59	Oldham 1964-66
Colin Whitaker	Wednesday 1951-52	Oldham 1962-64
Bobby Craig	Wednesday 1959-62	Oldham 1963-65
Brian Woodall	Wednesday 1967-70	Oldham 1969-70
Rodger Wylde	Wednesday 1972-80	Oldham 1979-83
Ken Knighton	Oldham 1966-68	Wednesday 1973-76
Martin Hodge	Oldham 1982-83	Wednesday 1983-88
John Ryan	Oldham 1981-83/85-87	Wednesday 1984-85
Simon Stainrod	Oldham 1978-81	Wednesday 1984-86
Glynn Snodin	Wednesday 1985-87	Oldham 1991-92
David Reeves	Wednesday 1988-89	Oldham 2001-02
John Sheridan	Wednesday 1989-97	Oldham 1998-2004
Paul Warhurst	Oldham 1988-91	Wednesday 1990-93
Manuel Agogo	Wednesday 1997-99	Oldham 1999-2000
Earl Barrett	Oldham 1987-92	Wednesday 1997-99
Paul Smith	Oldham 2000-01	Wednesday 2003-04
Mickael Antoine-Curier	Oldham 2003-04	Wednesday 2003-04

Imre Varadi was on target five
times for Wednesday against
the Latics.

v. Oxford United

Season	League	Date	Result	Home Wed'day	Oxford	Date	Result	Away Wed'day	Oxford	Final Positions Wed'day	Oxford
1970-71	Division 2	9 December	Drew	1	1	22 August	Drew	1	1	15th	14th
1971-72	Division 2	3 April	Drew	0	0	25 September	Lost	0	1	14th	15th
1972-73	Division 2	11 November	Lost	0	1	20 September	Lost	0	1	10th	8th
1973-74	Division 2	24 November	Lost	0	1	6 April	Lost	0	1	19th	18th
1974-75	Division 2	19 April	Drew	1	1	12 October	Lost	0	1	22ndR	11th
1976-77	Division 3	14 May	Won	2	0	18 December	Drew	1	1	8th	17th
1977-78	Division 3	8 April	Won	2	1	12 November	Lost	0	1	14th	18th
1978-79	Division 3	17 October	Drew	1	1	25 April	Drew	1	1	14th	11th
1979-80	Division 3	20 October	Drew	2	2	1 March	Won	2	0	3rdP	17th
1985-86	Division 1	18 January	Won	2	1	31 August	Won	1	0	5th	18th
1986-87	Division 1	4 October	Won	6	1	28 March	Lost	1	2	13th	18th
1987-88	Division 1	18 August	Drew	1	1	13 April	Won	3	0	11th	21stR
1990-91	Division 2	1 April	Lost	0	2	22 December	Drew	2	2	3rdP	10th

FA Cup

										Division	
1983-84	Round 5					18 February	Won	3	0	Div 2	Div 3

League Cup

1996-97	Round 2	18 September	Drew	1	1	24 September	Lost	0	1	Prem	Div 1

Summary	P	W	D	L	F	A
Wednesday's home league record:	13	4	6	3	18	13
Wednesday's away league record:	13	3	4	6	12	12
Wednesday's cup record:	3	1	1	1	4	2
TOTAL:	**29**	**8**	**11**	**10**	**34**	**27**

Nigel Jemson

FACT FILE

● **Wednesday failed to win in their first 11 meetings with Oxford, scoring only four goals in the process.**

● **Between 1975 and 1987, Wednesday were unbeaten in eight home games in the series.**

Wednesday's top scorers vs Oxford
Lee Chapman 5
Rodger Wylde 4
Brian Hornsby 3

Played for both clubs

David Grant	Wednesday 1977-82	Oxford 1982-84
Andy McCulloch	Oxford 1974-76	Wednesday 1979-83
Gary Bannister	Wednesday 1981-84	Oxford 1991-92
Gary Shelton	Wednesday 1981-87	Oxford 1987-89
Imre Varadi	Wednesday 1983-85/88-90	Oxford 1992-93
Nigel Jemson	Wednesday 1991-94	Oxford 1996-98/99-2000
Mike Williams	Wednesday 1992-97	Oxford 1998-99
O'Neill Donaldson	Wednesday 1994-98	Oxford 1997-98
Guy Whittingham	Wednesday 1994-99	Oxford 2000-01
Jim Magilton	Oxford 1990-94	Wednesday 1997-99
Dean Windass	Oxford 1998-99	Wednesday 2001-02
Garry Monk	Oxford 2000-01	Wednesday 2002-03
Robbie Mustoe	Oxford 1986-90	Wednesday 2003-04

Gary Shelton was a bargain buy for Wednesday from Aston Villa for £50,000 in 1982. He moved to Oxford five years later.

v. Peterborough United

Season	League	Date	Result	Home Wed'day P'boro	Date	Result	Away Wed'day P'boro	Final Positions Wed'day P'boro
1975-76	Division 3	4 October	Drew	2 2	10 March	Drew	2 2	20th 10th
1976-77	Division 3	30 April	Won	4 0	27 November	Won	2 1	8th 16th
1977-78	Division 3	24 September	Lost	0 1	22 February	Lost	1 2	14th 4th
1978-79	Division 3	27 March	Won	3 0	19 August	Lost	0 2	14th 21stR
2003-04	Division 2	24 January	Won	2 0	23 August	Won	1 0	16th 18th

FA Cup

								Division
1959-60	Round 4	30 January	Won	2 0				Div 1 Non L

Summary	P	W	D	L	F	A
Wednesday's home league record:	5	3	1	1	11	3
Wednesday's away league record:	5	2	1	2	6	7
Wednesday's cup record:	1	1	0	0	2	0
TOTAL:	**11**	**6**	**2**	**3**	**19**	**10**

Wednesday's top scorers vs Peterborough
Paul Bradshaw, Bobby Craig, Tommy Tynan,
Rodger Wylde 2

Played for both clubs
Tom McAnearney	Wednesday 1952-65	Peterborough 1965-66
Peter Johnson	Wednesday 1957-65	Peterborough 1965-67
Eddie Holliday	Wednesday 1961-64	Peterborough 1969-70
Graham Birks	Wednesday 1962-63	Peterborough 1964-66
Peter Eustace	Wednesday 1962-70/72-75	Peterborough 1975-76
Frank Noble	Wednesday 1963-66	Peterborough 1967-72
Kenny Burton	Wednesday 1968-72	Peterborough 1972-73
Ian Nimmo	Wednesday 1975-79	Peterborough 1976-77
Graham Hyde	Wednesday 1991-99	Peterborough 2002-03
Mike Williams	Wednesday 1992-97	Peterborough 1996-97
Guy Whittingham	Wednesday 1994-99	Peterborough 2000-01
Mark McKeever	Peterborough 1996-97	Wednesday 1998-2000
Ian Hendon	Wednesday 2000-03	Peterborough 2002-03

Peter Eustace was
around for a long time
at Hillsborough in two
spells. He also had a
period at Peterborough.

v. Plymouth Argyle

Season	League	Date (Home)	Result	Wed'day	Plymouth	Date (Away)	Result	Wed'day	Plymouth	Final Positions Wed'day	Plymouth
1937-38	Division 2	27 December	Drew	1	1	25 December	Won	4	2	17th	13th
1938-39	Division 2	3 December	Lost	1	2	8 April	Drew	1	1	3rd	15th
1939-40	Division 2	2 September	Lost	0	1						
1946-47	Division 2	7 September	Won	2	1	4 January	Lost	1	4	20th	19th
1947-48	Division 2	28 February	Drew	1	1	11 October	Won	2	0	4th	17th
1948-49	Division 2	2 April	Won	2	1	6 November	Lost	2	3	8th	20th
1949-50	Division 2	14 January	Lost	2	4	10 September	Won	1	0	2ndP	21stR
1955-56	Division 2	20 August	Won	5	2	17 December	Drew	1	1	1stP	21stR
1977-78	Division 3	27 September	Drew	1	1	4 April	Drew	1	1	14th	19th
1978-79	Division 3	23 September	Lost	2	3	27 January	Lost	0	2	14th	15th
1979-80	Division 3	12 January	Lost	0	1	1 September	Won	3	1	3rdP	15th
1990-91	Division 2	13 October	Won	3	0	19 March	Drew	1	1	3rdP	18th
2003-04	Division 2	22 October	Lost	1	3	2 March	Lost	0	2	16th	1stP

FA Cup

		Date (Home)	Result	Wed'day	Plymouth	Date (Away)	Result	Wed'day	Plymouth	Division Wed'day	Plymouth
1903-04	Round 1	10 February	Won	2	0	6 February	Drew	2	2	Div 1	Non L
1967-68	Round 3	27 January	Won	3	0					Div 1	Div 2

Summary

	P	W	D	L	F	A
Wednesday's home league record:	13	4	3	6	21	21
Wednesday's away league record:	12	4	4	4	17	18
Wednesday's cup record:	3	2	1	0	7	2
TOTAL:	**28**	**10**	**8**	**10**	**45**	**41**

FACT FILE

- The longest run either side has had without winning is five matches (by Plymouth in 1955-78). Generally, it has been a very even series.

Lee Chapman's early career at Stoke City included a loan spell to Plymouth Argyle where he played four games. He then joined Arsenal, Sunderland and Sheffield Wednesday, and left the Owls for Niort. He returned to England to play for Nottingham Forest, Leeds United, Portsmouth, West Ham, Southend and Ipswich Town. He is married to actress Lesley Ash.

Tommy Tynan scored goals wherever he went and had a good record at Wednesday with 37 goals from 107 starts. At Plymouth Tynan was a hero, consistently topping the goalscoring charts, with over 120 goals over six seasons in the 1980s.

Wednesday's top scorers vs Plymouth
Eddie Quigley, Jackie Sewell, Rodger Wylde 3

Wednesday hat-tricks vs Plymouth
20 Aug 1955 Jackie Sewell

Played for both clubs

Vic Wright	Wednesday 1931-32	Plymouth 1937-38
Bernard Oxley	Wednesday 1933-35	Plymouth 1935-36
Hugh McJarrow	Wednesday 1949-52	Plymouth 1953-56
Keith Thomas	Wednesday 1950-52	Plymouth 1953-56
Jim McAnearney	Wednesday 1953-59	Plymouth 1959-64
George Kirby	Wednesday 1959-60	Plymouth 1959-63
Neil Ramsbottom	Wednesday 1975-76	Plymouth 1976-77
Tommy Tynan	Wednesday 1976-79	Plymouth 1983-90
Jimmy Hinch	Plymouth 1970-74	Wednesday 1977-78
Mark Smith	Wednesday 1977-87	Plymouth 1987-90
Gary Megson	Plymouth 1977-80	Wednesday 1981-84/85-89
Martin Hodge	Plymouth 1977-79/94-95	Wednesday 1983-88
Lee Chapman	Plymouth 1978-79	Wednesday 1984-88
Steve McCall	Wednesday 1987-91	Plymouth 1991-96/98-2000
John Beswetherick	Plymouth 1997-2002	Wednesday 2002-04

v. Port Vale

Season	League	Date	Result	Wed'day	Port Vale	Date	Result	Wed'day	Port Vale	Wed'day	Port Vale
1899-00	Division 2	14 April	Won	4	0	12 February	Won	3	0	1stP	11th
1920-21	Division 2	22 January	Won	1	0	15 January	Lost	0	1	10th	17th
1921-22	Division 2	3 April	Won	2	0	18 March	Lost	0	1	10th	18th
1922-23	Division 2	28 April	Won	2	0	5 May	Drew	2	2	8th	17th
1923-24	Division 2	3 September	Won	2	1	27 August	Lost	0	2	8th	16th
1924-25	Division 2	14 March	Lost	0	1	8 November	Lost	0	1	14th	8th
1925-26	Division 2	20 March	Lost	0	2	7 November	Lost	3	4	1stP	8th
1955-56	Division 2	3 March	Won	4	0	22 October	Won	1	0	1stP	12th
1975-76	Division 3	8 November	Lost	0	3	16 February	Lost	0	1	20th	12th
1976-77	Division 3	5 February	Lost	1	2	28 August	Lost	0	2	8th	19th
1977-78	Division 3	11 February	Won	3	1	17 September	Drew	0	0	14th	21stR
1990-91	Division 2	20 October	Drew	1	1	6 May	Drew	1	1	3rdP	15th
2003-04	Division 2	26 December	Lost	2	3	7 February	Lost	0	3	16th	7th

FA Cup										Division	
1936-37	Round 3	16 January	Won	2	0					Div 1	Div 3N

Summary

	P	W	D	L	F	A
Wednesday's home league record:	13	7	1	5	22	14
Wednesday's away league record:	13	2	3	8	10	18
Wednesday's cup record:	1	1	0	0	2	0
TOTAL:	27	10	4	13	34	32

FACT FILE

● Wednesday won their first five home games against Port Vale.

● Wednesday have won once in their last 12 away games in the series.

Wednesday's top scorers vs Port Vale
Jocky Wright 4
Harry Millar, Charlie Petrie, Albert Quixall 2

Wednesday hat-tricks vs Port Vale
14 Apr 1900 Jocky Wright

Played for both clubs

Len Armitage	Wednesday 1919-20	Port Vale 1932-34
Harry Anstiss	Wednesday 1926-27	Port Vale 1926-31
Arthur Prince	Port Vale 1922-24	Wednesday 1924-28
Alf Strange	Port Vale 1924-27	Wednesday 1926-35
Walter Aveyard	Wednesday 1946-47	Port Vale 1948-52
Andy Proudlove	Wednesday 1975-76	Port Vale 1978-79
Jeff Johnson	Wednesday 1976-81	Port Vale 1985-86
Mark Smith	Wednesday 1977-87	Port Vale 1992-93
Simon Mills	Wednesday 1982-85	Port Vale 1987-93
Mark Chamberlain	Port Vale 1978-82	Wednesday 1985-88
Colin West	Wednesday 1987-89	Port Vale 1991-92
Mark Bright	Port Vale 1981-84	Wednesday 1992-97
Ian Taylor	Port Vale 1992-94	Wednesday 1994-95
Jon McCarthy	Port Vale 1995-98/2002-03	Wednesday 2001-02

v. Portsmouth

Season	League	Date	Result	Wed'day	Portsm'th	Date	Result	Wed'day	Portsm'th	Wed'day	Portsm'th
			Home				**Away**			*Final Positions*	
1924-25	Division 2	13 December	Won	5	2	18 April	Drew	1	1	14th	4th
1925-26	Division 2	26 September	Won	4	2	6 February	Won	2	1	1stP	11th
1927-28	Division 1	21 April	Won	2	0	10 December	Drew	0	0	14th	20th
1928-29	Division 1	4 March	Won	2	1	6 October	Lost	2	3	1st	20th
1929-30	Division 1	28 December	Drew	1	1	31 August	Won	4	0	1st	13th
1930-31	Division 1	11 April	Drew	2	2	6 December	Won	4	2	3rd	4th
1931-32	Division 1	9 April	Won	3	1	28 November	Lost	0	2	3rd	8th
1932-33	Division 1	12 November	Won	2	1	25 March	Lost	0	3	3rd	9th
1933-34	Division 1	18 November	Lost	1	2	31 March	Won	2	0	11th	10th
1934-35	Division 1	9 February	Won	3	0	29 September	Lost	1	2	3rd	14th
1935-36	Division 1	12 February	Lost	0	1	21 September	Lost	2	3	20th	10th
1936-37	Division 1	26 September	Drew	0	0	3 February	Lost	0	1	22ndR	9th
1950-51	Division 1	21 August	Won	2	1	30 August	Lost	1	4	21stR	7th
1952-53	Division 1	15 November	Lost	3	4	4 April	Lost	2	5	18th	15th
1953-54	Division 1	24 October	Drew	4	4	7 April	Lost	1	2	19th	14th
1954-55	Division 1	12 February	Lost	1	3	25 September	Lost	1	2	22ndR	3rd
1956-57	Division 1	9 April	Won	3	1	25 August	Lost	1	3	14th	19th
1957-58	Division 1	11 January	Won	4	2	7 September	Lost	2	3	22ndR	20th
1970-71	Division 2	30 March	Won	3	1	5 September	Lost	0	2	15th	16th
1971-72	Division 2	4 September	Drew	1	1	18 December	Won	2	1	14th	16th
1972-73	Division 2	9 September	Won	2	1	27 January	Lost	0	1	10th	17th
1973-74	Division 2	13 October	Lost	1	2	20 February	Drew	1	1	19th	15th
1974-75	Division 2	18 January	Lost	0	2	30 November	Lost	0	1	22ndR	17th
1976-77	Division 3	4 September	Drew	1	1	12 February	Won	3	0	8th	20th
1977-78	Division 3	25 February	Drew	0	0	1 October	Drew	2	2	14th	24thR
1983-84	Division 2	7 April	Won	2	0	15 October	Won	1	0	2ndP	16th
1987-88	Division 1	19 March	Won	1	0	31 October	Won	2	1	11th	19thR
1990-91	Division 2	29 December	Won	2	1	6 April	Lost	0	2	3rdP	17th
2000-01	Division 1	7 March	Drew	0	0	14 October	Lost	1	2	17th	20th
2001-02	Division 1	3 November	Lost	2	3	23 March	Drew	0	0	20th	17th
2002-03	Division 1	23 November	Lost	1	3	12 April	Won	2	1	22ndR	1stP

FA Cup										*Division*	
1904-05	Round 2	18 February	Won	2	1					Div 1	Non L
1908-09	Round 2	11 February	Won	3	0	6 February	Drew	2	2	Div 1	Non L
1948-49	Round 4					29 January	Lost	1	2	Div 2	Div 1

Summary	P	W	D	L	F	A
Wednesday's home league record:	31	15	8	8	58	43
Wednesday's away league record:	31	9	5	17	40	51
Wednesday's cup record:	4	2	1	1	8	5
TOTAL:	**66**	**26**	**14**	**26**	**106**	**99**

FACT FILE

- Portsmouth won 11 home games in a row from 1934 to 1970.
- Wednesday were unbeaten in their first 10 home games against Pompey.
- Between 1976 and 1988, Wednesday were unbeaten for eight games in a row.

Wednesday's top scorers vs Portsmouth
Jimmy Trotter 8
Ellis Rimmer 5
Jack Allen, Redfern Froggatt, Mark Hooper 4

Wednesday hat-tricks vs Portsmouth
13 Dec 1924 Jimmy Trotter (5)

Played for both clubs

Frank Stringfellow	Wednesday 1908-11	Portsmouth 1920-22
John Smelt	Portsmouth 1920-21	Wednesday 1920-22
Joe Armstrong	Portsmouth 1920-21	Wednesday 1921-22
Ernie Thompson	Portsmouth 1920-21	Wednesday 1921-22
Alf Strange	Portsmouth 1922-24	Wednesday 1926-35
Jack Surtees	Portsmouth 1932-33	Wednesday 1934-37
John Collins	Portsmouth 1971-74	Wednesday 1976-77
Steve Bryant	Wednesday 1976-77	Portsmouth 1978-82
Jeff King	Portsmouth 1975-76	Wednesday 1979-82
Lee Chapman	Wednesday 1984-88	Portsmouth 1993-94
Mark Chamberlain	Wednesday 1985-88	Portsmouth 1988-94
Guy Whittingham	Portsmouth 1989-93/98-2001	Wednesday 1994-99
Barry Horne	Portsmouth 1987-89	Wednesday 1999-2000
Ian Hendon	Portsmouth 1991-92	Wednesday 2000-03
Darryl Powell	Portsmouth 1988-95	Wednesday 2002-03
Lee Bradbury	Portsmouth 1995-97/1999-2003	Wednesday 2002-03
Carl Robinson	Wednesday 2002-03	Portsmouth 2002-04
Mark Burchill	Portsmouth 2002-03	Wednesday 2003-04

Former England winger Mark Chamberlain dazzled Wednesday fans on an inconsistent basis in the mid-1980s and later served Portsmouth for six years.

v. Preston North End

Season	League	Date (Home)	Result	Wed'day	Preston NE	Date (Away)	Result	Wed'day	Preston NE	Final Wed'day	Final Preston NE
1892-93	Division 1	14 January	Lost	0	5	12 September	Lost	1	4	12th	2nd
1893-94	Division 1	6 February	Won	3	0	26 March	Lost	0	1	12th	14th
1894-95	Division 1	3 September	Won	3	1	13 April	Lost	1	3	8th	4th
1895-96	Division 1	1 January	Drew	1	1	6 April	Won	1	0	7th	9th
1896-97	Division 1	2 January	Won	1	0	20 February	Drew	2	2	6th	4th
1897-98	Division 1	11 December	Won	2	1	18 December	Lost	0	2	5th	12th
1898-99	Division 1	19 September	Won	2	1	22 April	Drew	1	1	18thR	15th
1900-01	Division 1	6 October	Lost	0	1	5 April	Lost	2	3	8th	17thR
1904-05	Division 1	2 January	Won	2	0	22 April	Lost	0	1	9th	8th
1905-06	Division 1	27 January	Drew	1	1	23 September	Won	1	0	3rd	2nd
1906-07	Division 1	22 September	Won	2	1	26 January	Lost	0	1	13th	14th
1907-08	Division 1	5 October	Won	1	0	2 September	Drew	1	1	5th	12th
1908-09	Division 1	24 October	Won	1	0	27 February	Lost	1	4	5th	10th
1909-10	Division 1	2 October	Won	4	1	12 February	Lost	0	1	11th	12th
1910-11	Division 1	21 January	Drew	0	0	17 September	Won	3	1	6th	14th
1911-12	Division 1	2 September	Lost	0	1	30 December	Won	3	2	5th	19thR
1913-14	Division 1	20 September	Won	2	1	17 January	Lost	0	5	18th	19thR
1919-20	Division 1	7 February	Lost	0	1	14 February	Lost	0	3	22ndR	19th
1925-26	Division 2	12 September	Won	5	1	23 January	Won	3	0	1stP	12th
1934-35	Division 1	17 November	Won	2	1	30 March	Lost	1	2	3rd	11th
1935-36	Division 1	28 September	Won	1	0	1 February	Won	1	0	20th	7th
1936-37	Division 1	3 October	Lost	0	1	6 February	Drew	1	1	22ndR	14th
1949-50	Division 2	11 March	Lost	0	1	22 October	Won	1	0	2ndP	6th
1952-53	Division 1	27 September	Drew	1	1	14 February	Lost	0	1	18th	2nd
1953-54	Division 1	2 September	Won	4	2	26 August	Lost	0	6	19th	11th
1954-55	Division 1	19 March	Won	2	0	30 October	Lost	0	6	22ndR	14th
1956-57	Division 1	22 April	Won	3	1	19 April	Lost	0	1	14th	3rd
1957-58	Division 1	25 December	Drew	4	4	26 December	Lost	0	3	22ndR	2nd
1959-60	Division 1	12 December	Drew	2	2	19 March	Won	4	3	5th	9th
1960-61	Division 1	4 February	Won	5	1	17 September	Drew	2	2	2nd	22ndR
1971-72	Division 2	4 March	Won	1	0	13 November	Lost	0	1	14th	18th
1972-73	Division 2	3 March	Won	2	1	7 October	Drew	1	1	10th	19th
1973-74	Division 2	15 April	Won	1	0	12 April	Drew	0	0	19th	21stR
1975-76	Division 3	20 December	Drew	2	2	30 March	Lost	2	4	20th	8th
1976-77	Division 3	16 April	Won	1	0	29 March	Lost	1	4	8th	6th
1977-78	Division 3	18 April	Won	1	0	4 October	Lost	1	2	14th	3rdP
1980-81	Division 2	30 August	Won	3	0	14 April	Lost	1	2	10th	20thR
2000-01	Division 1	23 September	Lost	1	3	24 February	Lost	0	2	17th	4th
2001-02	Division 1	16 October	Lost	1	2	5 February	Lost	2	4	20th	8th
2002-03	Division 1	1 March	Lost	0	1	14 September	Drew	2	2	22ndR	12th

FA Cup

Season	League	Date (Home)	Result	Wed'day	Preston NE	Date (Away)	Result	Wed'day	Preston NE	Division Wed'day	Division Preston NE
1887-88	Q'ter final	30 January	Lost	1	3						
1904-05	Q'ter final	9 March	Won	3	0	4 March	Drew	1	1	Div 1	Div 1

| | | | | Home | | | Away | | Final Positions | |
Season	League	Date	Result	Wed'day Preston NE	Date	Result	Wed'day Preston NE		Wed'day	Preston NE
1946-47	Round 5	20 February	Lost	0 2					Div 2	Div 1
1953-54	Semi-Final	27 March		Maine Road		Lost	0 2		Div 1	Div 1
1956-57	Round 3	9 January	Drew*	2 2	5 January	Drew	0 0		Div 1	Div 1
		14 January		Goodison Park (2nd replay)		Lost	1 5			
1991-92	Round 3				4 January	Won	2 0		Div 1	Div 3

League Cup

1983-84	Round 3				8 November	Won	2 0		Div 2	Div 3

Summary	P	W	D	L	F	A
Wednesday's home league record:	40	24	7	9	67	40
Wednesday's away league record:	40	8	8	24	40	82
Wednesday's cup record:	10	3	3	4	12	15
TOTAL:	**90**	**35**	**18**	**37**	**119**	**137**

FACT FILE

- From 1952 to 1980, Wednesday were unbeaten in 15 home games against Preston.
- Wednesday have not won in their last 11 league visits to Deepdale, although they have won two cup matches there in that time.
- Wednesday's last-ever Christmas Day fixture was against Preston in 1957. The 4-4 draw meant Wednesday's first four matches in December 1957 produced 31 goals.
- Between 1953 and 1957, Wednesday failed to score in six games at Deepdale, conceding 17 along the way.

Martin Hodge had two loan spells at Deepdale from Everton before moving to Hillsborough. He was a model of consistency and was on stand-by for England's World Cup squad for Mexico '86.

Wednesday's top scorers vs Preston

Andrew Wilson 9
Harry Chapman 6
Keith Ellis, Jimmy Trotter 5
Albert Quixall, Fred Spiksley 4

Wednesday hat-tricks vs Preston

12 Sep 1925 Jimmy Trotter (4)

Played for both clubs

Harry Millar	Preston 1893-94	Wednesday 1899-1901
Jimmy Melia	Wednesday 1896-98	Preston 1901-02
Walter Holbern	Wednesday 1906-11	Preston 1913-15
David McLean	Preston 1909-11	Wednesday 1910-20
Ted Harper	Wednesday 1927-29	Preston 1931-34
George Stephenson	Wednesday 1930-33	Preston 1933-34
George Bargh	Preston 1928-35	Wednesday 1935-36
Jackie Palethorpe	Preston 1933-35	Wednesday 1934-36
Eddie Quigley	Wednesday 1947-50	Preston 1949-52
Tony Coleman	Preston 1964-65	Wednesday 1969-70
Eric Potts	Wednesday 1970-77	Preston 1978-81
Jimmy Mullen	Wednesday 1970-80	Preston 1981-82
Danny Cameron	Wednesday 1973-76	Preston 1975-81
Ken Knighton	Preston 1967-69	Wednesday 1973-76
John Lowey	Wednesday 1978-80	Preston 1987-88
Trevor Matthewson	Wednesday 1980-83	Preston 1993-94
Martin Hodge	Preston 1981-83	Wednesday 1983-88
Greg Fee	Wednesday 1987-90	Preston 1990-91
David Reeves	Wednesday 1988-89	Preston 1996-98
Dean Barrick	Wednesday 1988-90	Preston 1995-98
Nigel Jemson	Preston 1985-89	Wednesday 1991-94
Lee Briscoe	Wednesday 1993-2000	Preston 2003-04
Richard Cresswell	Wednesday 1998-2001	Preston 2000-04
Kevin Gallacher	Wednesday 2001-02	Preston 2001-02
Marlon Broomes	Wednesday 2001-02	Preston 2002-04
Brian Barry-Murphy	Preston 1999-2003	Wednesday 2002-04
David Lucas	Preston 1995-2004	Wednesday 2003-04

Peter Springett

v. Queen's Park Rangers

				Home				**Away**		*Final Positions*	
Season	*League*	*Date*	*Result*	Wed'day	QPR	*Date*	*Result*	Wed'day	QPR	Wed'day	QPR
1948-49	Division 2	27 November	Won	2	0	23 April	Won	3	1	8th	13th
1949-50	Division 2	15 October	Won	1	0	4 March	Drew	0	0	2ndP	20th
1951-52	Division 2	15 March	Won	2	1	27 October	Drew	2	2	1stP	22ndR
1968-69	Division 1	14 December	Won	4	0	12 October	Lost	2	3	15th	22ndR
1970-71	Division 2	12 September	Won	1	0	6 April	Lost	0	1	15th	11th
1971-72	Division 2	16 October	Drew	0	0	14 August	Lost	0	3	14th	4th
1972-73	Division 2	30 December	Won	3	1	19 August	Lost	2	4	10th	2ndP
1980-81	Division 2	20 September	Won	1	0	28 February	Won	2	1	10th	8th
1981-82	Division 2	14 November	Lost	1	3	29 March	Lost	0	2	4th	5th
1982-83	Division 2	19 April	Lost	0	1	18 September	Won	2	0	6th	1stP
1984-85	Division 1	23 April	Won	3	1	10 November	Drew	0	0	8th	19th
1985-86	Division 1	8 April	Drew	0	0	2 November	Drew	1	1	5th	13th
1986-87	Division 1	2 May	Won	7	1	29 November	Drew	2	2	13th	16th
1987-88	Division 1	28 November	Won	3	1	23 April	Drew	1	1	11th	5th
1988-89	Division 1	25 March	Lost	0	2	17 September	Lost	0	2	15th	9th
1989-90	Division 1	16 December	Won	2	0	21 April	Lost	0	1	18thR	11th
1991-92	Division 1	31 August	Won	4	1	28 December	Drew	1	1	3rd	11th
1992-93	Premiership	19 December	Won	1	0	11 May	Lost	1	3	7th	5th
1993-94	Premiership	9 April	Won	3	1	1 January	Won	2	1	7th	9th
1994-95	Premiership	17 December	Lost	0	2	24 August	Lost	2	3	13th	8th
1995-96	Premiership	17 February	Lost	1	3	9 September	Won	3	0	15th	19thR
2000-01	Division 1	2 December	Won	5	2	25 October	Won	2	1	17th	23rdR
2003-04	Division 2	8 May	Lost	1	3	29 November	Lost	0	3	16th	2ndP

FA Cup | | | | | | | | | | *Division* | |

										Division	
1966-67	Round 3	28 January	Won	3	0					Div 1	Div 3

League Cup

										Division	
1973-74	Round 3					6 November	Lost	2	8	Div 2	Div 1
1992-93	Round 4	2 December	Won	4	0					Prem	Prem
1993-94	Round 4					1 December	Won	2	1	Prem	Prem

Summary	P	W	D	L	F	A
Wednesday's home league record:	23	15	2	6	45	23
Wednesday's away league record:	23	6	7	10	28	36
Wednesday's cup record:	4	3	0	1	11	9
TOTAL:	50	24	9	17	84	68

FACT FILE

- Wednesday won eight and drew one of their first nine home games in the series.
- Wednesday failed to win in eight games at Loftus Road from 1984 to 1993.

Wednesday's top scorers vs QPR

Mark Bright 8
David Hirst 5
Clarrie Jordan, Carlton Palmer 4

Wednesday hat-tricks vs QPR

28 Jan 1967 John Ritchie (cup)
31 Aug 1991 Carlton Palmer
2 Dec 2000 Gerald Sibon

Played for both clubs

Jimmy Lofthouse	Wednesday 1920-23	QPR 1926-28
Norman Smith	Wednesday 1927-28	QPR 1930-32
Colin Whitaker	Wednesday 1951-52	QPR 1960-61
Peter Baker	Wednesday 1957-58	QPR 1960-63
Mike Pinner	Wednesday 1957-59	QPR 1959-60
Ron Springett	QPR 1955-58/67-69	Wednesday 1957-67
Vic Mobley	Wednesday 1963-70	QPR 1969-71
Peter Springett	QPR 1962-67	Wednesday 1967-75
Andy McCulloch	QPR 1970-73	Wednesday 1979-83
Gary Bannister	Wednesday 1981-84	QPR 1984-88
Simon Stainrod	QPR 1980-85	Wednesday 1984-86
Garry Thompson	Wednesday 1985-86	QPR 1991-93
Trevor Francis	QPR 1987-90	Wednesday 1989-94
Chris Woods	QPR 1979-81	Wednesday 1991-96
Andy Sinton	QPR 1988-93	Wednesday 1993-96
Marlon Broomes	QPR 2000-01	Wednesday 2001-02
Danny Maddix	QPR 1987-2001	Wednesday 2001-03
Leon Knight	QPR 2000-01	Wednesday 2002-03

Andy McCulloch found the net regularly for the Owls but had begun his career at QPR in the early 1970s.

Ron Springett

v. Reading

			Home				**Away**		*Final Positions*	
Season	League	Date	Result	Wed'day	Reading	Date	Result	Wed'day	Reading	Wed'day Reading
1976-77	Division 3	26 March	Won	2	1	16 October	Won	1	0	8th 21stR
1979-80	Division 3	1 April	Drew	1	1	21 December	Won	2	0	3rdP 7th
2002-03	Division 1	11 January	Won	3	2	13 August	Lost	1	2	22ndR 4th

FA Cup *Division*

				Date	Result	Wed'day	Reading	Division
1928-29	Round 4			26 January	Lost	0	1	Div 1 Div 2
1965-66	Round 3			22 January	Won	3	2	Div 1 Div 3

Summary

	P	W	D	L	F	A
Wednesday's home league record:	3	2	1	0	6	4
Wednesday's away league record:	3	2	0	1	4	2
Wednesday's cup record:	2	1	0	1	3	3
TOTAL:	**8**	**5**	**1**	**2**	**13**	**9**

FACT FILE

● **Wednesday won four games in a row from 1966 to 1979.**

Wednesday's top scorers vs Reading
Terry Curran, John Fantham, Gerald Sibon 2

Played for both clubs

Bert Eggo	Wednesday 1919-21	Reading 1921-29
Tom Hodgkiss	Wednesday 1927-28	Reading 1930-32
Dick Mellors	Wednesday 1926-31	Reading 1931-34
George Johnson	Wednesday 1930-31	Reading 1932-37
Jackie Palethorpe	Reading 1930-33	Wednesday 1934-36
Jack Whitham	Wednesday 1966-70	Reading 1975-76
Andy Proudlove	Reading 1971-72	Wednesday 1975-76
Ian Porterfield	Reading 1976-77	Wednesday 1977-80
Chris Woods	Wednesday 1991-96	Reading 1995-96
Mark McKeever	Reading 1998-99	Wednesday 1998-2000
Lloyd Owusu	Wednesday 2002-04	Reading 2003-04
Eric Nixon	Reading 1995-96	Wednesday 2003-04
Mark Robins	Reading 1997-98	Wednesday 2003-04

v. Rochdale

		Home					
							Division

League Cup	Date	Result	Wed'day	R'hdale			Wed'day	R'hdale
2002-03 Round 1	11 September	Won	**1**	**0**			Div 1	Div 3

Summary	P	W	D	L	F	A
Wednesday's cup record:	1	1	0	0	1	0
TOTAL:	**1**	**1**	**0**	**0**	**1**	**0**

FACT FILE

- Gerald Sibon scored the goal.

Played for both clubs

David Parkes	Wednesday 1913-20	Rochdale 1922-28
Arthur Hinchcliffe	Wednesday 1919-20	Rochdale 1921-23
Harry Anstiss	Rochdale 1924-26	Wednesday 1926-27
Dickie Rhodes	Wednesday 1935-38	Rochdale 1939-40
Jimmy Dailey	Wednesday 1946-49	Rochdale 1957-58
Albert Morton	Wednesday 1947-51	Rochdale 1953-57
Colin Whitaker	Wednesday 1951-52	Rochdale 1961-63
Donald Watson	Wednesday 1954-57	Rochdale 1962-64
Jack Martin	Wednesday 1954-61	Rochdale 1962-64
Malcolm Darling	Rochdale 1971-74	Wednesday 1977-78
David Grant	Wednesday 1977-82	Rochdale 1984-87
Gary Shelton	Wednesday 1977-82	Rochdale 1984-87
Martin Hodge	Wednesday 1983-88	Rochdale 1993-94
John Ryan	Wednesday 1984-85	Rochdale 1991-94
Simon Coleman	Wednesday 1993-95	Rochdale 2000-02
Grant Holt	Wednesday 2002-04	Rochdale 2003-04
Mickael Antoine-Curier	Rochdale 2003-04	Wednesday 2003-04

v. Rotherham United

Season	League		Home Date	Result	Wed'day	Roth'ham	Away Date	Result	Wed'day	Roth'ham	Final Positions Wed'day	Roth'ham
1920-21	Division 2	28 March	Won	2	0		1 November	Lost	0	2	10th	19th
1921-22	Division 2	8 October	Won	1	0		15 October	Drew	0	0	10th	16th
1922-23	Division 2	2 September	Won	1	0		26 August	Won	2	1	8th	21stR
1951-52	Division 2	22 September	Lost	3	5		26 January	Drew	3	3	1stP	9th
1955-56	Division 2	10 December	Lost	0	2		10 March	Won	3	2	1stP	19th
1958-59	Division 2	1 November	Won	5	0		21 March	Lost	0	1	1stP	20th
1975-76	Division 3	29 November	Drew	0	0		20 March	Lost	0	1	20th	16th
1976-77	Division 3	2 November	Lost	1	3		12 April	Won	1	0	8th	4th
1977-78	Division 3	27 December	Won	1	0		25 March	Won	2	1	14th	20th
1978-79	Division 3	7 May	Won	2	1		7 October	Won	1	0	14th	17th
1979-80	Division 3	23 February	Won	5	0		13 October	Won	2	1	3rdP	13th
1981-82	Division 2	8 September	Won	2	0		4 May	Drew	2	2	4th	7th
1982-83	Division 2	28 December	Lost	0	1		2 April	Won	3	0	6th	20thR
2001-02	Division 1	23 February	Lost	1	2		25 September	Drew	1	1	20th	21st
2002-03	Division 1	24 August	Lost	1	2		1 January	Won	2	0	22ndR	15th

FA Cup

											Division	
1933-34	Round 3						13 January	Won	3	0	Div 1	Div 3N

League Cup

											Division	
1966-67	Round 2	14 September	Lost	0	1						Div 1	Div 2
1971-72	Round 1						17 August	Won	2	0	Div 2	Div 3

Summary

	P	W	D	L	F	A
Wednesday's home league record:	15	8	1	6	25	16
Wednesday's away league record:	15	8	4	3	22	15
Wednesday's cup record:	3	2	0	1	5	1
TOTAL:	**33**	**18**	**5**	**10**	**52**	**32**

Wednesday's top scorers vs Rotherham
Gary Bannister, Andy McCulloch 4
Jackie Sewell, Rodger Wylde 3

Wednesday hat-tricks vs Rotherham
23 Feb 1980 Andy McCulloch

FACT FILE

- Wednesday, in common with some other major clubs, declined to enter the League Cup for the first few years of competition, starting in 1960-61. When they did finally enter six years later, they lost at home to second division Rotherham in their first match.
- Wednesday have lost their last three home matches in the series, but are unbeaten in their last eight away from home.

Played for both clubs

Ted Glennon	Wednesday 1910-15	Rotherham 1919-21
Jimmy Lofthouse	Wednesday 1920-23	Rotherham 1922-24
Tom Brelsford	Wednesday 1919-24	Rotherham 1925-26
Andy Smailes	Wednesday 1922-24	Rotherham 1929-32
Vic Wright	Rotherham 1929-31/32-34	Wednesday 1931-32
George Bratley	Rotherham 1929-34	Wednesday 1932-33
Mark Hooper	Wednesday 1926-38	Rotherham 1939-40
Joe Cockroft	Rotherham 1930-33	Wednesday 1946-49
Charlie Tomlinson	Wednesday 1946-51	Rotherham 1950-52
Walter Rickett	Wednesday 1949-53	Rotherham 1952-53
Brian Slater	Wednesday 1952-53	Rotherham 1956-57
Jack Shaw	Rotherham 1946-53	Wednesday 1953-58
Albert Broadbent	Wednesday 1955-58	Rotherham 1957-59
Peter Johnson	Rotherham 1953-58	Wednesday 1957-65
John Fantham	Wednesday 1957-70	Rotherham 1969-71
Billy Griffin	Wednesday 1958-63	Rotherham 1968-70
John Quinn	Wednesday 1959-68	Rotherham 1967-72
Robin Hardy	Wednesday 1961-64	Rotherham 1964-66
David Layne	Rotherham 1957-59	Wednesday 1962-64
Peter Eustace	Wednesday 1962-70/72-75	Rotherham 1971-72
Andy Burgin	Wednesday 1964-65	Rotherham 1967-68
Harold Wilcockson	Rotherham 1964-68	Wednesday 1969-71
Steve Downes	Rotherham 1967-70	Wednesday 1969-72
Jimmy Mullen	Wednesday 1970-80	Rotherham 1980-82
Rodger Wylde	Wednesday 1972-80	Rotherham 1987-88
Phil Henson	Wednesday 1974-77	Rotherham 1979-84
Barry Watling	Rotherham 1975-76	Wednesday 1975-76
Dave Cusack	Wednesday 1975-78	Rotherham 1987-88
Tommy Tynan	Wednesday 1976-79	Rotherham 1985-87
Gordon Owen	Wednesday 1977-83	Rotherham 1979-80
Mike Pickering	Wednesday 1978-83	Rotherham 1983-86
John Pearson	Wednesday 1980-85	Rotherham 1990-91
Tony Simmons	Wednesday 1981-83	Rotherham 1983-87
Pat Heard	Wednesday 1982-85	Rotherham 1988-90
Tony Cunningham	Wednesday 1983-84	Rotherham 1991-93
Imre Varadi	Wednesday 1983-85/88-90	Rotherham 1992-95
Glynn Snodin	Wednesday 1985-87	Rotherham 1991-92
Dave Tomlinson	Wednesday 1986-87	Rotherham 1987-88
Des Hazel	Wednesday 1987-88	Rotherham 1988-95
Wayne Jacobs	Wednesday 1987-88	Rotherham 1993-94
Dean Barrick	Wednesday 1988-90	Rotherham 1990-93
Nigel Jemson	Wednesday 1991-94	Rotherham 1995-96
Julian Watts	Rotherham 1990-92	Wednesday 1992-96
Adem Poric	Wednesday 1993-98	Rotherham 1997-98
Matt Clarke	Rotherham 1992-96	Wednesday 1996-98
Robbie Stockdale	Wednesday 2000-01	Rotherham 2003-04
Carl Robinson	Wednesday 2002-03	Rotherham 2003-04
Mark Robins	Rotherham 2000-04	Wednesday 2003-04

v. Rushden & Diamonds

			Home			Away		Final Positions	
Season	League	Date	Result	Wed'day Rushden	Date	Result	Wed'day Rushden	Wed'day	Rushden
2003-04	Division 2	18 October	Drew	0 0	21 February	Won	2 1	16th	22ndR

Summary	P	W	D	L	F	A
Wednesday's home league record:	1	0	1	0	0	0
Wednesday's away league record:	1	1	0	0	2	1
TOTAL:	2	1	1	0	2	1

Wednesday's top scorers vs Rushden & Diamonds
Guylain Ndumbu-Nsungu 2

Played for both clubs
Paul Evans   Wednesday 2002-03   Rushden & Diamonds 2003-04

v. Salisbury City

		Home				*Division*
FA Cup	*Date*	*Result*	Wed'day Salisbury			Wed'day Salisbury
2003-04 Round 1	9 November	Won	**4** **0**			Div 2 Non L

Summary	P	W	D	L	F	A
Wednesday's cup record:	1	1	0	0	4	0
TOTAL:	1	1	0	0	4	0

Wednesday's top scorers vs Salisbury

Adam Proudlock 3

Wednesday hat-tricks vs Salisbury

9 Nov 2003 Adam Proudlock (cup)

v. Scunthorpe United

			Home			Away		Final Positions	
Season	League	Date	Result	Wed'day Scunth'pe	Date	Result	Wed'day Scunth'pe	Wed'day	Scunth'pe
1958-59	Division 2	14 February	Won	2 0	27 September	Won	4 1	1stP	18th

FA Cup								Division	
1969-70	Round 4	24 January	Lost	1 2				Div 1	Div 4
1978-79	Round 1	28 November	Won	1 0	25 November	Drew	1 1	Div 3	Div 4
2003-04	Round 2	17 December	Drew*	0 0	6 December	Drew	2 2	Div 2	Div 3

(lost 1-3 pens)

League Cup									
1974-75	Round 1				20 August	Lost	0 1	Div 2	Div 4

Summary	P	W	D	L	F	A	
Wednesday's home league record:	1	1	0	0	2	0	
Wednesday's away league record:	1	1	0	0	4	1	
Wednesday's cup record:	6	1	3	2	5	6	
TOTAL:	**8**	**3**	**3**	**2**	**11**	**7**	(+one penalty shoot-out defeat)

Wednesday's top scorers vs Scunthorpe
Roy Shiner 3

Ian Nimmo, Derek Wilkinson 2

Wednesday hat-tricks vs Scunthorpe
27 Sep 1958 Roy Shiner

Played for both clubs
Jack Marriott	Wednesday 1946-55	Scunthorpe 1957-64
Doug Fletcher	Wednesday 1948-50	Scunthorpe 1956-58
Keith Ellis	Wednesday 1954-64	Scunthorpe 1963-64
Graham Pugh	Wednesday 1965-72	Scunthorpe 1979-81
Archie Irvine	Wednesday 1968-70	Scunthorpe 1975-76
Allan Thompson	Wednesday 1970-76	Scunthorpe 1981-82
Ronnie Ferguson	Wednesday 1974-75	Scunthorpe 1975-76
Derek Bell	Wednesday 1975-76	Scunthorpe 1983-85
Dennis Leman	Wednesday 1976-82	Scunthorpe 1982-84
Kevin Taylor	Wednesday 1978-84	Scunthorpe 1987-91
Imre Varadi	Wednesday 1983-85/88-90	Scunthorpe 1995-96
Ian Knight	Wednesday 1985-89	Scunthorpe 1989-90
Carl Bradshaw	Wednesday 1986-89	Scunthorpe 2001-02
David Reeves	Scunthorpe 1986-88	Wednesday 1988-89
Craig Shakespeare	Wednesday 1989-90	Scunthorpe 1997-98
Danny Wilson	Scunthorpe 1983-84	Wednesday 1990-93
Ryan Jones	Wednesday 1992-95	Scunthorpe 1995-96
Richie Humphreys	Wednesday 1995-2001	Scunthorpe 1999-2000
David Lucas	Scunthorpe 1996-97	Wednesday 2003-04

v. Sheffield Heeley

Home

FA Cup		Date	Result	Wed'day	Sheff H
1881-82	Round 4	21 January	Won	**3**	**1**

Summary	P	W	D	L	F	A
Wednesday's cup record:	1	1	0	0	3	1
TOTAL:	**1**	**1**	**0**	**0**	**3**	**1**

FACT FILE

- Sheffield Heeley is one of the oldest football clubs in the world, having been formed in 1860.

Graham Pugh appeared for Scunthorpe some years after his Hillsborough career.

v. Sheffield Providence

FA Cup		Date					Away Result	Wed'day	Sheff P
1881-82	Round 1	5 November	Quibell's Field				Won	2	0

Summary	P	W	D	L	F	A
Wednesday's cup record:	1	1	0	0	2	0
TOTAL:	**1**	**1**	**0**	**0**	**2**	**0**

FACT FILE

● Sheffield Providence entered the FA Cup three times (1879-82) but never won a match.

v. Sheffield United

		Home					Away			Final Positions	
Season	League	Date	Result	Wed'day	Sheff Utd	Date	Result	Wed'day	Sheff Utd	Wed'day	Sheff Utd
1893-94	Division 1	13 November	Lost	1	2	16 October	Drew	1	1	12th	10th
1894-95	Division 1	27 October	Lost	2	3	12 January	Lost	0	1	8th	6th
1895-96	Division 1	7 September	Won	1	0	26 December	Drew	1	1	7th	12th
1896-97	Division 1	2 March	Drew	1	1	26 December	Lost	0	2	6th	2nd
1897-98	Division 1	16 October	Lost	0	1	27 December	Drew	1	1	5th	1st
1898-99	Division 1	3 October	Drew	1	1	26 December	Lost	1	2	18thR	16th
1900-01	Division 1	29 April	Won	1	0	15 December	Lost	0	1	8th	14th
1901-02	Division 1	2 November	Won	1	0	1 March	Lost	0	3	9th	10th
1902-03	Division 1	11 October	Lost	0	1	1 September	Won	3	2	1st	4th
1903-04	Division 1	9 April	Won	3	0	12 December	Drew	1	1	1st	7th
1904-05	Division 1	10 December	Lost	1	3	8 April	Lost	2	4	9th	6th
1905-06	Division 1	18 April	Won	1	0	21 October	Won	2	0	3rd	13th
1906-07	Division 1	3 November	Drew	2	2	4 April	Lost	1	2	13th	4th
1907-08	Division 1	7 March	Won	2	0	9 November	Won	3	1	5th	17th
1908-09	Division 1	25 December	Won	1	0	26 December	Lost	1	2	5th	12th
1909-10	Division 1	19 March	Lost	1	3	6 November	Drew	3	3	11th	6th
1910-11	Division 1	22 October	Won	2	0	25 February	Won	1	0	6th	9th
1911-12	Division 1	9 March	Drew	1	1	4 November	Drew	1	1	5th	14th
1912-13	Division 1	26 October	Won	1	0	1 March	Won	2	0	3rd	15th
1913-14	Division 1	28 February	Won	2	1	25 October	Won	1	0	18th	10th
1914-15	Division 1	2 January	Drew	1	1	5 September	Won	1	0	7th	6th
1919-20	Division 1	27 September	Won	2	1	4 October	Lost	0	3	22ndR	14th
1926-27	Division 1	28 August	Lost	2	3	15 January	Lost	0	2	16th	8th
1927-28	Division 1	4 February	Drew	3	3	24 September	Drew	1	1	14th	13th
1928-29	Division 1	22 September	Won	5	2	2 February	Drew	1	1	1st	11th
1929-30	Division 1	1 February	Drew	1	1	28 September	Drew	2	2	1st	20th
1930-31	Division 1	3 January	Lost	1	3	6 September	Drew	1	1	3rd	15th
1931-32	Division 1	21 November	Won	2	1	2 April	Drew	1	1	3rd	7th
1932-33	Division 1	24 September	Drew	3	3	4 February	Won	3	2	3rd	10th
1933-34	Division 1	21 October	Lost	0	1	3 March	Lost	1	5	11th	22ndR
1937-38	Division 2	16 October	Lost	0	1	26 February	Lost	1	2	17th	3rd
1938-39	Division 2	4 March	Won	1	0	29 October	Drew	0	0	3rd	2ndP
1949-50	Division 2	17 September	Won	2	1	21 January	Lost	0	2	2ndP	3rd
1951-52	Division 2	5 January	Lost	1	3	8 September	Lost	3	7	1stP	11th
1953-54	Division 1	23 January	Won	3	2	12 September	Lost	0	2	19th	20th
1954-55	Division 1	5 February	Lost	1	2	18 September	Lost	0	1	22ndR	13th
1958-59	Division 2	4 October	Won	2	0	21 February	Lost	0	1	1stP	3rd
1961-62	Division 1	3 February	Lost	1	2	16 September	Lost	0	1	6th	5th
1962-63	Division 1	15 May	Won	3	1	6 October	Drew	2	2	6th	10th
1963-64	Division 1	18 January	Won	3	0	14 September	Drew	1	1	6th	12th
1964-65	Division 1	5 September	Lost	0	2	2 January	Won	3	2	8th	19th
1965-66	Division 1	12 March	Drew	2	2	18 September	Lost	0	1	17th	9th
1966-67	Division 1	24 September	Drew	2	2	4 February	Lost	0	1	11th	10th
1967-68	Division 1	6 January	Drew	1	1	1 September	Won	1	0	19th	21stR

				Home				Away		Final Positions	
Season	League	Date	Result	Wed'day	Sheff Utd	Date	Result	Wed'day	Sheff Utd	Wed'day	Sheff Utd
1970-71	Division 2	12 April	Drew	0	0	3 October	Lost	2	3	15th	2ndP
1979-80	Division 3	26 December	Won	4	0	5 April	Drew	1	1	3rdP	12th
1991-92	Division 1	11 March	Lost	1	3	17 November	Lost	0	2	3rd	9th
1992-93	Premiership	21 April	Drew	1	1	8 November	Drew	1	1	7th	14th
1993-94	Premiership	22 January	Won	3	1	23 October	Drew	1	1	7th	20thR
2000-01	Division 1	1 April	Lost	1	2	16 December	Drew	1	1	17th	10th
2001-02	Division 1	7 October	Drew	0	0	29 January	Drew	0	0	20th	13th
2002-03	Division 1	1 September	Won	2	0	17 January	Lost	1	3	22ndR	3rd

FA Cup

										Division	
1899-00	Round 2	19 February	Lost	0	2	17 February	Drew	1	1	Div 2	Div 1
1924-25	Round 2					31 January	Lost	2	3	Div 2	Div 1
1927-28	Round 5	18 February	Drew	1	1	22 February	Lost	1	4	Div 1	Div 1
1953-54	Round 3	9 January	Drew	1	1	13 January	Won	3	1	Div 1	Div 1
1959-60	Q'ter final					12 March	Won	2	0	Div 1	Div 2
1992-93	Semi-Final	3 April		Wembley			Won*	2	1	Prem	Prem

League Cup

										Division	
1980-81	Round 1	9 August	Won	2	0	12 August	Drew	1	1	Div 2	Div 3
2000-01	Round 3	1 November	Won*	2	1					Div 1	Div 1

Summary

	P	W	D	L	F	A
Wednesday's home league record:	52	22	14	16	79	64
Wednesday's away league record:	52	10	19	23	54	81
Wednesday's cup record:	12	5	4	3	18	16
TOTAL:	**116**	**37**	**37**	**42**	**151**	**161**

FA Cup semi-final drama as Mark Bright heads home an extra-time John Harkes corner past Kelly to clinch a final place in the Sheffield Wembley derby on 3 April 1993.

FACT FILE

- Fred Spiksley was the Owls' first league goalscorer against their big city rivals.
- United currently lead the series of league matches 39-32. United have led the series since September 1951. Neither side has ever led the series by more than seven.
- The sides have won three ties each in the FA Cup, but Wednesday have won both League Cup ties.
- Wednesday have not won at Bramall Lane since 1967.
- The most famous meeting of the sides took place at Wembley in 1993. Chris Waddle gave Wednesday the perfect start with a goal from a free kick, and although United took the game to extra time, Mark Bright fired home the winner and Wednesday were on their way to Wembley again. In total they played four matches at Wembley in April and May 1993. The win over United remains Wednesday's most recent FA Cup win over Premiership opposition.
- United's longest run of consecutive wins is four, last achieved from 1950 to 1953. Wednesday won five in a row from 1912 to 1914.
- Wednesday have achieved five league doubles, most recently in 1913-14.
- United have achieved nine league doubles, most recently in 1991-92.
- Six of the last 10 league meetings have been drawn, and both cup ties from this period went to extra-time as well.

David Hirst chips United keeper Alan Kelly for an 84th-minute equaliser on 8 November 1992 at Bramall Lane.

Wednesday's top scorers vs Sheffield United
Andrew Wilson 11
Harry Chapman 7
Jack Ball, Mark Hooper, David Layne, Jimmy Trotter 5
John Fantham, Ted Glennon, Fred Spiksley,
Jimmy Stewart, Derek Wilkinson 4

Played for both clubs
Billy Mellor	Sheffield U 1892-93	Wednesday 1893-94
Ollie Tummon	Wednesday 1905-10	Sheffield U 1919-20
Charles Taylor	Wednesday 1919-20	Sheffield U 1923-24
Bernard Oxley	Sheffield U 1928-34	Wednesday 1933-35
Joe Cockroft	Wednesday 1946-49	Sheffield U 1948-49
Walter Rickett	Sheffield U 1946-48	Wednesday 1949-53
David Ford	Wednesday 1965-70	Sheffield U 1970-73
Alan Warboys	Wednesday 1968-71	Sheffield U 1972-73
Bernard Shaw	Sheffield U 1962-69	Wednesday 1973-76
Neil Ramsbottom	Wednesday 1975-76	Sheffield U 1979-80
Terry Curran	Wednesday 1978-82	Sheffield U 1982-83
Jeff King	Wednesday 1979-82	Sheffield U 1981-83
Imre Varadi	Sheffield U 1978-79	Wednesday 1983-85/88-90
Simon Stainrod	Sheffield U 1975-79	Wednesday 1984-86
Brian Marwood	Wednesday 1984-88	Sheffield U 1990-92
Carl Bradshaw	Wednesday 1986-89	Sheffield U 1989-94
Wilf Rostron	Wednesday 1988-89	Sheffield U 1989-91
Franz Carr	Wednesday 1989-90	Sheffield U 1992-94
Earl Barrett	Sheffield U 1997-98	Wednesday 1997-99
Owen Morrison	Wednesday 1998-2003	Sheffield U 2002-03
Dean Windass	Wednesday 2001-02	Sheffield U 2002-03
Carl Robinson	Wednesday 2002-03	Sheffield U 2003-04

Action in the Owls' goalmouth as Kevin Pressman gathers the ball in the Bramall Lane Premiership derby on 23 October 1993.

v. Shrewsbury Town

Season	League	Date	Result	Wed'day	Shrewsb'y	Date	Result	Wed'day	Shrewsb'y	Wed'day	Shrewsb'y
			Home					**Away**		*Final Positions*	
1975-76	Division 3	25 October	Drew	**1**	**1**	13 April	Drew	**0**	**0**	20th	9th
1976-77	Division 3	23 October	Lost	**0**	**1**	2 April	Drew	**1**	**1**	8th	10th
1977-78	Division 3	10 September	Lost	**0**	**1**	28 February	Drew	**0**	**0**	14th	11th
1978-79	Division 3	3 March	Drew	**0**	**0**	21 October	Drew	**2**	**2**	14th	1stP
1980-81	Division 2	26 December	Drew	**1**	**1**	21 April	Lost	**0**	**2**	10th	14th
1981-82	Division 2	2 March	Drew	**0**	**0**	10 April	Won	**1**	**0**	4th	18th
1982-83	Division 2	26 March	Drew	**0**	**0**	13 November	Lost	**0**	**1**	6th	9th
1983-84	Division 2	3 December	Drew	**1**	**1**	5 May	Lost	**1**	**2**	2ndP	8th

FA Cup — *Division*

1962-63	Round 3	3 March	Won*	**2**	**1**	21 February	Drew	**1**	**1**	Div 1	Div 3

League Cup

1987-88	Round 2	6 October	Won	**2**	**1**	22 September	Drew	**1**	**1**	Div 1	Div 2

Summary	P	W	D	L	F	A
Wednesday's home league record:	8	0	6	2	3	5
Wednesday's away league record:	8	1	4	3	5	8
Wednesday's cup record:	4	2	2	0	6	4
TOTAL:	**20**	**3**	**12**	**5**	**14**	**17**

FACT FILE

- Most of the league matches between the sides came during one of the blackest periods in Wednesday's illustrious history. Nonetheless, Wednesday's record of one win in 16 is extraordinarily bad.
- In every season the sides have met, there has been at least one draw.

Wednesday's top scorers vs Shrewsbury
Gary Bannister, Colin West, Rodger Wylde 2

Played for both clubs

Colin Whitaker	Wednesday 1951-52	Shrewsbury 1956-61
Brian Hornsby	Shrewsbury 1976-78	Wednesday 1977-82
Gary Megson	Wednesday 1981-84/85-89	Shrewsbury 1995-96
Nigel Pearson	Shrewsbury 1982-88	Wednesday 1987-94
Dave Bennett	Wednesday 1988-90	Shrewsbury 1991-92
Mark Taylor	Wednesday 1989-90	Shrewsbury 1990-98
Steve MacKenzie	Wednesday 1990-92	Shrewsbury 1991-94
Nigel Jemson	Wednesday 1991-94	Shrewsbury 2000-03
Simon Stewart	Wednesday 1992-93	Shrewsbury 1995-96
Julian Watts	Shrewsbury 1992-93	Wednesday 1992-96
O'Neill Donaldson	Shrewsbury 1991-94	Wednesday 1994-98
Carl Robinson	Shrewsbury 1995-96	Wednesday 2002-03

v. Southampton

		Home				Away				Final Positions	
Season	League	Date	Result	Wed'day	So'ton	Date	Result	Wed'day	So'ton	Wed'day	So'ton
1922-23	Division 2	1 January	Drew	0	0	2 April	Drew	1	1	8th	11th
1923-24	Division 2	8 September	Drew	1	1	15 September	Lost	0	3	8th	5th
1924-25	Division 2	6 September	Won	1	0	3 January	Lost	0	1	14th	7th
1925-26	Division 2	12 December	Won	2	1	24 April	Won	2	1	1stP	14th
1937-38	Division 2	19 February	Drew	0	0	9 October	Lost	2	5	17th	15th
1938-39	Division 2	18 February	Won	2	0	15 October	Lost	3	4	3rd	18th
1946-47	Division 2	14 December	Won	3	0	19 April	Lost	1	3	20th	14th
1947-48	Division 2	1 September	Lost	1	2	27 August	Lost	1	3	4th	3rd
1948-49	Division 2	25 September	Won	2	0	19 February	Lost	0	1	8th	3rd
1949-50	Division 2	12 November	Drew	2	2	15 April	Lost	0	1	2ndP	4th
1951-52	Division 2	1 September	Won	3	1	29 December	Won	4	1	1stP	13th
1966-67	Division 1	11 February	Won	4	1	1 October	Lost	2	4	11th	19th
1967-68	Division 1	4 November	Won	2	0	30 March	Lost	0	2	19th	16th
1968-69	Division 1	28 December	Drew	0	0	26 October	Drew	1	1	15th	7th
1969-70	Division 1	11 October	Drew	1	1	7 February	Lost	0	4	22ndR	19th
1974-75	Division 2	31 March	Lost	0	1	28 December	Won	1	0	22ndR	13th
1984-85	Division 1	4 September	Won	2	1	29 December	Won	3	0	8th	5th
1985-86	Division 1	23 November	Won	2	1	26 April	Won	3	2	5th	14th
1986-87	Division 1	8 November	Won	3	1	22 April	Drew	1	1	13th	12th
1987-88	Division 1	6 February	Won	2	1	5 September	Drew	1	1	11th	12th
1988-89	Division 1	18 February	Drew	1	1	22 October	Won	2	1	15th	13th
1989-90	Division 1	7 April	Lost	0	1	30 December	Drew	2	2	18thR	7th
1991-92	Division 1	21 September	Won	2	0	18 April	Won	1	0	3rd	16th
1992-93	Premiership	12 April	Won	5	2	28 December	Won	2	1	7th	18th
1993-94	Premiership	18 September	Won	2	0	12 March	Drew	1	1	7th	18th
1994-95	Premiership	2 January	Drew	1	1	29 April	Drew	0	0	13th	10th
1995-96	Premiership	23 December	Drew	2	2	20 March	Won	1	0	15th	17th
1996-97	Premiership	2 November	Drew	1	1	22 February	Won	3	2	7th	16th
1997-98	Premiership	4 April	Won	1	0	29 November	Won	3	2	16th	12th
1998-99	Premiership	31 October	Drew	0	0	21 March	Lost	0	1	12th	17th
1999-00	Premiership	12 February	Lost	0	1	28 August	Lost	0	2	19thR	15th

FA Cup

										Division	
1895-96	Round 1					1 February	Won	3	2	Div 1	Non L
1906-07	Round 2	7 February	Won	3	1	2 February	Drew	1	1	Div 1	Non L
1948-49	Round 3	8 January	Won	2	1					Div 2	Div 2
1983-84	Q'ter final	11 March	Drew	0	0	20 March	Lost	1	5	Div 2	Div 1
2000-01	Round 4					27 January	Lost	1	3	Div 1	Prem

League Cup

1991-92	Round 3	30 October	Drew	1	1	20 November	Lost	0	1	Div 1	Div 1
1994-95	Round 3	26 October	Won	1	0					Prem	Prem

Summary	P	W	D	L	F	A
Wednesday's home league record:	31	16	11	4	48	23
Wednesday's away league record:	31	11	7	13	41	51
Wednesday's cup record:	10	4	3	3	13	15
TOTAL:	**72**	**31**	**21**	**20**	**102**	**89**

FACT FILE

- **Wednesday were unbeaten in 16 matches from 1991 to 1998. However, they have lost all four games since then.**
- **Wednesday lost only two of their first 24 home matches against the Saints.**
- **Between 1922 and 1968, Southampton won 10 out of 12 games at the Dell.**

Wednesday's top scorers vs Southampton
Lee Chapman, David Hirst 8
Chris Bart-Williams 5
Dennis Woodhead 4

Wednesday hat-tricks vs Southampton
15 Oct 1938 Charlie Napier
11 Feb 1967 John Fantham
12 Apr 1993 Chris Bart-Williams

Played for both clubs

Sam Taylor	Wednesday 1920-25	Southampton 1926-28
Charlie Petrie	Wednesday 1921-25	Southampton 1927-29
George Kirby	Wednesday 1959-60	Southampton 1962-64
Jim McCalliog	Wednesday 1965-69	Southampton 1974-77
Peter Rodrigues	Wednesday 1970-75	Southampton 1975-77
Terry Curran	Southampton 1978-79	Wednesday 1978-82
Mike Pickering	Southampton 1977-79	Wednesday 1978-83
David Hirst	Wednesday 1986-98	Southampton 1997-99
Carlton Palmer	Wednesday 1988-94/2000-02	Southampton 1997-99
Gordon Watson	Wednesday 1990-95	Southampton 1994-97
Chris Woods	Wednesday 1991-96	Southampton 1996-97
Dan Petrescu	Wednesday 1994-96	Southampton 2000-02
Jim Magilton	Southampton 1993-98	Wednesday 1997-99
Barry Horne	Southampton 1988-92	Wednesday 1999-2000
Stuart Ripley	Southampton 1998-2002	Wednesday 2000-01
Trond Egil Soltvedt	Southampton 1999-2001	Wednesday 2000-03
Garry Monk	Southampton 1998-2003	Wednesday 2002-03
Eric Nixon	Southampton 1986-87	Wednesday 2003-04

v. Southend United

		Home					Away			Final Positions	
Season	League	Date	Result	Wed'day	Southend	Date	Result	Wed'day	Southend	Wed'day	Southend
1975-76	Division 3	29 April	Won	2	1	16 August	Lost	1	2	20th	23rdR
1978-79	Division 3	9 September	Won	3	2	13 February	Lost	1	2	14th	13th
1979-80	Division 3	17 November	Won	2	0	29 March	Drew	1	1	3rdP	22ndR

FA Cup										Division	
1982-83	Round 3	11 January	Drew*	2	2	8 January	Drew	0	0	Div 2	Div 3
		24 January	Won	2	1	(2nd replay)					
1992-93	Round 5	13 February	Won	2	0					Prem	Div 1

Summary	P	W	D	L	F	A
Wednesday's home league record:	3	3	0	0	7	3
Wednesday's away league record:	3	0	1	2	3	5
Wednesday's cup record:	4	2	2	0	6	3
TOTAL:	**10**	**5**	**3**	**2**	**16**	**11**

FACT FILE

● None of the 10 meetings between the sides has ended in an away win.

Wednesday's top scorers vs Southend
Brian Hornsby, Ian Mellor, Mick Prendergast,
Kevin Taylor, Paul Warhurst 2

Played for both clubs
Arthur Price	Wednesday 1919-22	Southend 1922-23
Fred Lunn	Wednesday 1921-22	Southend 1923-24
Walter Lamb	Wednesday 1921-22	Southend 1925-26
Sid Binks	Wednesday 1922-25	Southend 1928-29
Billy Powell	Wednesday 1924-25	Southend 1930-31
Ernie Hatfield	Wednesday 1928-29	Southend 1931-33
Graham Birks	Wednesday 1962-63	Southend 1965-70
Kevin Johnson	Wednesday 1971-72	Southend 1972-74
Dave Cusack	Wednesday 1975-78	Southend 1978-83
Charles Williamson	Wednesday 1979-84	Southend 1984-85
Lee Chapman	Wednesday 1984-88	Southend 1994-95
Paul Williams	Wednesday 1990-93	Southend 1996-98
Simon Coleman	Wednesday 1993-95	Southend 1997-2000
Adem Poric	Wednesday 1993-98	Southend 1996-97
Steve Harkness	Southend 1994-95	Wednesday 2000-01
Danny Maddix	Southend 1986-87	Wednesday 2001-03
Brian Barry-Murphy	Southend 2001-02	Wednesday 2002-04

Season	League	Date	Result	Home Wed'day	South S	Date	Result	Away Wed'day	South S	Final Positions Wed'day	South S
1920-21	Division 2	19 February	Drew	1	1	12 February	Won	3	2	10th	8th
1921-22	Division 2	4 March	Lost	0	3	11 March	Drew	0	0	10th	6th
1922-23	Division 2	17 March	Won	2	0	24 March	Drew	1	1	8th	13th
1923-24	Division 2	5 April	Won	5	0	29 March	Drew	1	1	8th	9th
1924-25	Division 2	28 February	Lost	0	1	25 October	Won	1	0	14th	9th
1925-26	Division 2	16 January	Won	1	0	5 September	Drew	1	1	1stP	9th

FA Cup

										Division	
1926-27	Round 4	29 January	Drew	1	1	2 February	Lost	0	1	Div 1	Div 2
1930-31	Round 3					10 January	Won	6	2	Div 1	Div 3N

Summary	P	W	D	L	F	A
Wednesday's home league record:	6	3	1	2	9	5
Wednesday's away league record:	6	2	4	0	7	5
Wednesday's cup record:	3	1	1	1	7	4
TOTAL:	**15**	**6**	**6**	**3**	**23**	**14**

FACT FILE

- In 1930, South Shields moved to Gateshead and were renamed Gateshead AFC. The last of Wednesday's 15 matches in the series was thus against Gateshead.
- Wednesday never lost a league match in South Shields.

Wednesday's top scorers vs South Shields
Sam Taylor 7
Joe Harron, Jimmy Lofthouse, Ellis Rimmer,
Jimmy Trotter 2

Wednesday hat-tricks vs South Shields
5 Apr 1924 Sam Taylor

Played for both clubs

Ted Richardson	South Shields 1919-21	Wednesday 1924-25
Jack Allen	Wednesday 1926-31	Gateshead 1935-36
Bill Gowdy	Wednesday 1931-32	Gateshead 1932-33
John T. Smith	Wednesday 1934-35	Gateshead 1937-39
Derrick Goodfellow	Gateshead 1934-36	Wednesday 1936-47

v. Spilsby

Home

FA Cup		Date	Result	Wed'day	Spilsby
1882-83	Round 1	4 November	Won	**12**	**2**

Summary	P	W	D	L	F	A
Wednesday's cup record:	1	1	0	0	12	2
TOTAL:	1	1	0	0	12	2

FACT FILE

● The Lincolnshire side became the first to concede double figures in a match against Wednesday.

Wednesday's top scorers vs Spilsby
R. Gregory 5
T.E. Cawley, H. Newbould 3

Wednesday hat-tricks vs Spilsby
4 Nov 1882 R. Gregory (5) (cup)
4 Nov 1882 T.E. Cawley (cup)
4 Nov 1882 H. Newbould (cup)

Herbert Newbould scored a hat-trick in the thrashing of Spilsby.

v. Staveley

		Home					Away		
FA Cup		*Date*	*Result*	Wed'day Staveley	*Date*	*Result*	Wed'day Staveley		
1881-82	Round 3	28 December	Drew	**2 2**	7 January	Drew	**0 0**		
		Lockwood's Ground (2nd replay)			9 January	Won	**5 1**		
1883-84	Round 2				1 December	Lost	**1 3**		

Summary	P	W	D	L	F	A
Wednesday's cup record:	4	1	2	1	8	6
TOTAL:	4	1	2	1	8	6

Wednesday's top scorers vs Staveley
E. Rhodes 5

T.E. Cawley 2

Wednesday hat-tricks vs Staveley
9 Jan 1882 E. Rhodes (4)

v. Stockport County

				Home				Away		Final Positions	
Season	League	Date	Result	Wed'day	Stockport	Date	Result	Wed'day	Stockport	Wed'day	Stockport
1920-21	Division 2	26 March	Won	2	1	2 April	Won	1	0	10th	22ndR
1922-23	Division 2	10 February	Won	4	1	15 March	Won	1	0	8th	20th
1923-24	Division 2	1 March	Won	3	0	8 March	Lost	0	1	8th	13th
1924-25	Division 2	20 September	Won	3	0	24 January	Lost	0	1	14th	19th
1925-26	Division 2	21 September	Won	6	2	31 August	Won	2	0	1stP	22ndR
1937-38	Division 2	30 October	Drew	3	3	12 March	Lost	1	2	17th	22ndR
2000-01	Division 1	9 December	Lost	2	4	7 April	Lost	1	2	17th	19th
2001-02	Division 1	24 November	Won	5	0	13 April	Lost	1	3	20th	24thR
2003-04	Division 2	13 September	Drew	2	2	20 March	Lost	0	1	16th	19th

FA Cup

										Division	
1976-77	Round 1	20 November	Won	2	0					Div 3	Div 4
1998-99	Round 4	23 January	Won	2	0					Prem	Div 1

League Cup

										Division	
1967-68	Round 2					13 September	Won	5	3	Div 1	Div 3
1986-87	Round 2	23 September	Won	3	0	6 October	Won	7	0	Div 1	Div 4

1986-87 away leg played at Maine Road.

Summary

	P	W	D	L	F	A
Wednesday's home league record:	9	6	2	1	30	13
Wednesday's away league record:	9	3	0	6	7	10
Wednesday's cup record:	5	5	0	0	19	3
TOTAL:	**23**	**14**	**2**	**7**	**56**	**26**

FACT FILE

- **Wednesday have won nine out of 12 home matches against Stockport.**
- **The sides have never contested a goalless draw.**

Wednesday's top scorers vs Stockport
Jimmy Trotter 6
George Ayres, Sid Binks 4
Johnny McIntyre, Mel Sterland, Colin Walker 3

Wednesday hat-tricks vs Stockport
10 Feb 1923 Sid Binks
20 Sep 1924 George Ayres
21 Sep 1925 Jimmy Trotter (5)
6 Oct 1986 Colin Walker (cup)

Played for both clubs
Albert Kay	Wednesday 1897-99	Stockport 1903-04
Jack Earp	Wednesday 1893-1900	Stockport 1900-01
Tom Brittleton	Stockport 1902-04	Wednesday 1904-20
Henry Hibbert	Wednesday 1907-08	Stockport 1908-09
Oliver Levick	Wednesday 1920-24	Stockport 1926-27
Len Williams	Wednesday 1923-26	Stockport 1926-27

Harry Burgess	Stockport 1925-29	Wednesday 1929-35
Tony Leach	Wednesday 1926-34	Stockport 1936-37
Bernard Oxley	Wednesday 1933-35	Stockport 1936-38
Albert Quixall	Wednesday 1950-59	Stockport 1966-67
Ivor Seemley	Wednesday 1953-55	Stockport 1955-57
Ron Staniforth	Stockport 1946-52	Wednesday 1955-59
Tony Coleman	Wednesday 1969-70	Stockport 1974-75
Eddie Prudham	Wednesday 1970-75	Stockport 1977-80
Allan Thompson	Wednesday 1970-76	Stockport 1976-79
Dave Sunley	Wednesday 1970-76	Stockport 1979-82
John Holsgrove	Wednesday 1971-75	Stockport 1975-76
Rodger Wylde	Wednesday 1972-80	Stockport 1988-89
Phil Henson	Wednesday 1974-77	Stockport 1978-80
Peter Feely	Wednesday 1975-77	Stockport 1976-77
Malcolm Darling	Stockport 1976-77	Wednesday 1977-78
Mike Pickering	Wednesday 1978-83	Stockport 1987-89
Trevor Matthewson	Wednesday 1980-83	Stockport 1985-87
Paul Hart	Stockport 1970-73	Wednesday 1985-87
Kenny Brannigan	Wednesday 1986-87	Stockport 1986-87
Carlton Palmer	Wednesday 1988-94/2000-02	Stockport 2001-03
Wayne Collins	Wednesday 1996-98	Stockport 2003-04
Owen Morrison	Wednesday 1998-2003	Stockport 2003-04
Simon Grayson	Wednesday 2000-01	Stockport 2000-01
Aaron Lescott	Wednesday 2000-02	Stockport 2001-04
Shefki Kuqi	Stockport 2000-02	Wednesday 2001-04
Garry Monk	Stockport 1999-2000	Wednesday 2002-03
Eric Nixon	Stockport 1997-99	Wednesday 2003-04
Ola Tidman	Stockport 2002-03	Wednesday 2003-04

David Sunley played for Stockport
after he had moved on from
Sheffield Wednesday.

v. Stoke City

		Home				Away		Final Positions	
Season	League	Date	Result	Wed'day	Stoke	Date	Result	Wed'day	Stoke	Wed'day	Stoke
1892-93	Division 1	1 April	Lost	0	1	17 December	Lost	0	2	12th	7th
1893-94	Division 1	7 December	Won	4	1	7 October	Lost	1	4	12th	11th
1894-95	Division 1	17 April	Lost	2	4	8 December	Won	2	0	8th	14th
1895-96	Division 1	16 November	Won	2	1	21 February	Lost	0	5	7th	6th
1896-97	Division 1	26 September	Won	4	3	23 January	Drew	0	0	6th	13th
1897-98	Division 1	25 December	Won	4	0	26 March	Lost	1	2	5th	16th
1898-99	Division 1	27 March	Lost	1	3	19 November	Lost	0	1	18thR	12th
1900-01	Division 1	2 March	Won	4	0	27 October	Lost	1	2	8th	16th
1901-02	Division 1	30 November	Won	3	1	29 March	Won	2	1	9th	16th
1902-03	Division 1	28 March	Won	1	0	29 November	Lost	0	4	1st	6th
1903-04	Division 1	12 March	Won	1	0	14 November	Lost	1	3	1st	16th
1904-05	Division 1	15 October	Won	3	0	11 February	Lost	1	2	9th	12th
1905-06	Division 1	9 April	Won	2	0	4 November	Lost	0	4	3rd	10th
1906-07	Division 1	30 March	Lost	0	1	24 November	Drew	1	1	13th	20thR
1920-21	Division 2	11 September	Lost	1	3	18 September	Won	1	0	10th	20th
1921-22	Division 2	14 January	Lost	0	1	31 December	Drew	1	1	10th	2ndP
1923-24	Division 2	8 December	Won	3	0	1 December	Drew	1	1	8th	6th
1924-25	Division 2	14 February	Won	2	1	11 October	Won	2	0	14th	20th
1925-26	Division 2	26 April	Won	2	0	5 April	Won	1	0	1stP	21stR
1933-34	Division 1	5 May	Drew	2	2	23 December	Won	1	0	11th	12th
1934-35	Division 1	25 August	Won	4	1	29 December	Drew	1	1	3rd	10th
1935-36	Division 1	14 December	Lost	0	1	18 April	Won	3	0	20th	4th
1936-37	Division 1	24 October	Drew	0	0	5 April	Lost	0	1	22ndR	10th
1950-51	Division 1	4 September	Drew	1	1	11 September	Drew	1	1	21stR	13th
1952-53	Division 1	21 February	Won	1	0	4 October	Won	3	1	18th	21stR
1955-56	Division 2	24 December	Won	4	0	27 August	Lost	0	2	1stP	13th
1958-59	Division 2	3 September	Won	4	1	27 August	Lost	0	3	1stP	5th
1963-64	Division 1	8 April	Won	2	0	16 November	Drew	4	4	6th	17th
1964-65	Division 1	28 November	Drew	1	1	10 April	Lost	1	4	8th	11th
1965-66	Division 1	30 March	Won	4	1	4 May	Lost	1	3	17th	10th
1966-67	Division 1	8 October	Lost	1	3	25 February	Won	2	0	11th	12th
1967-68	Division 1	23 October	Drew	1	1	16 March	Won	1	0	19th	18th
1968-69	Division 1	30 November	Won	2	1	22 April	Drew	1	1	15th	19th
1969-70	Division 1	15 November	Lost	0	2	28 March	Lost	1	2	22ndR	9th
1984-85	Division 1	22 December	Won	2	1	1 September	Lost	1	2	8th	22ndR
2002-03	Division 1	10 August	Drew	0	0	28 December	Lost	2	3	22ndR	21st

FA Cup

										Division	
1893-94	Round 2	10 February	Won	1	0					Div 1	Div 1
1898-99	Round 1	28 January	Drew	2	2	2 February	Lost	0	2	Div 1	Div 1
1908-09	Round 1	16 January	Won	5	0					Div 1	Non L
1945-46	Round 5	11 February	Drew	0	0	9 February	Lost	0	2	Div 2	Div 1

			Home				Away		Division	
League Cup	Date	Result	Wed'day	Stoke	Date	Result	Wed'day	Stoke	Wed'day	Stoke
1967-68 Round 4	1 November	Drew	0	0	15 November	Lost	1	2	Div 1	Div 1
1983-84 Round 4					30 November	Won	1	0	Div 2	Div 1
1999-00 Round 2	22 September	Won	3	1	14 September	Drew	0	0	Prem	Div 2

Summary	P	W	D	L	F	A
Wednesday's home league record:	36	21	6	9	68	36
Wednesday's away league record:	36	10	8	18	39	61
Wednesday's cup record:	11	4	4	3	13	9
TOTAL:	83	35	18	30	120	106

FACT FILE

- Wednesday were unbeaten in 10 matches between 1923 and 1934.
- Between 1901 and 1906, Wednesday won six consecutive home matches, conceding only one goal in the process.
- Only one of the first 26 league matches in the series ended in a draw.
- On 15 October 1904, victory over Stoke brought Wednesday's winning run that season to nine games – a club record.

Wednesday's top scorers vs Stoke
Fred Spiksley 9
Andrew Wilson 7
Harry Chapman, John Fantham 5
Tommy Crawshaw, Neil Dewar, David Ford,
Redfern Froggatt 4

Played for both clubs

Tom Brittleton	Wednesday 1904-20	Stoke 1920-25
David Parkes	Wednesday 1913-20	Stoke 1920-21
Len Armitage	Wednesday 1919-20	Stoke 1923-32
Jackie Palethorpe	Stoke 1932-34	Wednesday 1934-36
Harry Ware	Stoke 1930-35	Wednesday 1937-38
John Ritchie	Stoke 1962-67/69-75	Wednesday 1966-69
Peter Fox	Wednesday 1972-77	Stoke 1978-93
Gary Bannister	Wednesday 1981-84	Stoke 1993-94
Nigel Worthington	Wednesday 1983-94	Stoke 1996-97
Simon Stainrod	Wednesday 1984-86	Stoke 1987-89
Lee Chapman	Stoke 1979-82	Wednesday 1984-88
Mark Chamberlain	Stoke 1982-86	Wednesday 1985-88
Kevin Pressman	Wednesday 1987-2004	Stoke 1991-92
Ian Cranson	Wednesday 1987-89	Stoke 1989-97
Paul Warhurst	Wednesday 1990-93	Stoke 2002-03
O'Neill Donaldson	Wednesday 1994-98	Stoke 1997-98
Mark Wilson	Stoke 2002-03	Wednesday 2003-04

v. Sunderland

Season	League	Date	Result	Home Wed'day	Sund'land	Date	Result	Away Wed'day	Sund'land	Final Positions Wed'day	Sund'land
1892-93	Division 1	29 October	Won	3	2	28 January	Lost	2	4	12th	1st
1893-94	Division 1	2 September	Drew	2	2	23 September	Drew	1	1	12th	2nd
1894-95	Division 1	23 March	Lost	1	2	26 February	Lost	1	3	8th	1st
1895-96	Division 1	19 October	Won	3	0	7 March	Lost	1	2	7th	5th
1896-97	Division 1	10 October	Drew	0	0	5 December	Drew	0	0	6th	15th
1897-98	Division 1	4 September	Lost	0	1	25 September	Lost	0	1	5th	2nd
1898-99	Division 1	18 February	Lost	0	1	22 October	Lost	0	2	18thR	7th
1900-01	Division 1	13 April	Won	1	0	8 December	Lost	0	1	8th	2nd
1901-02	Division 1	14 December	Drew	1	1	12 April	Won	2	1	9th	1st
1902-03	Division 1	22 November	Won	1	0	21 March	Won	1	0	1st	3rd
1903-04	Division 1	13 February	Drew	0	0	17 October	Won	1	0	1st	6th
1904-05	Division 1	27 December	Drew	1	1	22 October	Lost	0	3	9th	5th
1905-06	Division 1	7 April	Drew	3	3	2 December	Lost	0	2	3rd	14th
1906-07	Division 1	13 April	Won	2	1	8 December	Drew	1	1	13th	10th
1907-08	Division 1	26 December	Lost	2	3	17 April	Won	2	1	5th	16th
1908-09	Division 1	29 March	Lost	2	5	3 October	Lost	2	4	5th	3rd
1909-10	Division 1	30 April	Won	1	0	18 December	Lost	0	2	11th	8th
1910-11	Division 1	5 November	Drew	1	1	11 March	Won	2	1	6th	3rd
1911-12	Division 1	26 December	Won	8	0	1 January	Drew	0	0	5th	8th
1912-13	Division 1	25 December	Lost	1	2	26 December	Won	2	0	3rd	1st
1913-14	Division 1	29 November	Won	2	1	4 April	Won	1	0	18th	7th
1914-15	Division 1	7 November	Lost	1	2	13 March	Lost	1	3	7th	8th
1919-20	Division 1	13 December	Lost	0	2	6 December	Lost	1	2	22ndR	5th
1926-27	Division 1	19 February	Won	4	1	2 October	Lost	1	4	16th	3rd
1927-28	Division 1	17 December	Drew	0	0	28 April	Won	3	2	14th	15th
1928-29	Division 1	8 September	Won	2	1	19 January	Lost	3	4	1st	4th
1929-30	Division 1	12 October	Drew	1	1	30 April	Won	4	2	1st	9th
1930-31	Division 1	1 November	Won	7	2	7 March	Lost	1	5	3rd	11th
1931-32	Division 1	23 April	Won	3	2	12 December	Lost	1	3	3rd	13th
1932-33	Division 1	15 October	Won	3	1	25 February	Won	2	1	3rd	12th
1933-34	Division 1	7 April	Won	2	0	25 November	Lost	0	4	11th	6th
1934-35	Division 1	1 December	Drew	2	2	13 April	Drew	2	2	3rd	2nd
1935-36	Division 1	14 March	Drew	0	0	26 October	Lost	1	5	20th	1st
1936-37	Division 1	29 August	Won	2	0	26 December	Lost	1	2	22ndR	8th
1950-51	Division 1	24 March	Won	3	0	4 November	Lost	1	5	21stR	12th
1952-53	Division 1	25 April	Won	4	0	6 December	Lost	1	5	18th	9th
1953-54	Division 1	21 November	Drew	2	2	10 April	Won	4	2	19th	18th
1954-55	Division 1	15 January	Lost	1	2	4 September	Lost	0	2	22ndR	4th
1956-57	Division 1	6 October	Won	3	2	16 February	Lost	2	5	14th	20th
1957-58	Division 1	26 October	Drew	3	3	8 March	Drew	3	3	22ndR	21stR
1958-59	Division 2	17 September	Won	6	0	10 September	Drew	3	3	1stP	15th
1964-65	Division 1	13 February	Won	2	0	28 April	Lost	0	3	8th	15th
1965-66	Division 1	23 October	Won	3	1	26 January	Won	2	0	17th	19th
1966-67	Division 1	28 March	Won	5	0	24 March	Lost	0	2	11th	17th

| | | | **Home** | | | | | **Away** | | *Final Positions* | |
Season	League	Date	Result	Wed'day	Sund'land	Date	Result	Wed'day	Sund'land	Wed'day	Sund'land
1967-68	Division 1	3 February	Lost	0	1	23 September	Won	2	0	19th	15th
1968-69	Division 1	5 October	Drew	1	1	26 December	Drew	0	0	15th	17th
1969-70	Division 1	26 December	Won	2	0	23 August	Won	2	1	22ndR	21stR
1970-71	Division 2	24 April	Lost	1	2	19 September	Lost	1	3	15th	13th
1971-72	Division 2	18 September	Won	3	0	1 January	Lost	0	2	14th	5th
1972-73	Division 2	10 February	Won	1	0	16 September	Drew	1	1	10th	6th
1973-74	Division 2	23 February	Lost	0	1	6 October	Lost	1	3	19th	6th
1974-75	Division 2	2 October	Lost	0	2	15 October	Lost	0	3	22ndR	4th
1984-85	Division 1	6 October	Drew	2	2	16 April	Drew	0	0	8th	21stR
1996-97	Premiership	12 March	Won	2	1	23 November	Drew	1	1	7th	18thR
1999-00	Premiership	22 April	Lost	0	2	25 September	Lost	0	1	19thR	7th

FA Cup

										Division	
1895-96	Round 2	15 February	Won	2	1					Div 1	Div 1
1897-98	Round 1					29 January	Won	1	0	Div 1	Div 1
1901-02	Round 1					25 January	Lost	0	1	Div 1	Div 1
1906-07	Round 3	23 February	Drew	0	0	27 February	Won	1	0	Div 1	Div 1
1971-72	Round 3					15 January	Lost	0	3	Div 2	Div 2
1992-93	Round 4	24 January	Won	1	0					Prem	Div 1

League Cup

2001-02	Round 2	12 September	Won*	4	2					Div 1	Prem

Summary

	P	W	D	L	F	A
Wednesday's home league record:	55	26	15	14	106	62
Wednesday's away league record:	55	14	11	30	64	110
Wednesday's cup record:	8	5	1	2	9	7
TOTAL:	**118**	**45**	**27**	**46**	**179**	**179**

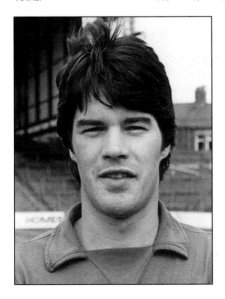

Past and future Owl Chris Turner pictured after signing for Sunderland in 1979 (wearing an old jersey!). Turner would return to Hillsborough as both player and in a managerial capacity.

FACT FILE

- On Boxing Day 1911, Wednesday won a league match by eight goals. They achieved this feat on only one other occasion (against Birmingham in 1930).
- Between 1927 and 1953, Wednesday were unbeaten in 14 home games in the series.
- Wednesday have not won in their last nine games in Sunderland. Their last win there was in 1969.
- Between 1896 and 1900, Wednesday failed to score in seven consecutive league matches against Sunderland.

Wednesday's top scorers vs Sunderland

Mark Hooper 11
Redfern Froggatt 10
Andrew Wilson 8
Jack Ball, David McLean 7
Jackie Sewell 6
Jimmy Trotter 5

Wednesday hat-tricks vs Sunderland

26 Dec 1911 David McLean (4)
19 Feb 1927 Jimmy Trotter
1 Nov 1930 Jack Ball
25 Apr 1953 Jackie Sewell
17 Sep 1958 Redfern Froggatt

Played for both clubs

John Smith	Sunderland 1890-92	Wednesday 1893-94
English McConnell	Sunderland 1905-08	Wednesday 1908-10
Billy Marsden	Sunderland 1920-24	Wednesday 1924-30
Len Hargreaves	Sunderland 1927-29	Wednesday 1928-29
Jackie Robinson	Wednesday 1934-47	Sunderland 1946-49
Brian Usher	Sunderland 1963-65	Wednesday 1965-68
Colin Symm	Wednesday 1966-69	Sunderland 1969-72
Rodger Wylde	Wednesday 1972-80	Sunderland 1984-85
Fred McIver	Sunderland 1971-72	Wednesday 1974-76
Chris Turner	Wednesday 1976-79/88-91	Sunderland 1979-85
Ian Porterfield	Sunderland 1967-76	Wednesday 1977-80
Bob Bolder	Wednesday 1977-83	Sunderland 1985-86
Terry Curran	Wednesday 1978-82	Sunderland 1986-87
Lee Chapman	Sunderland 1983-84	Wednesday 1984-88
Colin West	Sunderland 1981-85	Wednesday 1987-89
Mark Proctor	Sunderland 1982-88	Wednesday 1987-89
Wilf Rostron	Sunderland 1977-80	Wednesday 1988-89
David Hodgson	Sunderland 1984-86	Wednesday 1988-89
Paul Williams	Wednesday 1990-93	Sunderland 1994-95
Chris Waddle	Wednesday 1992-96	Sunderland 1996-97
Emerson Thome	Wednesday 1997-2000	Sunderland 2000-03
Alan Quinn	Wednesday 1997-2004	Sunderland 2003-04
Terry Cooke	Sunderland 1995-96	Wednesday 2000-01/03-04
Allan Johnston	Sunderland 1996-99	Wednesday 2002-03
Carl Robinson	Wednesday 2002-03	Sunderland 2003-04
Michael Reddy	Sunderland 1999-2001	Wednesday 2002-04

v. Swansea City

			Home				Away		Final Positions	
Season	League	Date	Result	Wed'day	Swansea	Date	Result	Wed'day	Swansea	Wed'day	Swansea
1925-26	Division 2	10 October	Won	3	1	11 March	Drew	2	2	1stP	5th
1937-38	Division 2	4 September	Drew	1	1	15 January	Drew	1	1	17th	18th
1938-39	Division 2	24 September	Drew	1	1	28 January	Won	1	0	3rd	19th
1946-47	Division 2	2 November	Won	3	0	10 May	Lost	0	2	20th	21stR
1949-50	Division 2	29 October	Won	3	0	18 March	Won	2	1	2ndP	8th
1951-52	Division 2	12 April	Drew	1	1	24 November	Won	2	1	1stP	19th
1955-56	Division 2	17 September	Drew	2	2	21 January	Lost	1	2	1stP	10th
1958-59	Division 2	23 August	Won	2	1	20 December	Lost	0	4	1stP	11th
1978-79	Division 3	7 April	Drew	0	0	2 December	Lost	2	4	14th	3rdP
1980-81	Division 2	21 February	Won	2	0	27 September	Won	3	2	10th	3rdP
1983-84	Division 2	14 January	Won	6	1	27 August	Won	1	0	2ndP	21stR

FA Cup
							Division
1961-62	Round 3	9 January	Won	1	0		Div 1 Div 2

Summary	P	W	D	L	F	A
Wednesday's home league record:	11	6	5	0	24	8
Wednesday's away league record:	11	5	2	4	15	19
Wednesday's cup record:	1	1	0	0	1	0
TOTAL:	**23**	**12**	**7**	**4**	**40**	**27**

Tommy Craig,
who had stints at
Wednesday and
Swansea.

FACT FILE

- **Wednesday have never lost at home to Swansea.**
- **Wednesday have won their last four matches against Swansea.**

Wednesday's top scorers vs Swansea
Matt Barrass 3

Played for both clubs

William Stapleton	Wednesday 1919-20	Swansea 1920-22
John Edmondson	Wednesday 1919-20	Swansea 1920-23
Joe Sykes	Wednesday 1919-24	Swansea 1924-35
Walter Lamb	Wednesday 1921-22	Swansea 1923-25
Len Williams	Wednesday 1923-26	Swansea 1929-31
Harry Anstiss	Wednesday 1926-27	Swansea 1931-33
Fred Marson	Wednesday 1926-28	Swansea 1928-29
Harry Hanford	Swansea 1927-36	Wednesday 1935-40
Jim Wright	Wednesday 1934-36	Swansea 1937-38
Dickie Rhodes	Wednesday 1935-38	Swansea 1938-39
Idris Lewis	Swansea 1935-38	Wednesday 1938-40
Sydney Chedgzoy	Wednesday 1937-38	Swansea 1938-39
Mike Pinner	Wednesday 1957-59	Swansea 1961-62
George Kirby	Wednesday 1959-60	Swansea 1964-65
Tommy Craig	Wednesday 1968-75	Swansea 1979-81
Phil Henson	Swansea 1972-73	Wednesday 1974-77
Tommy Tynan	Swansea 1975-76	Wednesday 1976-79
David Rushbury	Wednesday 1976-79	Swansea 1979-81
Jeff Johnson	Swansea 1972-73	Wednesday 1976-81
Lee Chapman	Wednesday 1984-88	Swansea 1995-96
Colin West	Wednesday 1987-89	Swansea 1992-93
David Hodgson	Wednesday 1988-89	Swansea 1991-92
Mark Wilson	Swansea 2003-04	Wednesday 2003-04

Tommy Craig

v. Swifts

			Home							Division	
FA Cup		*Date*	*Result*	Wed'day	Swifts					Wed'day	Swifts
1889-90	Round 1	20 January	Won	6	1					Non L	Non L

Summary	*P*	*W*	*D*	*L*	*F*	*A*
Wednesday's cup record:	1	1	0	0	6	1
TOTAL:	1	1	0	0	6	1

FACT FILE

● Swifts, based in Slough, reached three FA Cup semi-finals in their time, but were past their best by 1890.

Wednesday's top scorers vs Swifts
W. Bennett, T.E. Cawley, Albert Mumford 2

v. Swindon Town

Season	League	Date	Result	Home Wed'day	Swindon	Date	Result	Away Wed'day	Swindon	Final Positions Wed'day	Swindon
1970-71	Division 2	30 January	Drew	2	2	28 November	Lost	0	3	15th	12th
1971-72	Division 2	23 October	Won	1	0	12 February	Lost	0	1	14th	11th
1972-73	Division 2	16 August	Won	2	1	29 August	Lost	0	1	10th	16th
1973-74	Division 2	19 January	Won	2	1	25 August	Lost	1	3	19th	22ndR
1975-76	Division 3	24 January	Lost	0	2	13 September	Lost	1	2	20th	19th
1976-77	Division 3	19 February	Won	3	1	11 September	Lost	2	5	8th	11th
1977-78	Division 3	20 August	Drew	1	1	14 January	Drew	2	2	14th	10th
1978-79	Division 3	11 May	Won	2	1	30 September	Lost	0	3	14th	5th
1979-80	Division 3	22 September	Won	4	2	9 February	Won	2	1	3rdP	10th
1990-91	Division 2	17 November	Won	2	1	19 February	Lost	1	2	3rdP	21st
1993-94	Premiership	29 December	Drew	3	3	4 April	Won	1	0	7th	22ndR
2003-04	Division 2	10 January	Drew	1	1	9 August	Won	3	2	16th	5th

FA Cup

										Division	
1927-28	Round 4					28 January	Won	2	1	Div 1	Div 3S
1967-68	Round 4	17 February	Won	2	1					Div 1	Div 3

League Cup

										Division	
1985-86	Round 3					29 October	Lost	0	1	Div 1	Div 4
1990-91	Round 3	31 October	Drew	0	0	6 November	Won	1	0	Div 2	Div 2

Summary

	P	W	D	L	F	A
Wednesday's home league record:	12	7	4	1	23	16
Wednesday's away league record:	12	3	1	8	13	25
Wednesday's cup record:	5	3	1	1	5	3
TOTAL:	29	13	6	10	41	44

Wally Dickinson, a 1920s
player, briefly at Wednesday
and then in Wiltshire for
Swindon.

FACT FILE

- Wednesday have been beaten at home by Swindon only once in 14 meetings.
- Swindon won their first six league matches at home in the series.

Wednesday's top scorers vs Swindon
Gordon Watson, Rodger Wylde 3

Played for both clubs

Tommy Bolland	Wednesday 1907-09	Swindon 1920-21
Harry Bentley	Wednesday 1913-20	Swindon 1922-24
Fred Dent	Wednesday 1920-21	Swindon 1929-30
Harry O'Neill	Wednesday 1919-22	Swindon 1923-28
Wally Dickinson	Wednesday 1922-23	Swindon 1923-30
Charlie Petrie	Wednesday 1921-25	Swindon 1925-27
Alec Cruickshank	Wednesday 1926-27	Swindon 1930-31
Dan Kirkwood	Wednesday 1926-28	Swindon 1933-34
Walter Bingley	Wednesday 1955-57	Swindon 1957-60
David Layne	Swindon 1959-61	Wednesday 1962-64
Colin Prophett	Wednesday 1969-73	Swindon 1974-78
Brian Marwood	Wednesday 1984-88	Swindon 1992-93
Tony Galvin	Wednesday 1987-89	Swindon 1989-90
Dave Bennett	Wednesday 1988-90	Swindon 1990-91
Phil King	Swindon 1986-90/96-97	Wednesday 1989-94
Juan Cobian	Wednesday 1998-99	Swindon 2000-02
Marlon Broomes	Swindon 1996-97	Wednesday 2001-02
Paul Heald	Swindon 1993-94	Wednesday 2001-02
John Beswetherick	Wednesday 2002-04	Swindon 2002-03
Michael Reddy	Swindon 2000-01	Wednesday 2002-04

v. Torquay United

FA Cup		Date	Result	Home Wed'day	Torquay	Date	Result	Away Wed'day	Torquay	Division Wed'day	Torquay
1982-83	Round 4					29 January	Won	3	2	Div 2	Div 4
1988-89	Round 3	7 January	Won	5	1					Div 1	Div 4

Summary	P	W	D	L	F	A
Wednesday's cup record:	2	2	0	0	8	3
TOTAL:	2	2	0	0	8	3

Wednesday's top scorers vs Torquay
Imre Varadi 2

Played for both clubs

Jimmy Trotter	Wednesday 1921-29	Torquay 1930-32
Jim Wright	Torquay 1930-32	Wednesday 1934-36
Albert Shelley	Wednesday 1936-37	Torquay 1937-39
Tommy Tynan	Wednesday 1976-79	Torquay 1990-91
Colin Walker	Wednesday 1986-87	Torquay 1987-88
Steve McCall	Wednesday 1987-91	Torquay 1996-98
Phil King	Torquay 1986-87	Wednesday 1989-94
Paul Williams	Wednesday 1990-93	Torquay 1995-96
Chris Waddle	Wednesday 1992-96	Torquay 1998-99
O'Neill Donaldson	Wednesday 1994-98	Torquay 1998-2000
Mark Platts	Wednesday 1995-96	Torquay 1998-2001
Garry Monk	Torquay 1995-96/98-99	Wednesday 2002-03
Ryan Green	Torquay 2000-01	Wednesday 2002-03

Siggi Jonsson scored in the
5-1 FA Cup win over Torquay
in January 1989.

v. Tottenham Hotspur

			Home				Away			Final Positions	
Season	League	Date	Result	Wed'day	Spurs	Date	Result	Wed'day	Spurs	Wed'day	Spurs
1909-10	Division 1	14 March	Drew	1	1	25 September	Lost	0	3	11th	15th
1910-11	Division 1	31 December	Won	2	1	3 September	Lost	1	3	6th	15th
1911-12	Division 1	30 September	Won	4	0	4 September	Lost	1	3	5th	12th
1912-13	Division 1	28 December	Won	2	1	7 September	Won	4	2	3rd	17th
1913-14	Division 1	25 April	Won	2	0	20 December	Drew	1	1	18th	17th
1914-15	Division 1	25 December	Won	3	2	26 December	Lost	1	6	7th	20thR
1926-27	Division 1	28 December	Won	3	1	30 August	Lost	3	7	16th	13th
1927-28	Division 1	10 April	Won	4	2	6 April	Won	3	1	14th	21thR
1933-34	Division 1	16 December	Won	2	1	28 April	Lost	3	4	11th	3rd
1934-35	Division 1	6 April	Won	4	0	24 November	Lost	2	3	3rd	22ndR
1937-38	Division 2	16 September	Lost	0	3	7 May	Won	2	1	17th	5th
1938-39	Division 2	29 April	Won	1	0	29 August	Drew	3	3	3rd	8th
1946-47	Division 2	1 March	Won	5	1	26 October	Lost	0	2	20th	6th
1947-48	Division 2	3 January	Won	1	0	30 August	Lost	1	5	4th	8th
1948-49	Division 2	18 December	Won	3	1	21 August	Lost	2	3	8th	5th
1949-50	Division 2	6 May	Drew	0	0	5 September	Lost	0	1	2ndP	1stP
1950-51	Division 1	9 December	Drew	1	1	28 April	Lost	0	1	21stR	1st
1952-53	Division 1	13 September	Won	2	0	24 January	Lost	1	2	18th	10th
1953-54	Division 1	22 August	Won	2	1	19 December	Lost	1	3	19th	16th
1954-55	Division 1	11 September	Drew	2	2	22 January	Lost	2	7	22ndR	16th
1956-57	Division 1	17 November	Won	4	1	30 March	Drew	1	1	14th	2nd
1957-58	Division 1	1 February	Won	2	0	21 September	Lost	2	4	22ndR	3rd
1959-60	Division 1	17 October	Won	2	1	5 March	Lost	1	4	5th	3rd
1960-61	Division 1	12 November	Won	2	1	17 April	Lost	1	2	2nd	1st
1961-62	Division 1	18 November	Drew	0	0	7 April	Lost	0	4	6th	3rd
1962-63	Division 1	8 April	Won	3	1	17 November	Drew	1	1	6th	2nd
1963-64	Division 1	13 April	Won	2	0	30 November	Drew	1	1	6th	4th
1964-65	Division 1	17 April	Won	1	0	5 December	Lost	2	3	8th	6th
1965-66	Division 1	9 April	Drew	1	1	13 November	Won	3	2	17th	8th
1966-67	Division 1	19 November	Won	1	0	15 April	Lost	1	2	11th	3rd
1967-68	Division 1	17 January	Lost	1	2	9 September	Lost	1	2	19th	7th
1968-69	Division 1	12 May	Drew	0	0	24 August	Won	2	1	15th	6th
1969-70	Division 1	30 March	Lost	0	1	1 November	Lost	0	1	22ndR	11th
1984-85	Division 1	8 September	Won	2	1	14 May	Lost	0	2	8th	3rd
1985-86	Division 1	22 February	Lost	1	2	21 September	Lost	1	5	5th	10th
1986-87	Division 1	7 April	Lost	0	1	18 October	Drew	1	1	13th	3rd
1987-88	Division 1	27 February	Lost	0	3	3 October	Lost	0	2	11th	13th
1988-89	Division 1	20 November	Lost	0	2	12 April	Drew	0	0	15th	6th
1989-90	Division 1	31 March	Lost	2	4	21 October	Lost	0	3	18thR	3rd
1991-92	Division 1	2 November	Drew	0	0	14 March	Won	2	0	3rd	15th
1992-93	Premiership	27 September	Won	2	0	16 January	Won	2	0	7th	8th
1993-94	Premiership	3 January	Won	1	0	5 February	Won	3	1	7th	15th
1994-95	Premiership	20 August	Lost	3	4	10 December	Lost	1	3	13th	7th
1995-96	Premiership	16 September	Lost	1	3	24 February	Lost	0	1	15th	8th

| | | | Home | | | | Away | | | Final Positions | |
Season	League	Date	Result	Wed'day	Spurs	Date	Result	Wed'day	Spurs	Wed'day	Spurs
1996-97	Premiership	9 April	Won	2	1	21 December	Drew	1	1	7th	10th
1997-98	Premiership	21 February	Won	1	0	19 October	Lost	2	3	16th	14th
1998-99	Premiership	9 January	Drew	0	0	22 August	Won	3	0	12th	11th
1999-00	Premiership	21 August	Lost	1	2	22 January	Won	1	0	19thR	10th

FA Cup

										Division	
1903-04	Q'ter final	9 March	Won	2	0	5 March	Drew	1	1	Div 1	Non L
1931-32	Round 3	13 January	Won	3	1	9 January	Drew	2	2	Div 1	Div 2
1970-71	Round 3					2 January	Lost	1	4	Div 2	Div 1

Summary	P	W	D	L	F	A
Wednesday's home league record:	48	28	9	11	79	49
Wednesday's away league record:	48	10	8	30	64	111
Wednesday's cup record:	5	2	2	1	9	8
TOTAL:	101	40	19	42	152	168

FACT FILE

- Wednesday won 10 in a row at Hillsborough between 1910 and 1935.
- Spurs won only once in their first 32 visits to Hillsborough, up to 1966.
- Wednesday failed to win in 12 games from 1985 to 1991, a run which included five successive home defeats.
- Between 1992 and 1994, Wednesday beat Spurs five times in a row.
- Wednesday failed to win at White Hart Lane in 17 matches between 1938 and 1964, including eight successive defeats.
- In 1960-61, Spurs had dropped only one point in their first 16 matches on their way to the double. Wednesday, however, beat them 2-1 with John Fantham scoring the winner.
- The final day 0-0 draw with Tottenham in 1950 clinched promotion, pipping Sheffield United and Southampton to glory on goal average. The final goal averages were this close: Wednesday 1.396, United 1.388, Southampton 1.333. Incidentally, Wednesday's task was not easy as Spurs were runaway winners of the division.

Wednesday's top scorers vs Spurs
Alan Finney, Mark Hooper 6
Mark Bright, John Fantham, David Hirst,
Jackie Sewell 5

Wednesday hat-tricks vs Spurs
10 Apr 1928 Mark Hooper
1 Mar 1947 Jimmy Dailey
17 Nov 1956 Alan Finney

Played for both clubs

Findlay Weir	Wednesday 1909-12	Spurs 1912-15
Jimmy Seed	Spurs 1919-27	Wednesday 1927-31
Arthur Lowdell	Wednesday 1921-27	Spurs 1927-30
Billy Felton	Wednesday 1922-29	Spurs 1931-34
Ted Harper	Wednesday 1927-29	Spurs 1928-32
Doug Hunt	Spurs 1934-37	Wednesday 1937-40
George Hunt	Spurs 1930-37	Wednesday 1946-48
Johnny Jordan	Spurs 1947-48	Wednesday 1950-51
John Collins	Spurs 1965-66	Wednesday 1976-77
Tony Galvin	Spurs 1978-87	Wednesday 1987-89
Chris Waddle	Spurs 1985-89	Wednesday 1992-96
Andy Sinton	Wednesday 1993-96	Spurs 1995-99
Andy Booth	Wednesday 1996-2001	Spurs 2000-01
Ian Hendon	Spurs 1990-92	Wednesday 2000-03

Doug Hunt
served Spurs and
Wednesday
before World
War Two.

v. Tranmere Rovers

Season	League	Date	Result	Home Wed'day	Tranmere	Date	Result	Away Wed'day	Tranmere	Final Positions Wed'day	Tranmere
1938-39	Division 2	10 September	Won	2	0	14 January	Won	4	1	3rd	22ndR
1976-77	Division 3	4 December	Won	3	1	6 May	Lost	0	1	8th	14th
1977-78	Division 3	27 March	Won	1	0	26 December	Lost	1	3	14th	12th
1978-79	Division 3	21 April	Lost	1	2	19 February	Drew	1	1	14th	23rdR
2000-01	Division 1	13 February	Won	1	0	16 September	Lost	0	2	17th	24thR
2003-04	Division 2	6 September	Won	2	0	28 December	Drew	2	2	16th	8th

FA Cup — Division

Season	Round	Date	Result	Home		Date	Result	Away		Division	
1978-79	Round 2	19 December	Won	4	0	16 December	Drew	1	1	Div 3	Div 3

Summary	P	W	D	L	F	A
Wednesday's home league record:	6	5	0	1	10	3
Wednesday's away league record:	6	1	2	3	8	10
Wednesday's cup record:	2	1	1	0	5	1
TOTAL:	**14**	**7**	**3**	**4**	**23**	**14**

FACT FILE

● **Wednesday have won six out of seven home matches in the series.**

Wednesday's top scorers vs Tranmere
Idris Lewis, Rodger Wylde 3

Played for both clubs

Archie Ratcliffe	Wednesday 1921-22	Tranmere 1922-23
Ellis Rimmer	Tranmere 1924-28	Wednesday 1927-38
Tommy Jones	Tranmere 1926-29	Wednesday 1929-34
Jack Roy	Wednesday 1936-38	Tranmere 1938-39
Tony Coleman	Tranmere 1962-64	Wednesday 1969-70
Jimmy Hinch	Tranmere 1969-71	Wednesday 1977-78
Gavin Oliver	Wednesday 1980-85	Tranmere 1982-83
Mark Proctor	Wednesday 1987-89	Tranmere 1992-94
Ian Nolan	Tranmere 1991-94	Wednesday 1994-2000
Adam Proudlock	Wednesday 2002-04	Tranmere 2002-03
Eric Nixon	Tranmere 1987-98/99-2003	Wednesday 2003-04

v. Turton

FA Cup				Date		Result	Wed'day	Turton
1880-81 Round 3				8 January		Won	2	0

Summary	P	W	D	L	F	A
Wednesday's cup record:	1	1	0	0	2	0
TOTAL:	1	1	0	0	2	0

FACT FILE

● Turton were based in Bolton.

v. Upton Park

Home

FA Cup	Date	Result	Wed'day	Upton P
1881-82 Q'ter final	7 February	Won	**6**	**0**

Summary	P	W	D	L	F	A
Wednesday's cup record:	1	1	0	0	6	0
TOTAL:	1	1	0	0	6	0

FACT FILE

● Upton Park were based in East London, and won the gold medal for football in the 1900 Olympics as representatives of Great Britain.

Wednesday's top scorers vs Upton Park
T.E. Cawley 3
W.H. Mosforth 2

Wednesday hat-tricks vs Upton Park
7 Feb 1882 T.E. Cawley (cup)

Craig Shakespeare had seven years with the Saddlers before signing for Wednesday.

v. Walsall

Season	League	Date	Result	Home Wed'day	Walsall	Date	Result	Away Wed'day	Walsall	Final Positions Wed'day	Walsall
1899-00	Division 2	16 December	Won	2	0	21 April	Drew	1	1	1stP	12th
1975-76	Division 3	6 March	Won	2	1	2 December	Drew	2	2	20th	7th
1976-77	Division 3	21 August	Drew	0	0	22 January	Lost	1	5	8th	15th
1977-78	Division 3	27 August	Drew	0	0	25 April	Drew	1	1	14th	6th
1978-79	Division 3	28 October	Lost	0	2	10 March	Won	2	0	14th	22ndR
2001-02	Division 1	20 October	Won	2	1	9 February	Won	3	0	20th	18th
2002-03	Division 1	4 May	Won	2	1	28 September	Lost	0	1	22ndR	17th

League Cup

Season	Round	Date	Result			Division
1977-78	Round 3	25 October	Won	2	1	Div 3 Div 3

Summary

	P	W	D	L	F	A
Wednesday's home league record:	7	4	2	1	8	5
Wednesday's away league record:	7	2	3	2	10	10
Wednesday's cup record:	1	1	0	0	2	1
TOTAL:	15	7	5	3	20	16

Wednesday's top scorers vs Walsall

Mick Prendergast, Gerald Sibon, Tommy Tynan, Rodger Wylde 2

Played for both clubs

Arthur Prince	Wednesday 1924-28	Walsall 1929-30
Lewis Bedford	Walsall 1922-30	Wednesday 1925-26
George Beeson	Wednesday 1929-34	Walsall 1938-40
Fred Walker	Walsall 1936-37	Wednesday 1937-40
Allenby Driver	Wednesday 1937-46	Walsall 1952-53
Frank Slynn	Wednesday 1946-51	Walsall 1953-54
George Kirby	Wednesday 1959-60	Walsall 1965-67
Jeff King	Walsall 1977-79	Wednesday 1979-82
Gary Shelton	Walsall 1975-78	Wednesday 1981-87
Craig Shakespeare	Walsall 1982-89	Wednesday 1989-90
Mark Taylor	Walsall 1984-89	Wednesday 1989-90
Danny Sonner	Wednesday 1998-2000	Walsall 2002-03
Barry Horne	Wednesday 1999-2000	Walsall 2000-01
Dean Smith	Walsall 1988-94	Wednesday 2002-03
Carl Robinson	Wednesday 2002-03	Walsall 2002-04
Lee Bradbury	Wednesday 2002-03	Walsall 2003-04
Mark Robins	Walsall 1999-2000	Wednesday 2003-04

v. Watford

			Home				Away		Final Positions	
Season	League	Date	Result	Wed'day	Watford	Date	Result	Wed'day	Watford	Wed'day	Watford

Season	League	Date	Result	Wed'day	Watford	Date	Result	Wed'day	Watford	Wed'day	Watford
1970-71	Division 2	5 December	Won	2	1	6 February	Lost	0	3	15th	18th
1971-72	Division 2	19 February	Won	2	1	30 October	Drew	1	1	14th	22ndR
1978-79	Division 3	5 May	Lost	2	3	31 March	Lost	0	1	14th	2ndP
1980-81	Division 2	29 November	Won	1	0	2 May	Lost	1	2	10th	9th
1981-82	Division 2	28 November	Won	3	1	24 April	Lost	0	4	4th	2ndP
1984-85	Division 1	24 February	Drew	1	1	17 November	Lost	0	1	8th	11th
1985-86	Division 1	26 August	Won	2	1	1 February	Lost	1	2	5th	12th
1986-87	Division 1	28 February	Lost	0	1	20 September	Won	1	0	13th	9th
1987-88	Division 1	12 September	Lost	2	3	26 December	Won	3	1	11th	20thR
1990-91	Division 2	15 September	Won	2	0	2 February	Drew	2	2	3rdP	20th
1999-00	Premiership	6 November	Drew	2	2	18 March	Lost	0	1	19thR	20thR
2000-01	Division 1	3 February	Lost	2	3	9 November	Won	3	1	17th	9th
2001-02	Division 1	16 February	Won	2	1	13 October	Lost	1	3	20th	14th
2002-03	Division 1	29 March	Drew	2	2	26 October	Lost	0	1	22ndR	13th

FA Cup

										Division
1997-98	Round 3	14 January	Drew*	0	0	3 January	Drew	1	1	Prem Div 2
			(won 5-3 pens)							

League Cup

1976-77	Round 3	21 September	Won	3	1		Div 3 Div 4
1980-81	Round 3	23 September	Lost	1	2		Div 2 Div 2
2001-02	Q'ter final	19 December	Won	4	0		Div 1 Div 1

Summary	P	W	D	L	F	A	
Wednesday's home league record:	14	7	3	4	25	20	
Wednesday's away league record:	14	3	2	9	13	23	
Wednesday's cup record:	5	2	2	1	9	4	
TOTAL:	**33**	**12**	**7**	**14**	**47**	**47**	(+one penalty shoot-out victory)

FACT FILE

- The sides' only ever goalless draw ended in the excitement of a penalty shoot-out.
- Wednesday failed to win in their first seven matches at Vicarage Road.

Wednesday's top scorers vs Watford
Lee Chapman 3

Played for both clubs

Ted Worrall	Wednesday 1910-15	Watford 1924-25
George Toone	Watford 1920-24	Wednesday 1924-25
George Prior	Wednesday 1920-24	Watford 1924-30
Harry Anstiss	Watford 1923-24	Wednesday 1926-27
Billy Chapman	Wednesday 1923-25	Watford 1928-34
Jimmy Trotter	Wednesday 1921-29	Watford 1931-33
George Johnson	Wednesday 1930-31	Watford 1937-39
Tommy Jones	Wednesday 1929-34	Watford 1935-46
George Drury	Wednesday 1936-38	Watford 1948-50
Jim McAnearney	Wednesday 1953-59	Watford 1963-67
Sam Ellis	Wednesday 1965-71	Watford 1977-79
Garry Thompson	Wednesday 1985-86	Watford 1988-90
Colin West	Watford 1984-86	Wednesday 1987-89
Wilf Rostron	Watford 1979-89	Wednesday 1988-89
Carlton Palmer	Wednesday 1988-94/2000-02	Watford 2000-01
Nigel Jemson	Wednesday 1991-94	Watford 1994-95
Guy Whittingham	Wednesday 1994-99	Watford 1998-99
Patrick Blondeau	Wednesday 1997-98	Watford 2001-02
Craig Armstrong	Watford 1996-97	Wednesday 2001-04

Lee Chapman is
Wednesday's leading
marksman against the
Hornets.

Carlton Palmer

v. West Bromwich Albion

<table>
<tr><th rowspan="2">Season</th><th rowspan="2">League</th><th colspan="4">Home</th><th colspan="4">Away</th><th colspan="2">Final Positions</th></tr>
<tr><th>Date</th><th>Result</th><th>Wed'day</th><th>WBA</th><th>Date</th><th>Result</th><th>Wed'day</th><th>WBA</th><th>Wed'day</th><th>WBA</th></tr>
<tr><td>1892-93</td><td>Division 1</td><td>2 January</td><td>Won</td><td>6</td><td>0</td><td>18 March</td><td>Lost</td><td>0</td><td>3</td><td>12th</td><td>8th</td></tr>
<tr><td>1893-94</td><td>Division 1</td><td>25 September</td><td>Lost</td><td>2</td><td>4</td><td>27 November</td><td>Drew</td><td>2</td><td>2</td><td>12th</td><td>8th</td></tr>
<tr><td>1894-95</td><td>Division 1</td><td>1 April</td><td>Won</td><td>3</td><td>2</td><td>22 April</td><td>Lost</td><td>0</td><td>6</td><td>8th</td><td>13th</td></tr>
<tr><td>1895-96</td><td>Division 1</td><td>5 October</td><td>Won</td><td>5</td><td>3</td><td>26 October</td><td>Won</td><td>3</td><td>2</td><td>7th</td><td>16th</td></tr>
<tr><td>1896-97</td><td>Division 1</td><td>12 September</td><td>Won</td><td>3</td><td>1</td><td>3 October</td><td>Won</td><td>2</td><td>0</td><td>6th</td><td>12th</td></tr>
<tr><td>1897-98</td><td>Division 1</td><td>9 April</td><td>Won</td><td>3</td><td>0</td><td>12 March</td><td>Won</td><td>2</td><td>0</td><td>5th</td><td>7th</td></tr>
<tr><td>1898-99</td><td>Division 1</td><td>14 February</td><td>Lost</td><td>1</td><td>2</td><td>1 October</td><td>Lost</td><td>0</td><td>2</td><td>18thR</td><td>14th</td></tr>
<tr><td>1900-01</td><td>Division 1</td><td>16 March</td><td>Won</td><td>2</td><td>1</td><td>10 November</td><td>Drew</td><td>1</td><td>1</td><td>8th</td><td>18thR</td></tr>
<tr><td>1902-03</td><td>Division 1</td><td>18 April</td><td>Won</td><td>3</td><td>1</td><td>20 December</td><td>Won</td><td>3</td><td>2</td><td>1st</td><td>7th</td></tr>
<tr><td>1903-04</td><td>Division 1</td><td>24 October</td><td>Won</td><td>1</td><td>0</td><td>2 September</td><td>Won</td><td>1</td><td>0</td><td>1st</td><td>18thR</td></tr>
<tr><td>1911-12</td><td>Division 1</td><td>23 December</td><td>Won</td><td>4</td><td>1</td><td>27 April</td><td>Won</td><td>5</td><td>1</td><td>5th</td><td>9th</td></tr>
<tr><td>1912-13</td><td>Division 1</td><td>19 April</td><td>Won</td><td>3</td><td>2</td><td>14 December</td><td>Drew</td><td>1</td><td>1</td><td>3rd</td><td>10th</td></tr>
<tr><td>1913-14</td><td>Division 1</td><td>13 December</td><td>Lost</td><td>1</td><td>4</td><td>18 April</td><td>Drew</td><td>1</td><td>1</td><td>18th</td><td>5th</td></tr>
<tr><td>1914-15</td><td>Division 1</td><td>27 March</td><td>Drew</td><td>0</td><td>0</td><td>21 November</td><td>Drew</td><td>0</td><td>0</td><td>7th</td><td>10th</td></tr>
<tr><td>1919-20</td><td>Division 1</td><td>29 November</td><td>Lost</td><td>0</td><td>3</td><td>22 November</td><td>Won</td><td>3</td><td>1</td><td>22ndR</td><td>1st</td></tr>
<tr><td>1926-27</td><td>Division 1</td><td>9 October</td><td>Won</td><td>2</td><td>1</td><td>26 February</td><td>Drew</td><td>2</td><td>2</td><td>16th</td><td>22ndR</td></tr>
<tr><td>1931-32</td><td>Division 1</td><td>12 March</td><td>Lost</td><td>2</td><td>5</td><td>31 October</td><td>Drew</td><td>1</td><td>1</td><td>3rd</td><td>6th</td></tr>
<tr><td>1932-33</td><td>Division 1</td><td>1 October</td><td>Won</td><td>3</td><td>1</td><td>11 February</td><td>Lost</td><td>0</td><td>2</td><td>3rd</td><td>4th</td></tr>
<tr><td>1933-34</td><td>Division 1</td><td>26 December</td><td>Won</td><td>3</td><td>1</td><td>27 December</td><td>Drew</td><td>1</td><td>1</td><td>11th</td><td>7th</td></tr>
<tr><td>1934-35</td><td>Division 1</td><td>1 January</td><td>Won</td><td>2</td><td>1</td><td>22 April</td><td>Drew</td><td>1</td><td>1</td><td>3rd</td><td>9th</td></tr>
<tr><td>1935-36</td><td>Division 1</td><td>2 November</td><td>Lost</td><td>2</td><td>5</td><td>4 April</td><td>Drew</td><td>2</td><td>2</td><td>20th</td><td>18th</td></tr>
<tr><td>1936-37</td><td>Division 1</td><td>17 April</td><td>Lost</td><td>2</td><td>3</td><td>23 April</td><td>Won</td><td>3</td><td>2</td><td>22ndR</td><td>16th</td></tr>
<tr><td>1938-39</td><td>Division 2</td><td>18 March</td><td>Won</td><td>2</td><td>1</td><td>12 November</td><td>Lost</td><td>1</td><td>5</td><td>3rd</td><td>10th</td></tr>
<tr><td>1946-47</td><td>Division 2</td><td>16 November</td><td>Drew</td><td>2</td><td>2</td><td>22 March</td><td>Lost</td><td>1</td><td>2</td><td>20th</td><td>7th</td></tr>
<tr><td>1947-48</td><td>Division 2</td><td>13 December</td><td>Lost</td><td>1</td><td>2</td><td>1 May</td><td>Drew</td><td>1</td><td>1</td><td>4th</td><td>7th</td></tr>
<tr><td>1948-49</td><td>Division 2</td><td>27 December</td><td>Won</td><td>2</td><td>1</td><td>25 December</td><td>Lost</td><td>0</td><td>1</td><td>8th</td><td>2ndP</td></tr>
<tr><td>1950-51</td><td>Division 1</td><td>26 December</td><td>Won</td><td>3</td><td>0</td><td>25 December</td><td>Won</td><td>3</td><td>1</td><td>21stR</td><td>16th</td></tr>
<tr><td>1952-53</td><td>Division 1</td><td>26 December</td><td>Lost</td><td>4</td><td>5</td><td>27 December</td><td>Won</td><td>1</td><td>0</td><td>18th</td><td>4th</td></tr>
<tr><td>1953-54</td><td>Division 1</td><td>26 September</td><td>Lost</td><td>2</td><td>3</td><td>13 February</td><td>Lost</td><td>2</td><td>4</td><td>19th</td><td>2nd</td></tr>
<tr><td>1954-55</td><td>Division 1</td><td>30 April</td><td>Won</td><td>5</td><td>0</td><td>16 October</td><td>Won</td><td>2</td><td>1</td><td>22ndR</td><td>17th</td></tr>
<tr><td>1956-57</td><td>Division 1</td><td>18 August</td><td>Won</td><td>4</td><td>2</td><td>15 December</td><td>Won</td><td>4</td><td>1</td><td>14th</td><td>11th</td></tr>
<tr><td>1957-58</td><td>Division 1</td><td>14 September</td><td>Lost</td><td>1</td><td>2</td><td>18 January</td><td>Lost</td><td>1</td><td>3</td><td>22ndR</td><td>4th</td></tr>
<tr><td>1959-60</td><td>Division 1</td><td>31 October</td><td>Won</td><td>2</td><td>0</td><td>16 April</td><td>Lost</td><td>1</td><td>3</td><td>5th</td><td>4th</td></tr>
<tr><td>1960-61</td><td>Division 1</td><td>20 August</td><td>Won</td><td>1</td><td>0</td><td>17 December</td><td>Drew</td><td>2</td><td>2</td><td>2nd</td><td>10th</td></tr>
<tr><td>1961-62</td><td>Division 1</td><td>16 December</td><td>Won</td><td>2</td><td>1</td><td>19 August</td><td>Won</td><td>2</td><td>0</td><td>6th</td><td>9th</td></tr>
<tr><td>1962-63</td><td>Division 1</td><td>1 September</td><td>Won</td><td>3</td><td>1</td><td>12 January</td><td>Won</td><td>3</td><td>0</td><td>6th</td><td>14th</td></tr>
<tr><td>1963-64</td><td>Division 1</td><td>15 February</td><td>Drew</td><td>2</td><td>2</td><td>5 October</td><td>Won</td><td>3</td><td>1</td><td>6th</td><td>10th</td></tr>
<tr><td>1964-65</td><td>Division 1</td><td>31 October</td><td>Drew</td><td>1</td><td>1</td><td>24 April</td><td>Lost</td><td>0</td><td>1</td><td>8th</td><td>14th</td></tr>
<tr><td>1965-66</td><td>Division 1</td><td>19 February</td><td>Lost</td><td>1</td><td>2</td><td>4 September</td><td>Lost</td><td>2</td><td>4</td><td>17th</td><td>6th</td></tr>
<tr><td>1966-67</td><td>Division 1</td><td>19 April</td><td>Won</td><td>1</td><td>0</td><td>29 October</td><td>Won</td><td>2</td><td>1</td><td>11th</td><td>13th</td></tr>
<tr><td>1967-68</td><td>Division 1</td><td>18 November</td><td>Drew</td><td>2</td><td>2</td><td>13 April</td><td>Drew</td><td>1</td><td>1</td><td>19th</td><td>8th</td></tr>
<tr><td>1968-69</td><td>Division 1</td><td>5 March</td><td>Won</td><td>1</td><td>0</td><td>10 August</td><td>Drew</td><td>0</td><td>0</td><td>15th</td><td>10th</td></tr>
<tr><td>1969-70</td><td>Division 1</td><td>10 March</td><td>Won</td><td>2</td><td>0</td><td>22 November</td><td>Lost</td><td>0</td><td>3</td><td>22ndR</td><td>16th</td></tr>
<tr><td>1973-74</td><td>Division 2</td><td>12 September</td><td>Won</td><td>3</td><td>1</td><td>24 October</td><td>Lost</td><td>0</td><td>2</td><td>19th</td><td>8th</td></tr>
</table>

Season	League	Date	Result	Wed'day	WBA	Date	Result	Wed'day	WBA	Final Positions Wed'day	WBA
			Home				**Away**				
1974-75	Division 2	25 September	Drew	0	0	8 March	Lost	0	4	22ndR	6th
1984-85	Division 1	12 January	Won	2	0	15 September	Drew	2	2	8th	12th
1985-86	Division 1	26 October	Won	1	0	22 April	Drew	1	1	5th	22ndR
1990-91	Division 2	9 March	Won	1	0	24 November	Won	2	1	3rdP	23rdR
2000-01	Division 1	8 October	Lost	1	2	10 March	Won	2	1	17th	6th
2001-02	Division 1	25 August	Drew	1	1	22 December	Drew	1	1	20th	2ndP

FA Cup

Season	Round	Date	Result	Wed	WBA	Date	Result	Wed	WBA	Division (Wed)	(WBA)
1890-91	Q'ter final	14 February	Lost	0	2					Non L	Div 1
1891-92	Q'ter final	13 February	Lost	1	2					Non L	Div 1
1894-95	Semi-Final	16 March				Derby Cricket Ground	Lost	0	2	Div 1	Div 1
1897-98	Round 2					12 February	Lost	0	1	Div 1	Div 1
1934-35	Final	27 April				Wembley	Won	4	2	Div 1	Div 1
1958-59	Round 3	19 January	Lost	0	2					Div 2	Div 1
1969-70	Round 3	3 January	Won	2	1					Div 1	Div 1
1985-86	Round 3	13 January	Drew	2	2	16 January	Won	3	2	Div 1	Div 1

Summary	P	W	D	L	F	A
Wednesday's home league record:	50	30	7	13	106	72
Wednesday's away league record:	50	18	17	15	74	80
Wednesday's cup record:	9	3	1	5	12	16
TOTAL:	**109**	**51**	**25**	**33**	**192**	**168**

Charlie Wilson, who had lengthy spells at Albion and Wednesday in the 1920s and 1930s.

FACT FILE

- Sheffield Wednesday last won the FA Cup in 1935. In an exciting game, Ellis Rimmer scored twice in the last six minutes to secure victory for the Yorkshiremen.
- In April 1903, Wednesday completed their league programme with victory over West Brom, and then went to Plymouth where they made various promotional appearances. In their absence, Sunderland lost 1-0 at Newcastle, and thus Wednesday became league champions for the first time.
- From 1900 to 1931, Wednesday were unbeaten in 11 away games in the series.
- Wednesday were unbeaten in 11 home matches between 1967 and 1991.
- Wednesday have lost once in their last 12 games in the series.

Wednesday's top scorers vs West Brom
David McLean, Fred Spiksley 8
Ellis Rimmer 7
Alec Brady, Harry Davis, John Fantham 6
Redfern Froggatt, Mark Hooper 5

Wednesday hat-tricks vs West Brom
27 Apr 1912 David McLean

Played for both clubs

Laurie Bell	Wednesday 1895-97	West Brom 1904-05
George Simpson	Wednesday 1902-09	West Brom 1908-11
Harry Burton	Wednesday 1903-09	West Brom 1908-10
Lewis Bedford	West Brom 1920-22	Wednesday 1925-26
Charlie Wilson	West Brom 1921-28	Wednesday 1927-32
George Drury	Wednesday 1936-38	West Brom 1946-48
Doug Witcomb	West Brom 1938-47	Wednesday 1946-53
Bobby Hope	West Brom 1959-72	Wednesday 1976-78
David Rushbury	West Brom 1974-76	Wednesday 1976-79
Gary Bannister	Wednesday 1981-84	West Brom 1989-92
David Mills	West Brom 1978-83	Wednesday 1982-83
Imre Varadi	Wednesday 1983-85/88-90	West Brom 1985-86
Garry Thompson	West Brom 1982-85	Wednesday 1985-86
Gary Owen	West Brom 1979-86	Wednesday 1987-88
Colin West	Wednesday 1987-89	West Brom 1988-92
Carlton Palmer	Wednesday 1988-94/2000-02	West Brom 1985-89
Craig Shakespeare	Wednesday 1989-90	West Brom 1989-93
Franz Carr	Wednesday 1989-90	West Brom 1997-98
Phil King	Wednesday 1989-94	West Brom 1995-96
Steve MacKenzie	West Brom 1981-87	Wednesday 1990-92
Steve Nicol	Wednesday 1995-98	West Brom 1997-98
David Burrows	West Brom 1985-89	Wednesday 2001-03
Adam Chambers	West Brom 2000-04	Wednesday 2003-04

v. West Ham United

		Home					Away			Final Positions	
Season	League	Date	Result	Wed'day	WHU	Date	Result	Wed'day	WHU	Wed'day	WHU
1920-21	Division 2	6 November	Lost	0	1	13 November	Lost	0	4	10th	5th
1921-22	Division 2	8 April	Won	2	1	1 April	Lost	0	2	10th	4th
1922-23	Division 2	30 April	Lost	0	2	3 March	Lost	1	2	8th	2ndP
1926-27	Division 1	6 September	Won	1	0	4 October	Drew	1	1	16th	6th
1927-28	Division 1	3 December	Won	2	0	14 April	Won	2	1	14th	17th
1928-29	Division 1	13 April	Won	6	0	1 December	Lost	2	3	1st	17th
1929-30	Division 1	29 March	Won	2	1	23 November	Drew	1	1	1st	7th
1930-31	Division 1	31 January	Won	5	3	27 September	Drew	3	3	3rd	18th
1931-32	Division 1	28 March	Won	6	1	25 March	Won	2	1	3rd	22ndR
1937-38	Division 2	2 October	Won	1	0	12 February	Lost	0	1	17th	9th
1938-39	Division 2	31 December	Lost	1	4	3 September	Won	3	2	3rd	11th
1946-47	Division 2	1 January	Drew	1	1	3 May	Lost	1	2	20th	12th
1947-48	Division 2	26 December	Won	5	3	27 December	Won	4	1	4th	6th
1948-49	Division 2	23 August	Won	3	0	30 August	Drew	2	2	8th	7th
1949-50	Division 2	10 December	Won	2	1	29 April	Drew	2	2	2ndP	19th
1951-52	Division 2	20 April	Drew	2	2	8 December	Won	6	0	1stP	12th
1955-56	Division 2	26 November	Drew	1	1	7 April	Drew	3	3	1stP	16th
1959-60	Division 1	28 November	Won	7	0	30 April	Drew	1	1	5th	14th
1960-61	Division 1	3 September	Won	1	0	14 January	Drew	1	1	2nd	16th
1961-62	Division 1	17 March	Drew	0	0	28 October	Won	3	2	6th	8th
1962-63	Division 1	24 November	Lost	1	3	2 April	Lost	0	2	6th	12th
1963-64	Division 1	12 October	Won	3	0	22 February	Lost	3	4	6th	14th
1964-65	Division 1	6 March	Won	2	0	4 October	Won	2	1	8th	9th
1965-66	Division 1	18 December	Drew	0	0	16 October	Lost	2	4	17th	12th
1966-67	Division 1	17 September	Lost	0	2	21 January	Lost	0	3	11th	16th
1967-68	Division 1	16 December	Won	4	1	19 August	Won	3	2	19th	12th
1968-69	Division 1	5 April	Drew	1	1	28 September	Drew	1	1	15th	8th
1969-70	Division 1	10 January	Lost	2	3	20 September	Lost	0	3	22ndR	17th
1980-81	Division 2	8 May	Lost	0	1	6 December	Lost	1	2	10th	1stP
1984-85	Division 1	11 May	Won	2	1	15 December	Drew	0	0	8th	16th
1985-86	Division 1	7 September	Drew	2	2	22 March	Lost	0	1	5th	3rd
1986-87	Division 1	27 September	Drew	2	2	24 March	Won	2	0	13th	15th
1987-88	Division 1	2 April	Won	2	1	7 November	Won	1	0	11th	16th
1988-89	Division 1	9 May	Lost	0	2	10 December	Drew	0	0	15th	19thR
1990-91	Division 2	29 September	Drew	1	1	16 March	Won	3	1	3rdP	2ndP
1991-92	Division 1	22 February	Won	2	1	30 November	Won	2	1	3rd	22ndR
1993-94	Premiership	18 December	Won	5	0	25 August	Lost	0	2	7th	13th
1994-95	Premiership	19 November	Won	1	0	23 January	Won	2	0	13th	14th
1995-96	Premiership	28 October	Lost	0	1	5 May	Drew	1	1	15th	10th
1996-97	Premiership	30 November	Drew	0	0	3 May	Lost	1	5	7th	14th
1997-98	Premiership	13 April	Drew	1	1	13 December	Lost	0	1	16th	8th
1998-99	Premiership	15 August	Lost	0	1	16 January	Won	4	0	12th	5th
1999-00	Premiership	11 March	Won	3	1	21 November	Lost	3	4	19thR	9th

FA Cup		Date	Result	Home Wed'day	WHU	Date	Result	Away Wed'day	WHU	Division Wed'day	WHU
1920-21	Round 1	8 January	Won	1	0					Div 2	Div 2
1985-86	Q'ter final	12 March	Won	2	1					Div 1	Div 1
1986-87	Round 5	21 February	Drew	1	1	25 February	Won	2	0	Div 1	Div 1

League Cup											
2000-01	Round 4					29 November	Won	2	1	Div 1	Prem

Summary	P	W	D	L	F	A
Wednesday's home league record:	43	22	11	10	82	46
Wednesday's away league record:	43	14	12	17	69	73
Wednesday's cup record:	5	4	1	0	8	3
TOTAL:	91	40	24	27	159	122

FACT FILE

- The first of Wednesday's three five-goal victories in the Premiership came against West Ham in 1993.
- Wednesday's only four-goal away win in the Premiership came against West Ham in 1999.
- In December 1951, Wednesday won by six goals away from home in the league for the only time since World War Two.
- From 1926 to 1937, Wednesday won seven consecutive home games against West Ham.
- Between 1926 and 1982, Wednesday lost once in 17 home games in the series.

Wednesday's top scorers vs West Ham
John Fantham, Mark Hooper, Eddie Quigley 9
Jack Allen, Lee Chapman, Redfern Froggatt,
Ellis Rimmer 5
Derek Dooley 4

Wednesday hat-tricks vs West Ham
26 Dec 1947 Eddie Quigley (4)
8 Dec 1951 Derek Dooley

Played for both clubs
Joe Cockroft	West Ham 1932-39	Wednesday 1946-49
Peter Eustace	Wednesday 1962-70/72-75	West Ham 1969-72
John Sissons	West Ham 1962-70	Wednesday 1970-74
Bobby Ferguson	West Ham 1967-80	Wednesday 1973-74
Lee Chapman	Wednesday 1984-88	West Ham 1993-95
Steve Whitton	West Ham 1983-85	Wednesday 1988-91
Franz Carr	Wednesday 1989-90	West Ham 1990-91
John Harkes	Wednesday 1990-93	West Ham 1995-96
Paolo DiCanio	Wednesday 1997-99	West Ham 1998-2003
Niclas Alexandersson	Wednesday 1997-2000	West Ham 2003-04
Robbie Stockdale	Wednesday 2000-01	West Ham 2003-04
David Burrows	West Ham 1993-95	Wednesday 2001-03

v. Wigan Athletic

FA Cup	Date	Result	Home Wed'day Wigan A	Date	Result	Away Wed'day Wigan A	Division Wed'day Wigan A
1975-76 Round 2	13 December	Won	2 0				Div 3 Non L
1977-78 Round 2				17 December	Lost	0 1	Div 3 Non L

Summary	P	W	D	L	F	A
Wednesday's cup record:	2	1	0	1	2	1
TOTAL:	2	1	0	1	2	1

FACT FILE

- Wednesday's last two FA Cup ties against non-league opposition have both been against Wigan. Given that Wednesday lost the last match, they may not want another one for a while.

Played for both clubs

John Lowey	Wednesday 1978-80	Wigan 1986-87
Carl Bradshaw	Wednesday 1986-89	Wigan 1997-2001
Peter Atherton	Wigan 1987-92	Wednesday 1994-2000
Ian Nolan	Wednesday 1994-2000	Wigan 2001-02
Terry Cooke	Wigan 1999-2000	Wednesday 2000-01/03-04
Eric Nixon	Wigan 1998-99	Wednesday 2003-04
Mark Burchill	Wigan 2003-04	Wednesday 2003-04

Carl Bradshaw.

v. Wigan Borough

FA Cup					Date	Result	Away Wed'day Wigan B	Division Wed'day Wigan B
1928-29 Round 3					12 January	Won	3 1	Div 1 Div 3N

Summary	P	W	D	L	F	A
Wednesday's cup record:	1	1	0	0	3	1
TOTAL:	1	1	0	0	3	1

FACT FILE

● This is not the same team as Wigan Athletic. Borough folded in 1932.

Wednesday's top scorers vs Wigan Borough
Jack Allen 2

Played for both clubs
Len Armitage   Wednesday 1919-20   Wigan B 1923-24

v. Wimbledon

		Home				Away				Final Positions	
Season	League	Date	Result	Wed'day	Wimb'don	Date	Result	Wed'day	Wimb'don	Wed'day	Wimb'don
1979-80	Division 3	9 March	Won	3	1	27 October	Won	4	3	3rdP	24thR
1986-87	Division 1	9 May	Lost	0	2	13 December	Lost	0	3	13th	6th
1987-88	Division 1	12 December	Won	1	0	3 May	Drew	1	1	11th	7th
1988-89	Division 1	5 April	Drew	1	1	25 February	Lost	0	1	15th	12th
1989-90	Division 1	28 October	Lost	0	1	24 March	Drew	1	1	18thR	8th
1991-92	Division 1	21 December	Won	2	0	2 October	Lost	1	2	3rd	13th
1992-93	Premiership	24 March	Drew	1	1	28 November	Drew	1	1	7th	12th
1993-94	Premiership	16 October	Drew	2	2	15 January	Lost	1	2	7th	6th
1994-95	Premiership	11 March	Lost	0	1	27 August	Won	1	0	13th	9th
1995-96	Premiership	10 February	Won	2	1	30 August	Drew	2	2	15th	14th
1996-97	Premiership	19 April	Won	3	1	12 October	Lost	2	4	7th	8th
1997-98	Premiership	31 January	Drew	1	1	23 August	Drew	1	1	16th	15th
1998-99	Premiership	3 March	Lost	1	2	19 September	Lost	1	2	12th	16th
1999-00	Premiership	2 October	Won	5	1	12 April	Won	2	0	19thR	18thR
2000-01	Division 1	9 September	Lost	0	5	10 February	Lost	1	4	17th	8th
2001-02	Division 1	6 March	Lost	1	2	15 September	Drew	1	1	20th	9th
2002-03	Division 1	5 April	Won	4	2	30 November	Lost	0	3	22ndR	10th

FA Cup										Division	
1996-97	Q'ter final	9 March	Lost	0	2					Prem	Prem

League Cup											
1980-81	Round 2	2 September	Won	3	1	26 August	Lost	1	2	Div 2	Div 4
1993-94	Q'ter final					11 January	Won	2	1	Prem	Prem

Summary	P	W	D	L	F	A
Wednesday's home league record:	17	7	4	6	27	24
Wednesday's away league record:	17	3	6	8	20	31
Wednesday's cup record:	4	2	0	2	6	6
TOTAL:	38	12	10	16	53	61

FACT FILE

- In consecutive home games in 1999 and 2000, Wednesday went from winning 5-1 to losing 5-0.
- Wednesday have never gone more than three home games in a row without losing.

Wednesday's top scorers vs Wimbledon
Terry Curran 5
Gilles De Bilde 3

Played for both clubs
Andy Pearce	Wednesday 1993-96	Wimbledon 1995-96
Efan Ekoku	Wimbledon 1994-99	Wednesday 2000-02
Paul Heald	Wimbledon 1995-2004	Wednesday 2001-02

v. Wolverhampton Wanderers

Season	League	Date	Result	Home Wed'day	Wolves	Date	Result	Away Wed'day	Wolves	Final Positions Wed'day	Wolves
1892-93	Division 1	11 March	Lost	0	1	11 February	Lost	0	2	12th	11th
1893-94	Division 1	2 December	Lost	1	4	4 September	Lost	1	3	12th	9th
1894-95	Division 1	17 November	Won	3	1	13 October	Lost	0	2	8th	11th
1895-96	Division 1	12 October	Won	3	1	14 September	Lost	0	4	7th	14th
1896-97	Division 1	12 December	Drew	0	0	13 March	Lost	0	2	6th	10th
1897-98	Division 1	5 March	Won	2	0	16 April	Lost	0	5	5th	3rd
1898-99	Division 1	29 October	Won	3	0	25 February	Drew	0	0	18thR	8th
1900-01	Division 1	1 January	Won	2	0	26 December	Drew	1	1	8th	13th
1901-02	Division 1	5 October	Drew	1	1	1 February	Lost	0	1	9th	14th
1902-03	Division 1	27 September	Drew	1	1	24 January	Lost	1	2	1st	11th
1903-04	Division 1	1 January	Won	4	0	10 October	Lost	1	2	1st	8th
1904-05	Division 1	10 September	Won	4	0	7 January	Lost	0	1	9th	14th
1905-06	Division 1	26 December	Won	5	1	4 September	Drew	0	0	3rd	20thR
1920-21	Division 2	11 April	Won	6	0	12 March	Won	2	1	10th	15th
1921-22	Division 2	12 February	Won	3	1	28 January	Drew	0	0	10th	17th
1922-23	Division 2	31 March	Won	1	0	7 April	Lost	0	2	8th	22ndR
1924-25	Division 2	29 November	Won	2	0	4 April	Lost	0	1	14th	6th
1925-26	Division 2	13 February	Won	2	1	3 October	Won	2	1	1stP	4th
1932-33	Division 1	4 March	Won	2	0	22 October	Won	5	3	3rd	20th
1933-34	Division 1	10 March	Won	2	1	28 October	Lost	2	6	11th	15th
1934-35	Division 1	20 October	Won	3	1	4 March	Drew	2	2	3rd	17th
1935-36	Division 1	7 September	Drew	0	0	4 January	Lost	1	2	20th	15th
1936-37	Division 1	2 January	Lost	1	3	5 September	Lost	3	4	22ndR	5th
1950-51	Division 1	14 October	Drew	2	2	3 March	Lost	0	4	21stR	14th
1952-53	Division 1	13 December	Lost	2	3	31 January	Lost	1	3	18th	3rd
1953-54	Division 1	12 April	Drew	0	0	28 November	Lost	1	4	19th	1st
1954-55	Division 1	18 December	Drew	2	2	21 August	Lost	2	4	22ndR	2nd
1956-57	Division 1	9 March	Won	2	1	8 December	Lost	1	2	14th	6th
1957-58	Division 1	26 April	Won	2	1	14 December	Lost	3	4	22ndR	1st
1959-60	Division 1	2 September	Drew	2	2	26 August	Lost	1	3	5th	2nd
1960-61	Division 1	11 March	Drew	0	0	2 October	Lost	1	4	2nd	3rd
1961-62	Division 1	28 April	Won	3	2	9 December	Lost	0	3	6th	18th
1962-63	Division 1	23 March	Won	3	1	3 November	Drew	2	2	6th	5th
1963-64	Division 1	23 November	Won	5	0	4 April	Drew	1	1	6th	16th
1964-65	Division 1	26 September	Won	2	0	6 February	Lost	1	3	8th	21stR
1967-68	Division 1	30 September	Drew	2	2	19 March	Won	3	2	19th	17th
1968-69	Division 1	19 October	Lost	0	2	21 December	Won	3	0	15th	16th
1969-70	Division 1	16 August	Lost	2	3	8 October	Drew	2	2	22ndR	13th
1982-83	Division 2	9 October	Drew	0	0	1 March	Lost	0	1	6th	2ndP
1990-91	Division 2	26 December	Drew	2	2	30 March	Lost	2	3	3rdP	12th
2000-01	Division 1	23 December	Lost	0	1	13 August	Drew	1	1	17th	12th
2001-02	Division 1	21 April	Drew	2	2	18 November	Drew	0	0	20th	3rd
2002-03	Division 1	1 February	Lost	0	4	27 August	Drew	2	2	22ndR	5thP

FA Cup		Date	Result	Home Wed'day	Wolves	Date	Result	Away Wed'day	Wolves	Division Wed'day	Wolves
1888-89	Q'ter final					2 March	Lost	0	3	Non L	Div 1
1895-96	Final	18 April		Crystal Palace			Won	2	1	Div 1	Div 1
1906-07	Round 1	12 January	Won	3	2					Div 1	Div 2
1913-14	Round 2	4 February	Won	1	0	31 January	Drew	1	1	Div 1	Div 2
1914-15	Round 2	30 January	Won	2	0					Div 1	Div 2
1934-35	Round 4					26 January	Won	2	1	Div 1	Div 1
1989-90	Round 3					6 January	Won	2	1	Div 1	Div 2
1994-95	Round 4	30 January	Drew	0	0	8 February	Drew*	1	1	Prem	Div 1
						(lost 3-4 pens)					
1999-00	Round 4	8 January	Drew	1	1	18 January	Drew*	0	0	Prem	Div 1
						(won 4-3 pens)					

League Cup

		Date	Result	Wed'day	Wolves	Division Wed'day	Wolves
1972-73	Round 3	4 October	Lost	1	3	Div 2	Div 1
1976-77	Round 2	31 August	Won	2	1	Div 3	Div 2

Summary

	P	W	D	L	F	A
Wednesday's home league record:	43	22	13	8	84	47
Wednesday's away league record:	43	5	11	27	48	95
Wednesday's cup record:	14	7	5	2	18	15
TOTAL:	**100**	**34**	**29**	**37**	**150**	**157**

(+two penalty shoot-outs; one victory and one defeat)

Derek Jefferson, who had four years at Molineux and a briefer stay at Hillsborough.

FACT FILE

- Wednesday first won the FA Cup in 1896. All the goals came in the first 20 minutes, with Fred Spiksley scoring both for Wednesday.
- Wednesday went 23 home games unbeaten between 1894 and 1935. This run included 14 successive wins.
- Between 1936 and 1961, Wolves won 11 sucessive home games.
- Wednesday last won a league game against Wolves in 1968. They have played 12 league games since, but have won three cup ties against Wolves in this period.
- In 1995, Wednesday were the victims of possibly the greatest penalty shoot-out comeback of all time. The first five penalties all went Wednesday's way (three successes for Wednesday, two failures by Wolves). Just one of the next five penalties had to go Wednesday's way for them to win, but none of them did. That took the shoot-out to sudden death, where Wednesday missed again and Wolves scored to go through. Five years later, however, Wednesday got revenge.

Wednesday's top scorers vs Wolves

Jack Ball, Harry Davis 6
Alec Brady, Ellis Rimmer, Jimmy Stewart,
Derek Wilkinson, Andrew Wilson 5

Wednesday hat-tricks vs Wolves

29 Oct 1898 Albert Kaye
26 Dec 1905 Jimmy Stewart (4)
22 Oct 1932 Jack Ball (4)

Played for both clubs

Fred Marson	Wolves 1923-25	Wednesday 1926-28
Tommy Davison	Wolves 1923-25	Wednesday 1930-32
Len Williams	Wednesday 1923-26	Wolves 1927-30
Ernie Hatfield	Wednesday 1928-29	Wolves 1930-31
Dickie Rhodes	Wolves 1928-36	Wednesday 1935-38
Jim McCalliog	Wednesday 1965-69	Wolves 1969-74
John Holsgrove	Wolves 1965-71	Wednesday 1971-75
Michael Kent	Wolves 1969-72	Wednesday 1973-74
Ken Knighton	Wolves 1964-67	Wednesday 1973-76
Bernard Shaw	Wolves 1969-73	Wednesday 1973-76
Derek Jefferson	Wolves 1972-76	Wednesday 1976-77
Peter Shirtliff	Wednesday 1978-86/89-93	Wolves 1993-96
Lawrie Madden	Wednesday 1983-91	Wolves 1991-93
Andy Blair	Wolves 1983-84	Wednesday 1984-86
Simon Coleman	Wednesday 1993-95	Wolves 1997-98
Andy Sinton	Wednesday 1993-96	Wolves 1999-2002
Guy Whittingham	Wolves 1993-94/98-99	Wednesday 1994-99
Adam Proudlock	Wolves 2000-03	Wednesday 2002-04
Ryan Green	Wolves 1998-2001	Wednesday 2002-03
Carl Robinson	Wolves 1996-2002	Wednesday 2002-03
Eric Nixon	Wolves 1986-87	Wednesday 2003-04

v. Wrexham

Season	League	Date	Result	Home Wed'day	Wrexham	Date	Result	Away Wed'day	Wrexham	Final Positions Wed'day	Wrexham
1975-76	Division 3	6 September	Won	1	0	10 April	Lost	0	3	20th	6th
1976-77	Division 3	5 March	Won	3	1	25 September	Drew	2	2	8th	5th
1977-78	Division 3	3 May	Won	2	1	15 October	Drew	1	1	14th	1stP
1980-81	Division 2	8 November	Won	2	1	11 April	Lost	0	4	10th	16th
1981-82	Division 2	3 October	Lost	0	3	13 February	Won	1	0	4th	21stR
2003-04	Division 2	25 August	Lost	2	3	3 January	Won	2	1	16th	13th

Summary	P	W	D	L	F	A
Wednesday's home league record:	6	4	0	2	10	9
Wednesday's away league record:	6	2	2	2	6	11
TOTAL:	12	6	2	4	16	20

FACT FILE

- The only two away wins in the series have come in the last four matches.

Wednesday's top scorers vs Wrexham
Terry Curran, Alan Quinn, Tommy Tynan, Rodger Wylde 2

Played for both clubs
George Holmes	Wednesday 1921-22	Wrexham 1922-23
Dennis Leman	Wednesday 1976-82	Wrexham 1981-82
Barry Horne	Wrexham 1984-87	Wednesday 1999-2000
Terry Cooke	Wrexham 1998-99	Wednesday 2000-01/03-04
Mark Wilson	Wrexham 1997-98	Wednesday 2003-04

v. Wycombe Wanderers

Season	League	Date	Result	Home Wed'day Wycombe	Date	Result	Away Wed'day Wycombe	Final Positions Wed'day Wycombe
2003-04	Division 2	30 January	Drew	1 1	1 September	Won	2 1	16th 24thR

Summary	P	W	D	L	F	A
Wednesday's home league record:	1	0	1	0	1	1
Wednesday's away league record:	1	1	0	0	2	1
TOTAL:	**2**	**1**	**1**	**0**	**3**	**2**

Played for both clubs

| Tony Cunningham | Wednesday 1983-84 | Wycombe 1993-94 |
| Guy Whittingham | Wednesday 1994-99 | Wycombe 2000-01 |

v. Yeovil & Petters United

FA Cup		Home				Away		Division	
	Date	Result	Wed'day	Y&P Utd	Date	Result	Wed'day Y&P Utd	Wed'day	Y&P Utd
1938-39 Round 3	7 January	Drew	1	1	12 January	Won	2 1	Div 2	Non L

Summary	P	W	D	L	F	A
Wednesday's cup record:	2	1	1	0	3	2
TOTAL:	2	1	1	0	3	2

FACT FILE

● In 1946, United changed their name to Yeovil Town.

v. York City

Season	League	Date	Result	Home Wed'day	York	Date	Result	Away Wed'day	York	Final Positions Wed'day	York
1974-75	Division 2	9 November	Won	3	0	31 January	Lost	0	3	22ndR	15th
1976-77	Division 3	27 December	Won	3	2	11 April	Won	2	0	8th	24thR

FA Cup

Season	Round	Date	Result			Date	Result			Division	
1945-46	Round 4	26 January	Won	5	1	30 January	Won	6	1	Div 2	Div 3N

Summary	P	W	D	L	F	A
Wednesday's cup record:	6	5	0	1	19	7
TOTAL:	6	5	0	1	19	7

Wednesday's top scorers vs York
Allenby Driver, Charlie Tomlinson 3

Wednesday hat-tricks vs York
30 Jan 1946 Charlie Tomlinson (cup)

Played for both clubs

Tom Gale	Wednesday 1946-47	York 1947-49
Eric Kirby	Wednesday 1950-51	York 1952-53
Ron Greensmith	Wednesday 1954-58	York 1957-60
Walter Bingley	Wednesday 1955-57	York 1960-63
Paul Taylor	Wednesday 1971-73	York 1973-74
Eric McMordie	Wednesday 1974-75	York 1975-77
Graeme Hedley	Wednesday 1977-78	York 1981-82
Jimmy Hinch	York 1974-77	Wednesday 1977-78
John Lowey	Wednesday 1978-80	York 1986-87
Mike Pickering	Wednesday 1978-83	York 1986-87
Simon Mills	Wednesday 1982-85	York 1985-88
Richard Cresswell	York 1995-99	Wednesday 1998-2001
Marlon Beresford	Wednesday 2000-01	York 2002-03
Jon McCarthy	York 1990-95/2002-03	Wednesday 2001-02
Michael Reddy	Wednesday 2002-04	York 2002-03
Jon Shaw	Wednesday 2002-04	York 2003-04

Mike Pickering pictured at York some years after he left Wednesday.

v. Wednesday in Europe

Wednesday in Europe vs French clubs

Year	Round	versus	Date	Home Wed'day		Date	Away Wed'day		Aggregate	
1961-62	Round of 32	Lyon	4 October	Won	5 2	12 September	Lost	2 4	Won	7 6

	P	W	D	L	F	A
TOTAL:	2	1	0	1	7	6

Wednesday in Europe vs German clubs

Year	Round	versus	Date	Home Wed'day		Date	Away Wed'day		Aggregate	
1963-64	Round of 16	Cologne	27 November	Lost	1 2	6 November	Lost	2 3	Lost	3 5
1992-93	Round of 32	Kaiserslautern	4 November	Drew	2 2	20 October	Lost	1 3	Lost	3 5

	P	W	D	L	F	A
TOTAL:	4	0	1	3	6	10

Wednesday in Europe vs Dutch clubs

Year	Round	versus	Date	Home Wed'day		Date	Away Wed'day		Aggregate	
1963-64	Round of 32	DOS Utrecht	15 October	Won	4 1	25 September	Won	4 1	Won	8 2

	P	W	D	L	F	A
TOTAL:	2	2	0	0	8	2

Wednesday in Europe vs Italian clubs

Year	Round	versus	Date	Home Wed'day		Date	Away Wed'day		Aggregate	
1961-62	Round of 16	Roma	29 November	Won	4 0	13 December	Lost	0 1	Won	4 1

	P	W	D	L	F	A
TOTAL:	2	1	0	1	4	1

Wednesday in Europe vs Luxembourg clubs

Year	Round	versus	Date	Home Wed'day		Date	Away Wed'day		Aggregate	
1992-93	Round of 64	Spora Luxembourg	16 September	Won	8 1	1 October	Won	2 1	Won	10 2

	P	W	D	L	F	A
TOTAL:	2	2	0	0	10	2

Wednesday in Europe vs Spanish clubs

Year	Round	versus	Date	Home Wed'day		Date	Away Wed'day		Aggregate	
1961-62	Q'ter final	Barcelona	28 February	Won	3 2	28 March	Lost	0 2	Lost	3 4

	P	W	D	L	F	A
TOTAL:	2	1	0	1	3	4

FACT FILE

- Wednesday's first two European campaigns (1961-62 and 1963-64) took place in the Fairs Cup. The 1992-93 campaign was in the Fairs Cup's successor, the UEFA Cup. They qualified by finishing third in the league in 1991-92, an impressive achievement given that they'd only been promoted the previous year.
- The highlight of Wednesday's European campaigns is probably a 4-0 win over Italian giants Roma in 1961.
- Wednesday are the only club to have brought European football to South Yorkshire.

Wednesday's top scorers in Europe

John Fantham, David Layne 5
Gerry Young 4
Paul Warhurst 3

Wednesday hat-tricks in Europe

29 Nov 1961 Gerry Young (vs Roma)
15 Oct 1963 David Layne (vs DOS Utrecht)